A TASTE OF INDIA

Madhur Jaffrey, author and actress, grew up in
Delhi. She first came to London to study drama
at RADA, where she was awarded a diploma
with Honours, a rare distiction. She has sub-
sequently appeared in numerous radio and
television plays, acted on Broadway and in
several films. She is equally well known as a
writer and broadcaster, particularly on Eastern
food. She is the author of three best-selling
books on the subject, presented the highly
acclaimed BBC series *Indian Cookery* and has
recently published her first children's book
entitled *Seasons of Splendour*. She is married with
three children and lives in New York.

MADHUR JAFFREY

A TASTE OF INDIA

Food photography by Christine Hanscomb
Specially commissioned location photography
by Henry Wilson

PAN BOOKS
London, Sydney and Auckland

First published in Great Britain 1985 by
Pavilion Books Ltd. This edition published
1987 by Pan Books Ltd, Cavaye Place,
London SW10 9PG

7   9   8   6

Copyright text © Madhur Jaffrey 1985
Commissioned location photography
© 1985 Henry Wilson

ISBN 0 330 29394 x

Photoset by Parker Typesetting Service, Leicester
Reproduced, printed and bound in Great Britain by
BPCC Hazells Ltd
Member of BPCC Ltd

Measurements in this book are given in imperial,
metric and American cups. When measuring ingredients,
follow one system throughout, not a mixture.

All spoon measurements are level. Do not use
heaped teaspoonfuls.

CONTENTS

LIST OF ILLUSTRATIONS

LIST OF ILLUSTRATIONS

Batloo (millet bread).

A Gujarati woman making *chapatis*.

MAHARASHTRA

Rice with Tomatoes and Spinach (page 90), Prawns cooked in
the Maharashtrian manner (page 87).

Cucumbers with Fresh Coconut (page 90), Lamb cooked in the
Kolhapuri style (page 88).

Syrup-filled *jalebis*.

KASHMIR

Red Kidney Beans cooked with Turnips (page 109),
Aubergines with Apple (page 104).

Appearing between pages 86 and 87

BENGAL

Sealdah vegetable market, Calcutta.

Fish in a Bengali Sauce (page 123), Prawns with Mustard Seeds (page 125).

Okra with Mustard Seeds (page 121), Plain Rice (page 193),
Delicious Fried Morsels (page 120), Roasted Moong Dal with Spinach (page 122).

Fish on sale in Calcutta.

HYDERABAD

Chicken in a Green Sauce (page 139), Hyderabadi Pilaf of Rice and
Split Peas (page 142).

Flaky Pan Bread (page 143), Sesame Chutney and Yoghurt Chutney (page 144–5),
Quick Kebabs (page 140).

Kulcha, a popular Hyderabadi bread.

A market trader.

Sacks of dried beans and split peas.

A TASTE OF INDIA

Appearing between pages 118 and 119

TAMIL NADU AND KARNATAKA

A family enjoys a picnic of okra, *sambar* and *idlis*.

Fishermen taking to the sea at sunrise from the beach at Madras.

KERALA

NOTE: Page references in parentheses refer to recipe entries.

ACKNOWLEDGEMENTS

I would like to gratefully acknowledge the help given to me by the following: The Government of India, Departments of Tourism and External Affairs, Salman Haider, Vina Sanyal, Digvijay Sinh, Nandita Mason, Pallavi Shah, M. M. Chudasaman, Snigdha Mukerji, Suhas Patvardhan, Juji Dayal, Devika Nair, Indira Chatterji, Geeta Kumar, Norma Moss, Mrs S. Mathai, Mrs A. M. Jacob, Mrs Babu Abraham, Mrs B. F. Verghese, Kunya Amina, Mr Kodar and his family, Rani Vijaya Devi, Mrs B. V. Achar, Mrs Malati Srinivasan, Mrs Ratna Rama Rao, Saraswati Vishveshwar, Mani Mann, Naomi Meadows, Mrs Bidapa, Prasad Bidapa, Leela Nadhan, Prema Srinivasan, Sita Muthiah, Prem Chandrasekhar, Mrs Madhavan, Ananda Rau of Hotel Dasaprakash, Shanta Guhan, Shah Alam Khan and his family, Sakina Mehta, Mr and Mrs Anand Lal, Mr Maharaj Karan, Mrs Taki Bilgrami, Shivi Rajeshwar, Bilkiz Alladin, Mrs Yamini Ranga Rao, Mala Rihan, Nilima Chitnis, Tara Warrior, John and Zakiya Kurrien and Mrs Kurrien, Mrs Ramabhai Bakle, Mr and Mrs Kumur Raste, Mr and Mrs Arvind Joshi of the Raviraj Hotel, Mrs Kamal Gole, Meera Bondre, Mrs Anjali Khare, Mrs Sheila Jacob, Mr and Mrs Ratanlal Kaka, Indira Bahadur, Salome Parikh, Mrs Kulu Panth, Pearl Patel, Mrs Hilla Daruwalla, Mr and Mrs Naval Havaldar, Zehra and Hassan Tyabji, Hani Mucchala, Ayman Mucchala, Mumtaz Currim, Mrs Fatima Basrai, Mrs V. Rajadhyaksha, Tarini Rajadhyaksha, Mrs Jagannathan, Mrs Marve, Mrs Amee Mistri of the Faryas Hotel, Roshan Dotiwalla, Durga Khote, Tina and Bakul Khote, Geeta Sippy, Arjun Sajnani, Uday and Vimla Mallik, Esther Moses, Rajveer Rathore, Mr A. N. Cowdhury, Mr D. K. Burman, Shrimati Bina Devi Burman, Mr Shashi Gupta and family, Anita Agarwal, Mrs Chhabi Raman, The Maharaja of Benares, Saran Bhua, Ravi and Madhu Prakash, Rashid, Rashid's cook, Naseem, Sher Singh at the Carlton Hotel, Shameem, Mrs Naheed Anees and her entire family, Joya Dutt, The Bengal Club, Ruby Palchoudhuri, Sm Rama Chakravarty, Anjali Malik, Mr and Mrs T. K. Roy, Mrs Uma Ghosh, Mrs Lali Mazumdar, Mr Rabi Das, Mrs Kamala Bose, Sm Anjana Roy, Maya Bahadur, Mrs Kamal Tayebbhai, Maharaj Kumar Shivbhadrsinhji and Nalini Kumari, The Rajmata of Jasdan, Pramodbhai C. Kalyani, Khanakhbhai Parekh, Mrs Niranjan Desai, Maharana Rajsaheb Pratapsinhji of Wankaner and the Maharani Saheba, Shambhu Prasad Harprasad Desai, Nivedita, Nirmala Raol, Veena Ben, Mamta Raol, Mr Gulam and Jawajara Muhammad, Bakshi Bashir Ahmed and his wife, Yasmin, Sakina Aga,

A TASTE OF INDIA

Fareeda Kaul, Mrs Niranjan Nath Pandita, Mrs Manohar Nath Kaul, the Oberoi group of hotels, the Taj group of hotels, the Ashok group of hotels, the Welcome group of hotels, *Gourmet* and *Asia* magazines (where some of this material has appeared before), to say nothing of the hundreds of villagers and townspeople whom I maddened with my questions.

If there are any omissions or misspellings on this list, I beg forgiveness.

I would like, very especially, to thank my daughter, Sakina, who assisted me in my travels and who kept me – and my notes – organized.

MADHUR JAFFREY

FOOD FOR BODY AND SOUL

As a child growing up in Delhi, nothing excited me more than an announcement by my middle uncle that he had asked the *khomcha-wallah* over for our Saturday tea. That was akin to telling a Western child that he could have a whole sweet or candy shop for an entire afternoon.

A *khomcha-wallah*, as it happened, had nothing sweet to offer. His normal habitat was the street, usually busy thoroughfares. Here he wandered eternally, or so it seemed to me, a basket balanced on his sturdy head, a cane stool tucked into the crook of his free arm. Whenever the crowd seemed promising, he set his stool down, lowered his basket to rest on it, and then began hawking his wares.

The basket was a mini-shop, containing a category of foods unknown in the West – hot, sour and savoury snacks known through much of North India as *chaat*. The food was half-prepared and many permutations – of ingredients, seasonings, sauces and dressings – were possible. If one asked, say, for *dahi baras*, the *khomcha-wallah* would take split pea patties (they had already been fried and softened in warm water, which also got rid of their oiliness) and put them on a 'plate' of large, semi-dried leaves. Then he took some plain yoghurt, beaten to a creamy consistency, and spread it over the top. Over the yoghurt went the salt and one or more of the yellow, red and black spice mixtures that sat in wide bowls. Those who wanted a mild, cumin-black pepper-dried mango flavour got only the black mixture. Those who said gleefully like I did, 'Make it *very* hot,' also got the yellow and red mixtures, filled with several varieties of chillies. If we had an extra craving for a sweet-and-sour taste,

1

we could ask for a tamarind chutney. A wooden spoon would disappear into the depths of a brown sauce, as thick as melted chocolate. It would emerge only to drop a dark, satiny swirl over our *dahi baras*. As we ate them, the *dahi baras* would melt in our mouths with the minimum of resistance, the hot spices would bring tears to our eyes,the yoghurt would cool us down, and the tamarind would perk up our taste buds as nothing else could. This, to us, was heaven.

From childhood onwards, an Indian is exposed to more combinations of flavours and seasonings than perhaps anyone else in the world. Our cuisine is based on this variety, which, in flavours, encompasses hot-and-sour, hot-and-nutty, sweet-and-hot, bitter-and-hot, bitter-and-sour and sweet-and-salty; in seasonings, it stretches from the freshness and sweetness of highly aromatic curry leaves to the dark pungency of the resin, asafetida, whose earthy aroma tends to startle Westerners just as much as the smell of a strong, ripe cheese does Indians.

Our spice shelves often contain more than thirty seasonings. The Indian genius lies not only in squeezing several flavours out of the same spice by roasting it, grinding it or popping it whole into hot oil (a technique known as '*baghar*'), but in combining seasonings – curry leaves with popped mustard seeds, ground roasted cumin seeds with mint, ginger and garlic with green chillies – to create a vast spectrum of tastes. It is this total mastery over seasonings that makes Indian foods quite unique.

When I was growing up in India and there was plenty of help around, most kitchens (and I speak here only of affluent homes), aside from having cooks and bearers, also had a *masalchi*, an underling to whose lot fell the tedious task of grinding, on a heavy stone, twice a day, all the spices the cook deemed necessary. The *masalchi* would arrange little hills of yellows, browns and greens on a metal plate, sometimes single seasonings such as turmeric, fresh coriander and ginger, sometimes mixtures of, say, cloves, cinnamon, nutmeg, mace and black pepper, all ground in one lot for a specific dish. Once this chore was done, it was the job of the expert – either the housewife or the head cook – to combine different spices for different dishes – ground spices with whole ones, roasted spices with fresh herbs – and to cook them to just the necessary degree. My mother, when asked to comment on a dish (cooked in a house other than her own, needless to say), might venture the opinion, 'Well, it was alright, I suppose, but the spices did taste a bit raw.' For maximum effect, the spices needed to be not only expertly blended but expertly cooked as well.

If the choice of seasonings gives one kind of variety to Indian foods, regional traditions give it quite another. India is a large country. Its size came home to me for the first time when I was still in school. But it was not in the classroom. Our official school atlases (India was still a British colony then) had the British Isles on one page, India on another. To a child, they looked just about the same size. Then, one day an older cousin brought home an 'underground' book distributed secretly by Indian freedom fighters. There was much excitement as we poured over its illicit pages. One of the pages showed an outline of India and, fitted neatly inside it, as in a jigsaw puzzle, was not just the British Isles, but *all* of Europe except for Russia. We were very impressed.

The country is vast, and, rather like Europe, it is not homogeneous. Before independence, it consisted of about 600 semi-independent kingdoms ruled over by Hindu maharajas and Muslim nawabs under British supervision, as well as large tracts of land ruled directly by the British, land that the British had divided, as and when they acquired it, into governable provinces. There were about fifteen major languages spoken across the land, as well as 1,652 minor languages and dialects, and the people belonged to at least five major faiths.

With independence, the princely kingdoms were 'coaxed' into merging with India. When the Indian government began the task of dividing this huge land into states, it wisely followed the line of least resistance and divided the country up on a linguistic basis. Each area with a major language and culture was given its own state. The idea of forcing a common language on the country has been shelved time and time again. The people are just not amenable to being herded into a melting-pot. They are proud of their separate cultures. Many have traditions (as well as poetry and literature) that go back a thousand years, and they are not about to give them up. This is true of foods as well, which are as different from one state to the next as, say, French food is from that of its neighbours, Italy and Spain.

India is, in that sense, very similar to Europe, with each state, rather like each European nation, having not only its own language, culture and foods, but its own history, its own unique geography and its own set of dominant religions. There are, of course, features that link all the states. We do, after all, have one central government. The entire country was influenced by Muslim rule, which began in earnest around the eleventh century, and later, by British colonization. And, where foods are concerned, the whole country has in common the total command over spices and seasonings.

But these foods are quite different from state to state. It is a pity that most of the Indian restaurants scattered across the world do not reflect our richly varied cuisine. They could have been the perfect showcase. One can hardly blame them, though. India has had no long tradition of fine public dining such as exists in France or Japan. Upper-class Hindus, who rarely crossed the 'seven seas' for fear of losing caste and whose meals had to be cooked and served by freshly bathed Brahmins, could scarcely be expected to dine in public places where the food had been prepared and touched by God knows who. Even in my family, where we were quite liberal, I never took a sip from my sister's glass or a bite from her apple. At least not without my mother's disapproval. Any food eaten by someone else was considered 'unclean' or *jhoota*.

With such taboos, fine restaurants did not get going until after Indian independence in 1947. It just so happened that the first few were owned and run by Punjabis. The food they served was vaguely Punjabi, vaguely North Indian 'royal'. The menu stuck. Restaurant after restaurant copied it. Home-style foods were never served, as it was felt, quite rightly I suppose, that no Indian would want to go out and pay for something that he could get in his own house. Regional foods were never served, because no one wanted to risk altering a successful formula.

While Indian restaurant food can be quite good, it is a world unto itself. India hides its real food – and the best of its food – in millions of private homes, rich and poor, scattered across its provinces. In the temperate state of Kashmir, tucked into the highest mountains of the world, I have eaten a wonderful dish of dried turnip rings cooked with sun-dried tomatoes. Snow covers much of the land in the winter so, come autumn, everything that can be dried is festooned around rafters, ceilings and roofs. The local tea, a green tea similar to some Chinese teas, is served sprinkled with almonds and cinnamon, ingredients which are known to warm the body. In tropical Tamil Nadu, where the needs of the body are quite the opposite, I have dined on superb crabs poached in a tart tamarind broth. Tamarind is cooling. Much of the South uses its temperature very cleverly to take care of some of the culinary details. Many staple dishes here require fermentation. No yeasts are used, as the mean temperature of about 80 degrees F (25 degrees C) does the work quite effortlessly. *Idlis*, small, savoury rice cakes, made faintly sour by an overnight fermentation, are served up for millions of southern breakfasts. They rely almost entirely on the weather to change a batter of ground rice and split peas into a light froth which only requires a quick steaming to become a deliciously light, highly nutritious and very digestible breakfast dish.

The South does a great deal of its cooking over steam, as a result of which every single home is equipped with large and small steaming pots. The North, where I come from, does not do any steaming at all, though it does use a technique learnt from Muslim rulers known as 'doing a *dum*'. For this, half-cooked rice and meat dishes, usually liberally sprinkled with aromatic flavourings such as attars, saffron, *garam masala* and browned onions, are put into a pot and the lid clamped shut with a seal of dough. The pot is then placed over a thin layer of smouldering ashes. A few embers are placed on the lid as well. The dish 'bakes' thus, slowly and gently. When the lid is removed, the foods are not only cooked through, but quite impregnated with haunting aromas.

Even within states, some foods are common to most of the people while others are cooked only by special communities. In Tamil Nadu, for example, I have been served foods preceded by remarks such as 'this is a typical Iyer Brahmin dish,' or 'only we Chettiyars [a trading community] make this'. The Muslim Moplas of Kerala serve stunning rice pilafs, as most Muslims do throughout India. Pilafs, after all, came to us from the Middle East. Even the Indian word for pilaf, *pullao*, is a corruption of the Persian *polo*. But, as with everything in India, the Keralites have modified the pilaf to suit their own tastes and conditions. On this coastal strip, the most favoured pilaf is studded with fresh Arabian Sea prawns, subtly flavoured with coconut milk!

All Indian food is served with either rice or bread or both, following each other in succession. In the North, it is whole-wheat breads, such as *chapatis* and *parathas*, that are commonly eaten, and in the South it is plain rice. The traditional Indian bread used to be flat, baked on cast-iron griddles rather like tortillas. The Muslims introduced ovens where sour dough and plain breads – such as *naans* and *shirmals* – could be baked. Those with natural yeast managed to rise almost an inch (a couple of centimetres). The Europeans (Dutch, French, Portuguese and English) outdid the Muslims, coming in with fat, yeasty loaves. The first Indian to set his eyes on one must have been left quite stunned. The Indians called this new bread *dubble roti*, or 'the double bread', and happily used it to mop up the good juices of many spicy stews. No foreign food was discarded. It was just made Indian. I remember that one of our favourite treats as children was to come home from school, kick off our restricting shoes and socks and pad in our loose Indian sandals to the pantry, where an obliging oven kept the leftovers from our parents' lunch warm for our after-school snacks. Sometimes there were *chapatis*, into which we would roll up some *sookhe aloo*, dry, well-spiced potatoes, and then gobble them up. At other times we would slice off about 2 inches (5 cm) from an end of a crusty *dubble roti*. The soft, fluffy part of the slice would be dug out and discarded – usually fed to the parrots in the garden. The hollow that resulted was filled with meat *korma* or whatever dish happened to be in the oven. A little mango pickle was sprinkled over the top. We then carried this treasure over to the study. Homework suddenly became almost bearable. Of course when my mother yelled out, wanting to know who had cut off both ends of both loaves of bread, we just giggled hysterically and buried our heads in our books.

The meat served in most Indian homes is generally fresh goat meat. The English referred to it as 'mutton' and that is what Indians speaking in English call it to this day. I refer to it as 'lamb', simply because, in the recipes, Western lamb is the nearest equivalent to our goat and because phrases like 'leg of goat' sound somewhat less than felicitous. If the English could get away with 'mutton', I could, surely, get away with 'lamb'.

At most Indian meals, aside from the meat, vegetables, split peas and rice or bread that are served, there are invariably relishes, yoghurt dishes, pickles and chutneys. They round off the full cycle of flavours and textures, adding bite, pungency and often vital vitamins and minerals as well. They also perk up the appetite, which tends to get sluggish in the hot weather (though, I must add, I have never suffered from this alleged sluggishness).

We eat with our hands – with the right hand, specifically, the left being used to pick up glasses of water or to serve ourselves more food. Finicky Northerners use just the very tips of their fingers, while Southerners, rather impatient with Northern pretensions, think of the whole hand as an implement – rather like a spoon – and use any part of it they deem suitable.

Around the world, food is eaten to fill stomachs and to keep bodies strong and healthy. In India, there is, frequently, a shift in emphasis. We, like everyone else, eat to survive, but we also eat to keep our bodies finely tuned, physically and spiritually.

The physical fine-tuning is achieved by a series of weekly fasts to 'cleanse the system', and by careful selection of the seasoning used in daily meals. According to the ancient Indian system of Ayurvedic medicine, all spices and herbs have been assigned medical properties. Turmeric, for example, is an antiseptic, both internal and external. Perhaps that is why it is always applied to fish before it is fried. Asafetida is a digestive which combats flatulence. Hence it is always put into pots of dried beans and split peas. Garlic is good for circulatory ailments, coriander and tamarind for constipation, cloves for toning up the heart and black pepper for giving energy to new mothers. Indians, however subliminally, are aware of this as they cook. I remember arriving in the city of Lucknow recently with the most depressing cough and cold. My octogenarian aunt, whom I was visiting, had already noticed that I had my tea without milk and sugar, my toast without butter and that I declined offers of clotted cream (*malai*) that the city residents are very partial to. 'No wonder you are sick,' my aunt declared. 'But I will fix you up.' At that, she disappeared, returning with a special tea, made with fresh ginger, black peppercorns, cloves, holy basil leaves (*tulsi*) and a little sugar. I do not know if it was my aunt's gentle ministrations or the tea, but I did start to feel much better.

Fine-tuning the spirit is quite another matter which appeared, at first, very puzzling to me. Millions of Hindus are vegetarian.

Three thousand years ago however, our forebears were meat-eaters. They even ate beef. Somewhere, as the BCs were changing to the ADs, the cult, if one call it that, of vegetarianism began to take hold – and grow. It might have been influenced by Buddhism and Jainism, two very successful movements that preached *ahimsa* or the 'non-hurting of life'. Around this time, the cow also became sacred and its meat taboo. But Hindu vegetarianism today seemed, as I examined it, to have less to do with the hurting of animals than with advancing the individual spirit along its upward path. I discovered that on holy days and on days of partial fasts, it was considered acceptable for vegetarians to eat tubers, *moong dal* and rice. Aubergines and tomatoes were not acceptable. Neither was brandy. I did not have much hope for brandy but I did want to know just how it was decided that one vegetarian product was better than another.

Answers were either unavailable or were of the 'my mother and grandmother did it' variety. Finally, a friend, the author of a book on Hinduism, offered the explanation which I paraphrase here: in Hinduism, our earthly journey from birth to death is divided into four parts. At first we are students and our duty is to study the scriptures, arts and sciences. Then we are householders and our duty is to raise and look after our families. But throughout our journey on earth, our souls are seeking union with the Universal Soul, God. To achieve this, starting with the third stage, *vanaprasha* (literally, 'retiring to the forest'), we must move away from worldly things and from all 'negative forces' in order to allow our 'soul force' to rise upwards. By the fourth stage, which few achieve, we should be totally detached ascetics.

All things (my friend continued) have their own magnetic force: some are negative, some positive. This applies to everything we eat. The only foods that Hindus should eat on days of partial fasts – and during their later life – are the 'positive' ones.

But how does one know which foods are 'positive' and which 'negative'? For most Indians, tradition suffices. Patterns laid down by ancestors are followed without questioning. Those who, like myself, question endlessly, can resort to a 'test', devised, I was told by my friend, by a Swami Poornananda. If a certain seed, a *rudraksha*, were to be suspended by a thread over a given food, it would begin to swing clockwise if the food was 'positive', anticlockwise if the food was 'negative'.

Could we do the test, I wanted to know. We set up a time and place. All kinds of food, from salt to nuts, were laid out on a large table at some distance from each other. The *rudraksha* did, indeed, swing in circles, sometimes wildly, sometimes gently, sometimes clockwise, sometimes anticlockwise, each time confirming, as I later found out, the detailed calibrations of the Swami. Onions were very 'negative'. The seed seemed to show active anger as it swung. Ginger was as 'positive' as onions were 'negative'. Salt was on the 'negative' list, as were garlic cloves, sugar, aubergines, tomatoes and red chillies. On the 'positive' list were honey, *ghee, toovar dal, moong dal*, limes, almonds, apples, rice, turmeric, ginger and green chillies. Potatoes were neutral. They seemed to mesmerize the seed to a standstill.

You may make of this what you will. I know that Indian foods from all its different regions will thrill your palates. They may, if you play your cards right, even uplift your soul.

DELHI

WITH

PUNJAB AND HARYANA

It is probably at dawn and dusk that Delhi offers the most distilled aspect of itself.

I remember as a child going away from Delhi on holidays to hill stations. When we returned – it was always a night journey by train – my mother would shake us awake as we neared the Yamuna River. Delhi lay just beyond it.

Swarms of squawking mynas and parrots would be circling the pink sky as the steam train pulled in at Shahadra, the stop just before Delhi. Our servants, who travelled in an adjacent compartment, would come in to roll up our portable bedding and to serve us our morning tea.

Tea was a simple affair, bought off vendors who marched up and down the platform with large kettles chanting, '*Chai garam, chai garam*' ('hot tea, hot tea'). It was served in handleless, terracotta cups, *mutkainas*, that added to the sugary, milky tea a delicious flavour of their own, that of the local earth. We wrapped handkerchiefs around the hot cups and took quick, short sips. Tea was quite a treat for us children. Once home, we would be subjected to our daily regimen of milk – two tall glasses of it, one in the morning and one in the early evening.

As soon as we had our tea, my mother would pull out her purse and extract from it a generous amount of coins. This was a sign that the train was about to go over the Yamuna Bridge. Each child, armed with a handful of *paisas*, would choose a position by a window. What we did next was to take a *paisa* at a time and, avoiding girders and other constructional obstructions on the bridge, hurl it into the holy currents of the Yamuna. If the coin hit the water, we had our mother's assurance that we would be blessed. If it hit a washerman beating clothes on a sandy island or a mendicant rooted to a rock in a lotus position, or the bridge, then no blessings could be expected.

We would try to get our blessings in quickly because the approaching city called for our full attention. With a refreshed sun raining gold upon it, the domes, minarets and crenelated walls of a seventeenth-century Moghul capital shimmered as they might in a miniature painting.

This was my city – the city where I was born and the city of all my ancestors, as far back as family records went. My heart invariably skipped a beat. It still does, even though now I swoop in, quite unceremoniously, from the skies, without any blessings at all from the holy waters of our local river.

Delhi, India's capital city, is a composite of so many Delhis. For the last thousand years, as dynasties and rulers replaced each other, one Delhi was torn down to build another, often with the stones of its former self. Most of these cities were built within a relatively small triangle formed by the Yamuna River and two mountain ridges. These natural barriers proved to be quite ineffective, for Delhi was invaded, pillaged or conquered by Scythians, Parthians, Turks, Afghans, Mongols (or Moghuls as they were called in their more urbane incarnation) and Britons. Some came and went, taking with them India's weavers, stonemasons and sculptors, besides a tonnage of emeralds and rubies and diamonds. Others stayed to rule, leaving a treasure in mosques, tombs, temples, palaces and churches.

Besides antiquities, Delhi's varied rulers left another legacy. Coming from distant places, they yearned for their own climate and food. They could do little about the weather except build gardens, water tanks and canals (the Moghuls had carved, marble canals rippling through their palace bedrooms) and move up to the hills in the summer. But they could eat their own food. As the years went by, some of their dishes were absorbed into the city's repertoire, others gradually changed. Persian-style pilafs, or *pullaos* that combined meat and long-grain rice, remained very much the same but *samosas*, triangular, Middle Eastern pastries that were filled with dried fruit, nuts and minced (ground) lamb in medieval times, began to be stuffed with a mixture of tartly spiced potatoes and peas. English lamb chops were still grilled but only after they had first been perked up in a marinade of ginger, garlic and hot green chillies! A formal tea at my family home today might well consist of home-made sponge cake, small lemon-curd tartlets, delicate cucumber sandwiches, *samosas* (filled, needless to say, with very spicy potatoes), *pakoris* (deep-fried vegetable fritters), *pistay-ki-lauz* (an all-pistachio sweetmeat), and, of course, tea. Not one person would consider the spread eclectic or pause for a moment to think of the varied ethnic origins of any of the dishes.

Of all Delhi's conquerors in the last millennium, the Moghuls were perhaps the most glorious. Backed by vast wealth and superb taste, they built two cities of which the seventeenth-century Shahjahanabad (now called the 'Old City') became renowned throughout the world as the seat of the 'Grand Moghul'. Here the mighty emperors ruled from their Peacock Throne, designed by jewellers to be a showcase for dazzling rubies, emeralds, sapphires and pearls. Most subjects never saw the glittering throne. Even if they were allowed into the Hall of Private Audience within the Red Fort, they had to keep their heads bowed. Those who got an oblique glance at it were filled with awe and envy. What perhaps won over the Hindu masses to these Muslim potentates was the serious – and successful – effort they made to unite the country – they even married Hindu princesses to achieve this – and the fact that they stayed to rule as Indians, not foreigners.

While the Moghuls remained in power (the British banished the last Moghul king to Burma in the mid nineteenth century), they were able to introduce to India an extravagant style of living that galvanized all of India's craftsmen into producing the most exquisite carpets, brocades, shawls, paintings and jewellery in India's history. Persian delicacy and Indian know-how were fused to create everything from vases to waistbands.

The same thing happened with food. The royal chefs were all trained in Central Asian, Persian and Afghanistani techniques. The palace demanded that they excelled themselves. An evening might begin with the emperor lolling on his beautiful carpet, wrapped in brocades and Kashmiri shawls. Wine from Shiraz might be served in a large rock crystal or jade cup set upon a gold saucer enriched with rubies, diamonds and emeralds. Dishes of fruit would be scattered about – grapes from Kabul, musk melons from Samarkand and quinces from

Kashmir. Each fruit would be marked according to its degree of excellence to spare the emperor any undue aggravation.

Food, prepared in tin-lined copper pots (they were tinned twice a month), would be tasted by at least three people. It was then placed in gold and silver dishes with domed covers, wrapped and sealed. It would arrive before the emperor in a procession led by mace bearers. A cloth would be spread, the servants would taste the food once more and the emperor would then begin to pick with his royal fingers.

The tasting was done not just to, say, check the salt, but to eliminate the very real threat of poison. The emperors themselves indulged in this common practice. Shah Jahan (the builder of the Red Fort and the Taj Mahal) once caught his favourite daughter with an unapproved beau. He smiled and continued to be civil, even going to the length of offering the beau a betel leaf – a very high honour (and a custom learnt from Hindu India). Of course, the exquisitely wrapped leaf was laced with the fiercest poison. The poor beau had no choice but to thank the emperor profusely, put the betel leaf in his mouth and commence chewing. He did not survive.

The foods laid out before Moghul royalty might well have included an aromatic basmati rice *pullao* which a seventeenth-century Englishman described as 'Rice boiled so artificially that every grain lies singly without being added together, with Spices intermixt and a boil'd Fowl in the middle.' There might also be split peas cooked with ginger and cumin seeds, lamb prepared with crushed grains, spinach simmered quickly with onion, ginger, black pepper and cardamoms, a *do piaza*, that is meat cooked with a lot of fried onions, and a *dumpukht*, meat or chicken, smothered in almonds and raisins and then braised in butter and yoghurt. Aubergines (eggplants) cooked with ginger and lime juice, *sanbusa* (*samosas* stuffed with minced meat), various skewered and grilled or pan-fried *kababs*, stuffed, boned chickens, and assorted plates of yoghurt, sweet saffron rice, breads, pickles, lime wedges, ginger shreds and raw salads would also be decorously set out. The emperors drank only Ganges water, brought daily from the north in camel caravans. The food, however, could be cooked in Yamuna water.

Most of these dishes have survived, intact, to this present day. Little did the Moghuls know that they were giving to the city a cuisine that would be cooked through much of North India and that, three centuries later, when the city learnt to accept the idea of good restaurants for public dining, these restaurants would rely heavily on the fancies of old rulers.

The Hindus of Delhi never gave up their own favourite food though some, like my family, did develop a split personality. The men in my family, right down to my father's time, learnt Persian, the Moghul court language, and knew how to appreciate the finer nuances of Persian poetry, delicate *kababs* and fine wine (with the takeover of the British, the wine changed to whisky). The women, on the other hand, were kept at home where they spoke and read Hindi well enough to master many Hindu religious texts. Most of them did not have much formal education and those that insisted upon it, like two of my aunts, were driven to a boys' college (they were the first women at St Stephen's, a missionary college in Delhi) in a curtained phaeton and had to attend classes sitting on two chairs set out separately in a corner. When they wished to play tennis, the entire court area was cleared so that no male eyes could see them dashing about in flowing sarees and tennis shoes. These women cooked quail and venison quite lovingly for their husbands but some, like my grandmother, remained vegetarian. They knew how to pickle limes and stuff them with cardamom, cumin and black pepper; they pickled watermelon rinds with mustard seeds and cooked potatoes with ginger and sour mango powder. They patiently slit okra and stuffed them with cumin and coriander and they made chickpea flour dumplings to float in a soupy *karhi*.

Even though my grandfather, like his ancestors, had been brought up in the Old City, he decided upon returning from a stay in England that he would take his entire brood and move out into what was then a country orchard just to the north of the Old City walls. Here he would set up his own little kingdom. His house, like Shah Jahan's, would have turret rooms and crenelations on the roof for soldiers' guns. The roof was to provide a splendid playground for the only army he was to see, his army of grandchildren.

On cold winter evenings a wood fire was lit in the drawing room where three upholstered benches encircled the fireplace. Here the children, about two dozen of us, would sit, playing word games and munching freshly fried cashews or Kashmiri walnuts. We were never allowed to eat the walnuts without raisins, as walnuts by themselves, so we were told, would give us the sorest throats imaginable. Nobody tested this theory as we all loved the combination. Every now and then my grandmother would send over from the distant kitchen various kinds of *pakoris*, fritters made by dipping vegetables in a thin, chickpea flour batter and deep-frying them. We would dunk the *pakoris* into a mint and green coriander chutney and devour them while they were still crisp and hot.

Behind the benches for the children was a circle of sofas and over-stuffed chairs. It was from one of these chairs that my grandfather held court. Here he would sit every night, puffing on his hookah, a tall water pipe that his servant filled, as instructed, with a special musky tobacco. Below him, on the crimson Persian carpet, two ladies, usually my mother and an aunt, sat playing *chaupar*, a dice game rather like parcheesi. My grandfather would puff on his hookah, take sips of his Scotch and soda, and imperiously direct the next moves of the dice game.

Once dinner was announced, Grandfather, accompanied by the adults, would amble slowly towards the dining room annexe. No sooner did he leave the room than we children made a dash for the hookah, forming a queue behind it. Each of us would take a quick puff, look around furtively and move on. It tasted so sweet, exotic, and – forbidden. Within minutes Grandfather's servant would hear the give-away gurgling of the pipe and rush in to shoo us away.

During those cold winter days, my favourite food was game: black buck meatballs, roasted Siberian goose (it flies all the way to India in the winter though I am told that few people eat it nowadays as they fear it has been infected by Soviet nuclear testing) and duck or quail cooked with cinnamon, cardamom, cloves, bay leaf, nutmeg and yoghurt. We ate the game with aromatic basmati rice or with *roomali roti* (handkerchief bread), flat wholewheat bread that was as fine, soft and large as a man's handkerchief. These breads were rarely made at home. They were ordered in advance and just before dinner a servant was dispatched to the Old City in a car. Just south of Jama Masjid, Emperor Shah Jahan's mosque, was a Muslim section of town that specialized not only in *roomali rotis* but in *bakarkhani*, a sumptuous layered bread, *siripai*, a fiery stew made of the head and feet of goats, and *seekh kababs*, grilled kebabs made with finely minced meat that melted in the mouth. It was from this area that the *roomali rotis* were collected. They had to be wrapped instantly in slightly damp tea-towels lest they hardend.

Grandfather loved to lecture his grandchildren on Delhi's history and his best opportunities came at family picnics. These were held in the winter or the monsoon season, not in some glorious wilderness but in the well-tended garden of an eighteenth-century tomb or a twelfth-century palace. The entire family went on the picnic. During my childhood, it did not occur to me that families could come in sizes smaller than thirty people, swelling beatifically to a few thousand at the mere hint of a wedding.

Preparations for the picnic would begin in the wee hours of the morning. All the short ladies of the house – and they were all short – would begin scurrying around in the kitchen. One would be stirring potatoes in a gingery tomato sauce; another, sitting on a low stool, would be rolling out *pooris* (small, puffed breads) by the dozen; yet another would be forming meatballs with wetted palms. Pickles had to be removed from pickling jars, fruit packed in baskets, and disposable terracotta *mutkainas* – our tea cups – given a thorough rinse. Two cars, the gleaming Plymouth and the well-worn Ford, would stand at the ready in the brick driveway.

The art of getting thirty people into two cars had long been mastered. The first layer consisted of alternating teenagers and short ladies, with the teenagers sitting perched on the edge of the seat. On their laps went the second layer of slim ten to twelve year olds. The third layer, sitting on the laps of the second layer, consisted of those under ten. The tall men and servants sat in the front seat. On *their* laps sat the fat ten to twelve year olds holding all the baskets and pots that could not be stuffed into the trunk.

The cars would groan and grunt but always start. The Plymouth would lead the Ford through the northern Kashmiri Gate of the Old City, past the St James Church built by an early nineteenth-century Anglo Indian, past Shah Jahan's Red Fort and out of the Old City though its southern gate. Soon we would be travelling along the wide, tree-lined boulevards of New Delhi, yet another Delhi, designed as the British capital in 1911. It was from here that British governor generals and viceroys, known by the Indians as 'Lord Sahibs', ruled from their own pink sandstone palace in a setting that one Englishman has described as 'the court of the Great Moghul run with the quiet precision of the Court of St James'. Beneath the entire four and a half acre palatial building (the palace is now the official residence of the Indian President) ran a full Edwardian basement, replete with domestic offices, sculleries, bakeries, larders – even a press to spew out streams of menus. Bands played when these viceroys came down to dinner, with one particular ruler choosing 'The Roast Beef of Old England'.

Our cars would now head towards open fields of mustard and millet (the mustard and millet of my childhood had given way to concrete as the city has expanded). Far away in the distance could be seen the tower towards which we were heading, the Qutb Minar, built in the twelfth century by the first Muslim dynasty to rule Hindu India.

The cars would pull up beside the gardens and unload their passengers. The short ladies, coming out last, would inhale the fresh country air with some relief and, with their hands, try vainly to iron out their now very crushed sarees. While the children rushed to climb the tall sandstone tower, the short ladies would amble to the base of the tower and, feeling that they had exerted themselves enough, amble back to the garden to pick a site for the picnic. A large cotton duree – blue with a red edging – would be spread out and on it laid a slightly smaller white sheet.

From the top of the tower, we children could survey all the other Delhis – the thirteenth-century Delhi of the Khilji dynasty, the fourteenth-century fort of the Tughlak dynasty, the fifteenth-century tombs of the Lodhi dynasty, the sixteenth-century tomb of the Moghul emperor Humanun, Shah Jahan's seventeenth-century mosque, and then British India with its elegant avenues and round shopping centre.

Soon our eyes, impelled by our stomachs, would settle on something closer – the sight of a brightly edged cotton duree over which hovered some very familiar short ladies. We would think of the meatballs cooked with cumin, coriander and yoghurt and the juicy mangoes cooling in tubs of ice ...

and we would all come thundering down the hundreds of steps.

The beginning of summer inevitably meant the coming of examination time, a period that fell, inexorably, during late April and early May. This is when hot *loo* winds blow with the ferocity of furnaces gone wild, picking up sand from the deserts of Central India and scattering it over North Indian cities. We would sit up late, learning about Moghul architecture or Tudor intransigence (we studied as much British history as Indian history), our fevered, overworked brains sustained by watermelon from across the river, orange-fleshed, sweet-sweet *Dassheri* mangoes that an aunt parcelled to us from Lucknow, and *kakris*, pencil-thin – and just as long – skinless, seedless cucumbers that were hawked in the bazaar as '*Laila ki ungliyan, Majnu ki pasliyan*', or 'The fingers of Juliet, the ribs of Romeo!'

Early in the morning, before we left to take our exams, my mother would appear with a plate of *badaam-ki-golis*, small almond balls made by soaking the nuts overnight, grinding them with sugar and cardamom and finally covering them with real silver tissue, *varak*. My mother firmly believed that almonds were brain food and that any child sent off to write two examination papers for six hours unfortified with almond balls was surely suffering from the severest form of neglect.

We would return from our ordeal hot and sticky, our fingers stained with royal blue Quink, and either irritable or ecstatic, depending upon how we thought we had fared. Waiting in the refrigerator to restore and refresh us would be huge jugs of icy buttermilk, spiced lightly with salt, pepper and freshly roasted cumin seeds.

Once exams ended, there was a surge in our movie-going. We saw many, many films – American, English and, of course. Indian. It was the Indian films that were most conducive to whetting our appetites. For one thing, they went on for three or four hours. Whole families went to see them, infants included. The films could be described as mythological-historical-tragi-comic-musicals. While they went on, there was a great deal of yelling, crying, getting up, singing along – and certainly no one minded the noisy unwrapping of newspaper cones that held *chane jor garam*, flattened chickpeas that had been highly spiced with cumin, red pepper and sour mango powder. During the long intermission, we would leave to buy *aloo-ki-tikiyas*, potato

patties, from vendors who generally posted themselves just outside the cinema door. Each vendor carried a portable charcoal
stove topped with a cast-iron griddle. The patties were shaped
from mashed potatoes, stuffed with a dough of spicy lentils and
then browned slowly in just a few drops of oil. Once they were
golden and crisp on both sides, they were lifted on to a clean,
round leaf, split open and smothered in a sour tamarind chutney. We would carry these patties on their leaf-plates back into
the cinema house and eat them in the dark as we watched our
dear hero riding across an indigo sky, dotted equidistantly with
hundreds of five-pointed stars, all cut from the same stencil.

The foods of my childhood can still be found in Delhi: many
more have been layered on. Mornings still start in a haze of
familiar smoke sent skyward by millions of stoves and cookers.
In those early hours, potatoes, peas and cauliflower are combined with ginger, turmeric and green chillies. *Chapatis*, delicate
wholewheat breads, are slapped on to cast-iron griddles – *tavas*.
These *chapatis* will be buttered lovingly, stacked, and then,
together with the vegetables and a piece of green mango pickle,
ensconced inside the compartments of a million tiffin-carriers.

Most people carry their lunches to their schools and offices.
Some lunches get to their destination in school bags, others
dangling from the handlebars of bicycles. Women labourers,
who work on construction sites, might balance theirs on their
pretty heads. Yet others, businessmen like my brother, will have
their lunches riding beside them on the front seats of their cars.

My brother's lunch is quite predictable. He will eat three,
small, delicate *chapatis* with a meat and a vegetable. The meat
might be a superb *rogan josh*, cubes of goat – with bone – cooked
with cardamom, cinnamon, cumin and red chillies. The vegetable might be fresh peas cooked with tomatoes and onions.
There will be plain yoghurt and an onion relish. I am so familiar
with my brother's office lunches because whenever I am in that
mid-town area, I stop and share them with him.

Until recently Delhi had no history of fine public dining –
Hindus have traditionally considered all foods cooked by 'out-
siders' to be unclean – yet, since the forties, it has started the
world on the *tandoori*-food craze and given birth to hundreds of
eating places that serve everything from hamburgers to Chinese
food.

Tandoori food – dishes cooked in hot, clay ovens – was brought into Delhi after India's partition in 1947. Fleeing Hindu refugees from the North-West and the Punjab came with a few clothes, a few pots, and their *tandoors*. One such enterprising family set up business in the Old City, not far from Shah Jahan's Red Fort. Tandoori chickens, red and succulent, and very mildly spiced, took the city by storm. Delhi had seen nothing like it. I can remember many college picnics (with boys!) that included this rare and rather exotic fare. Today the standard menus in most of Delhi's better restaurants – and Indian restaurants around the world – have the quick-roasted tandoori kebabs, tandoori prawns and assorted tandoori breads such as the large, leaf-shaped *naans*. These restaurants also serve the more grace-ful pilafs and meat *kormas* of Moghul heritage.

With the partition of India and the ensuing holocaust, mil-lions of Punjabi refugees poured into Delhi, more than quad-rupling its population in one painful heave. Through these refugees, Delhi acquired yet another layer of culture, that of the adventurous, outgoing, eat well – drink well Punjabis.

Punjab, already split between Pakistan and India, was further divided into the Indian states of Punjab and Haryana. The city of Lahore, with all the glamour and vitality of Paris, was lost to Pakistan as were Gujranwala's orchards of gloriously juicy *mul-tas*, blood-red oranges. Sugar-sweet *sarda* melons, delicate seed-less grapes from which my grandfather used to make wine in his cellar, and sultanas (golden raisins) that came routinely from Afghanistan, disappeared from the markets. Still, Punjab man-aged to prosper. Perhaps it was the nature of her tenacious people. They took to tractors as they had once to horses and used nuclear energy where its power could be harnessed for agriculture, turning their vast wheat fields into the granaries of the nation.

Many Punjabis are farmers, and even those who are not have close ties to the farms that they or their relatives own. Some of Punjab's best food is hearty country fare, based on good milk, buttermilk, *ghee*, and freshly harvested produce. I have Punjabi cousins (by marriage) who think nothing of swallowing a tea-spoon of *ghee* every morning as if it were a vitamin pill. Ask them about it and they say that it fills them with energy. These cousins frown upon the rest of us effete, urban Delhiwallas.

Punjabi refugees have brought their exquisite country fare to Delhi: layered *parathas* – griddle breads – stuffed with grated radishes or pomegranate seeds; buttery mustard greens (*sarson da sag*) to be eaten with fresh corn bread and washed down with enormous glasses of buttermilk; black-eyed beans or red kidney beans simmered long over slow fires; and the *dhaba* (cheap storefront restaurant) special, beloved of all students looking for a tasty bargain, *chana-bhatura*, very spicily stewed chickpeas eaten with leavened, deep-fried breads.

In spite of the plethora of restaurants in Delhi, it is still impossible to find the best of traditional Hindu food outside traditional Hindu homes.

My mother's side of the family stayed on in the Old City which, with its narrow lanes and small shops, had become quite unfashionable. My mother would take me occasionally to visit her relatives there. The food was superb, amongst the best that Delhi's Hindus could offer. A duree was spread on the floor with a white sheet on top of it. All food was placed in the centre and had to be shared. My mouth would begin to water even before the dishes had been brought in from the kitchen. There were tiny monsoon mushrooms cooked with cumin, red chillies and turmeric, potatoes cooked with tomatoes and asafetida, okra cooked with slices of dried, green mango and, in the winter, red 'bleeding' carrots pickled with mustard seeds. I would eat and eat, dipping my bread into the common plates and perspiring with the heat of the food and the heat of the day. My aunt with large teeth would then say, 'Poor child, she is so hot. She is not used to the ways of the Old City.' And she would begin to fan me with a large wet fan perfumed with aromatic *khas* roots.

Kashmiri tourists settle down to enjoy a freshly cooked breakfast beneath the imposing red sandstone walls of Shah Jahan's Red Fort, in Delhi.

A typical Indian kitchen: a grater and a *karhai* hang from the wall; cups, saucers and spoons for the tea are stored on a neat rack. In the foreground are two large earthenware vessels in which water cools by the age-old process of condensation and evaporation.

Stuffed Okra, Skewered Lamb Kebabs made with Cooked Meat, Chickpea Flour Stew with Dumplings.

All manner of quick nourishing snacks can be bought in the
street. This vendor is selling freshly roasted nuts – various kinds
of peanuts and chickpeas – as well as puffed rice (*mur muras*) on
Barakhamba Road, one of the main streets radiating outwards
from Connaught Place, the 'hub' of New Delhi.

Moghlai Spinach, Moghlai Chicken braised with Almonds and
Raisins.

Typical North Indian foods on sale in the streets of Benares.

Samosas frying in a *karhai* (*above left*). *Khoya* (*above*), the base for hundreds of sweets, is made from milk cooked slowly until the water evaporates and it turns into a 'dough'. Yoghurts, sold in terracotta pots (*below*).

A vegetarian meal being prepared. On the left, onions and ginger are being ground and on the right, chillies, mint and fresh coriander are being ground for a chutney. The long, pale green vegetables near the tomatoes are *kakris*, skinless, seedless cucumbers. Lucknow's Whole Leg of Lamb (*below*), Flaky Oven Bread and Yoghurt with Apple.

Radishes, cooked with their leaves, Dry Cauliflower, Stir-fried
Aubergine, Carrots with Dill, Spicy Potatoes.

RECIPES FROM DELHI
WITH PUNJAB AND HARYANA

STUFFED OKRA
Bhari Hui Bhindi

This absolutely delicious dish is a great favourite with my family. The okra is stuffed very simply with coriander, cumin, and lots of *amchoor*, a tart, green mango powder that is sold in most Indian grocery shops. If, for some reason, you cannot find it, leave it out. Instead, sprinkle about 2 tsp/ 10 ml of lemon juice over the top of the okra just when you are ready to cover it for the final 5 minutes of cooking. Stuffed okra is very versatile and may be served with almost any meal.

Serves 6
¾ lb/350 g whole, fresh okra
1 tbs/15 ml ground coriander seeds
1 tbs/15 ml ground cumin seeds
1 tbs/15 ml ground *amchoor* or 2 tsp/
    10 ml lemon juice
¼ tsp red chilli powder (cayenne
    pepper)
½ tsp/2.5 ml salt
freshly ground black pepper
2 oz/50 g, 1 small onion, peeled, cut in
    half lengthwise and then cut
    crosswise into fine half rings
6 tbs/90 ml vegetable oil

Rinse off the okra and pat with absorbent kitchen paper (paper towels) until quite dry. Trim the okra by cutting off the bottom tip and the top cone. (I actually prefer to peel the cone, thus leaving a conical shape on the top of the okra pod.)

In a bowl, mix together the coriander, cumin, *amchoor*, chilli powder (cayenne pepper), salt and black pepper.

One at a time, hold an okra in one hand and with the other make a long slit in it using a sharp knife. The slit should stop at least ¼ in/0.5 cm short of the two ends and it should not go right through the pod. Stick a thumb into the slit to keep it open and with the other hand, take generous pinches of the stuffing and push them into the opening. Stuff all the okra this way. There should be just enough stuffing to fill the pods.

Over a medium-high flame, heat the oil in a frying pan that is large enough to hold all the okra in a single layer. (A 10-inch/25-cm pan is ideal though one that is a bit smaller will do.) Put in the onion. Stir and fry until the onion just begins to brown. Put the okra in a single layer and turn the heat to medium low. The okra should cook slowly, uncovered. Gently turn the okra pods around until all sides are very lightly browned. This should take about 15 minutes. Cover the pan, turn the heat to low and cook for another 5 minutes.

MOGHLAI SPINACH
Moghlai Saag

This wonderfully simple spinach dish is cooked according to a sixteenth-century Moghul recipe. You could serve it with almost any meat dish and rice or as part of a vegetarian meal.

Serves 6
3 lb/1.4 kg fresh spinach
fresh ginger, about 2 in/5 cm × 1 in/
    2.5 cm × 1 in/2.5 cm
4 tbs/60 ml vegetable oil
2 oz/50 g/4 tablespoons unsalted butter
½ tsp/2.5 ml whole fennel seeds
4 whole cardamom pods
10 oz/275 g, 3 medium-sized onions,
    peeled, cut in half lengthwise and
    then cut crosswise into fine half rings
1 tsp/5 ml salt
¼ tsp red chilli powder (cayenne
    pepper)
½ tsp/2.5 ml *garam masala* (page 200)

Wash the spinach well and set it aside.
    Peel the ginger and cut it into very fine slices. Stack a few slices together at a time and cut into fine julienne strips.
    Over a medium-high flame, heat the oil and butter in a pan large enough to hold all the spinach. When the fat is hot, put in the fennel seeds and cardamom pods. Stir once and add the onions and ginger. Stir and fry until the onions turn a rich, brown colour. Now put in all the spinach, stuffing it into the pan, if necessary. Cover, and allow the spinach to wilt completely. Stir every now and then. When the spinach has wilted, turn the heat to medium, add the salt and chilli powder (cayenne pepper), cover and cook for 25 minutes.

Remove the lid and add the *garam masala*. Stir and cook the spinach, uncovered, for another 5 minutes or until there is hardly any liquid left at the bottom of the pan.

POTATOES COOKED WITH GINGER
Labdharay Aloo

This popular potato dish, eaten at school lunches, picnics and simple home meals, is generally served with a bread, such as deep-fried *pooris*, and a selection of pickles. I have also been known to serve it with pitta bread, yoghurt, a green vegetable and a chicken or meat dish. Those who are cooking Western meals will find that these potatoes taste quite wonderful with simple roast lamb.

Serves 6
2¼ lb/1 kg potatoes
fresh ginger, about 3 in/7.5 cm × 1 in/
    2.5 cm × 1 in/2.5 cm
12 oz/350 g, 2 large tomatoes
4 tbs/60 ml vegetable oil
½ tsp/2.5 ml whole cumin seeds
¼ tsp nigella seeds (*kalonji*)
⅛ tsp fenugreek seeds (*methi*)
¼ tsp ground turmeric
1 tsp/5 ml ground cumin seeds
1 tsp/5 ml ground coriander seeds
¼ tsp or more red chilli powder
    (cayenne pepper)
¾–1 tsp/4–5 ml salt

Boil the potatoes in their skins. Drain them and let them cool. Peel them and cut them into 1-in/2.5-cm dice.

24

Peel the ginger and chop it coarsely. Place it with 4tbs/60ml of water into the container of a food processor or blender. Blend.

Chop the tomatoes into very small pieces. Heat the oil in a large frying pan, sauté pan or wide-based pan over a medium-high flame. When hot, put in the whole cumin seeds, nigella seeds, and fenugreek seeds. Stir once and put in the paste from the food processor or blender as well as the turmeric. Stir for 1 minute. Add the tomatoes. Continue to stir and cook until the tomatoes have turned paste-like. Add the ground cumin, ground coriander and chilli powder (cayenne pepper). Stir once or twice. Now put in the potatoes, ½pint/300ml/1¼cups of water and the salt. Mix well and bring to a boil. Turn heat to low, cover, and simmer gently for 15 minutes.

MOGHLAI CHICKEN BRAISED WITH ALMONDS AND RAISINS
Moghlai Murgh Dumpukht

When in the seventeenth century an English traveller encountered this dish in Moghul India, he referred to it as 'Dumpoked' fowl; this was his way of saying *dumpukht*, the Moghul word for slow braising in a tightly sealed pan. In India today, this word has now been shortened to *dum*. He also described it as fowl 'boiled in butter in any small Vessel and stuffed with Raisins and Almonds'.

This dish is easy to make, mild, and very elegant. It is best served with rice and perhaps Moghlai Spinach.

Serves 6
3½lb/1.6kg chicken, skinned and cut into serving pieces
1 tsp/5ml salt
freshly ground black pepper
2tbs/30ml vegetable oil
2oz/50g/4 tablespoons unsalted butter
7whole cardamom pods
8whole cloves
2-in/5-cm cinnamon stick
2bay leaves
1oz/25g/2½tablespoons blanched, slivered almonds
1oz/25g/2½tablespoons raisins or sultanas (golden raisins)
8fl oz/250ml/1 cup plain yoghurt
1 tsp/5ml ground cumin seeds
¼–½tsp red chilli powder (cayenne pepper)

When you cut the chicken into serving pieces divide whole legs into two and whole breasts into six pieces. Spread the chicken pieces out in a single layer and sprinkle with ¼tsp of salt and some freshly ground black pepper. Pat the salt and pepper in so they adhere. Turn the chicken pieces over and sprinkle with another ¼tsp of salt and some freshly ground black pepper. Pat this in as well.

Heat the oil and butter in a large, preferably non-stick, frying pan over a medium-high flame. When hot, put in the cardamom, cloves, cinnamon, bay leaves and as many of the chicken pieces as the pan will hold in a single layer. Brown the chicken on both sides. As soon as the pieces get browned, lift them up with a set of tongs or a slotted spoon and put them in an oven-proof, flame-proof, casserole pan. Do all the chicken this way.

Put the almonds into the hot oil left

in the frying pan. Stir them once or twice. As soon as they start to brown, put in the raisins and stir once. Quickly, before the raisins start to burn, pour the contents of the frying pan, fat and all, over the chicken in the casserole pan.

Preheat the oven to 350°F/180°C/gas mark 4.

Put the yoghurt in a bowl. Add the cumin, chilli powder, (cayenne pepper) and the remaining ½ tsp/2.5 ml of salt as well as some freshly ground black pepper. Beat lightly with a fork or whisk until smooth and creamy. Pour the yoghurt over the chicken and mix well. Cover the pan tightly and place in the oven. Bake for 20 minutes. Turn the chicken pieces over and baste with the juices surrounding them. Cover tightly and return to the oven for another 20–25 minutes or until the chicken is quite tender.

When you are ready to eat, reheat the chicken over a low flame. Lift out the chicken pieces and put them in a warm serving dish. Spoon off most of the fat left in the pan. If the remaining sauce is thin, reduce it by cooking it over a medium-high flame. Pour this thick sauce over the chicken pieces.

Beware! The large, whole spices are not meant to be eaten.

SKEWERED LAMB KEBABS MADE WITH COOKED MEAT
Pakay Gosht Ke Kebab

Traditionally, all of Delhi's cubed meat kebabs – what the world calls 'shish kebabs' – are made not with raw meat but with meat that has been partially cooked first. This way, the meat gets very tender (it never remains rare, something most Delhi-wallahs would not care for) and the flavour of the spices gets all the way inside.

Once the meat has been partially cooked, you have two options. You could skewer it and brown it over live charcoal – ideal to do in the summer – or you could spread the meat out on a grilling (broiling) tray and brown it under your kitchen grill (broiler).

These kebabs may be served with Indian or Middle Eastern breads or with rice. They should be accompanied by vegetables, salads and yoghurt dishes.

Serves 6
8 fl oz/250 ml 1 cup plain yoghurt
2 tbs/30 ml ground coriander seeds
2 tsp/10 ml peeled and very finely grated fresh ginger
½ tsp/2.5 ml red chilli powder (cayenne pepper)
2 tbs/30 ml lemon juice
2 tbs/30 ml vegetable oil
1 tsp/5 ml salt
2½ lb/1 kg boned lean meat from lamb shoulder or from lamb shoulder chops, cut into 2-in/5-cm × 1-in/2.5-cm pieces
8 oz/225 g, 2 large onions, peeled and very finely chopped
½ tsp/2.5 ml ground turmeric
½ tsp/2.5 ml *garam masala* (page 200)

Put half the yoghurt, the ground coriander, ginger, chilli powder (cayenne pepper), lemon juice, oil and salt in a large bowl. Beat lightly with a fork or a whisk until smooth and creamy. Add the meat and the onion to the bowl and mix well. Set aside to marinate for 1 hour.

Put the remaining yoghurt into a wide, heavy-based pan. Add the turmeric and *garam masala* and beat lightly with a fork or a whisk until the yoghurt is smooth and creamy. Add the contents of the meat bowl to the pan. Mix. Now bring the meat to a simmer slowly on a medium flame. Cover, turn the heat to low and cook for 30–40 minutes or until the meat is almost, but not quite, done. Remove the lid, turn up the heat and boil away most of the liquid. Only a thick sauce should cling to the pieces of meat.

If you wish to grill (broil) the meat over charcoal, heat your barbecue. Skewer the meat pieces, about 6 to a skewer, and place over not too hot a fire. Turn the skewer frequently so the meat just gets lightly browned. It should not get charred.

If you wish to brown the meat indoors in your kitchen, light your grill (broiler). If you can control the heat, try not to make it fiercely hot. Spread the meat pieces out in a single layer in a grilling (broiling) tray. Brown the meat on one side then turn the pieces over and do the other side.

MINCED/GROUND LAMB PATTIES
Shami Kabab

I associate *shami kababs* with joyous, festive times. They are often taken on picnics, packed for hunting trips, served with drinks, (when they are made half their normal size) and eaten at grand meals that also include *pullaos* or *biryanis*. At their best, *shamis* should be delicate and crumbly.

Makes 8 patties and serves 4
2 oz/50 g/⅓ cup skinned *chana dal* or yellow split peas (page 200)
1 lb/450 g minced (ground) lean lamb
10 whole cloves
1 tsp/5 ml whole black peppercorns
1¾-in/2-cm cinnamon stick
6 cardamom pods
3 bay leaves
about 1½ tsp/7.5 ml salt
1½ tsp/7.5 ml peeled, finely grated fresh ginger
1 large egg
2 tbs/30 ml very finely chopped onion
1 tbs/15 ml very finely chopped fresh mint leaves
1 tsp/5 ml very finely chopped fresh, hot, green chilli
vegetable oil

For the garnish:
1 onion, cut into paper-thin rounds
fresh mint sprigs (optional)

Soak the *dal* in 8 fl oz/250 ml/1 cup of water for 2 hours. Put the *dal*, the water it was soaking in, and the minced (ground) lamb into a heavy, preferably non-stick, pan. Add the cloves, peppercorns, cinnamon, cardamom, bay leaves and salt and bring to a boil. Cover, turn the heat to very low and simmer gently for 1 hour. Remove the lid and turn the heat to medium-high. Boil off all the liquid, stirring constantly. The meat must be very dry, with no hint of liquid. Turn off the heat and allow the meat to cool.

Turn the contents of the pan into the container of a food processor. Grind until you have a fine paste. No whole spices should be visible. Add the ginger and egg. Turn the processor on again briefly, just to mix all the ingredients. Taste and add more salt if necessary. The paste will look rather unmanageable at this stage. Do not worry. Put the contents of the processor into a bowl, cover and refrigerate for at least 2 hours or overnight.

Mix together the chopped onion, mint and green chillies. Divide into eight portions.

Divide the meat paste into eight parts. Form smooth balls out of all the parts. Take one ball at a time and make a deep depression in it with your thumb. Stuff one portion of the onion-mint mixture into the depression. Cover up the depression with the paste and flatten the ball into a smooth patty, about 2½ in/6.5 cm in diameter. Form all the patties this way.

Pour enough oil into a large, heavy, non-stick, frying pan so that it covers the base to a depth of ⅛ in/0.5 cm. Heat it over a medium flame. When hot, put in as many patties as will fit in easily and fry for 3–4 minutes on each side or until they are slightly crisp and a medium brown. As they get done, drain them on any absorbent paper. Make all the patties this way.

Arrange the patties in a single layer in a large serving plate. Separate the onion rings and lay them over the patties. Garnish the plate with the sprigs of fresh mint.

CHICKPEA FLOUR STEW WITH DUMPLINGS
Karhi

We often had this soupy stew, filled with bobbing dumplings, as part of our Sunday lunch. I still serve it, with plain Basmati rice, Skewered Lamb Kebabs, a vegetable such as spinach or okra, and a crunchy salad such as Tomato, Onion and Cucumber Relish.

Serves 6
¾ pint/450 ml/2 cups plain yoghurt
4 oz/100 g/1 cup chickpea flour (gram flour/*besan*)
2 tbs/30 ml vegetable oil
¼ tsp whole cumin seeds
¼ tsp whole fennel seeds
¼ tsp nigella seeds (*kalonji*)
15 fenugreek seeds (*methi*)
1–2 whole, dried, hot, red chillies
¼ tsp ground turmeric
1 tsp/5 ml salt

For the dumplings:
4 oz/100 g/1 cup chickpea flour (gram flour/*besan*)
¼ tsp salt
½ tsp/2.5 ml bicarbonate of soda (baking soda)
about 4 fl oz/125 ml/½ cup plain yoghurt
vegetable oil

Put the ¾ pint/450 ml/2 cups of yoghurt in a large bowl. Beat lightly with a fork or whisk until smooth and creamy. Slowly add 2 pints/1.1 litres/5 cups of water and mix.

Put 4 oz/100 g/1 cup of chickpea flour in another large bowl. Very slowly, add the yoghurt mixture, a little at a time, mixing well as you do so. If lumps form, remove them as you go along before adding more of the yoghurt mixture. If the final paste is a bit lumpy, just strain it.

Heat the 2 tbs/30 ml of oil in a large pan over a medium flame. When hot, put in the whole cumin seeds, fennel seeds, nigella seeds, fenugreek seeds and, last of all, the red chillies. When the chillies darken (this just takes seconds), put in the turmeric and, a moment later, the chickpea flour and yoghurt mixture. Add the salt and bring to a boil. Turn heat to low, cover partially and simmer gently for 25 minutes. Turn off the heat.

While the *karhi* is cooking, make the dumplings. Put the 4oz/100g/1 cup of chickpea flour for the dumplings in a bowl. Add the salt and the bicarbonate of soda. Mix. Add the 4floz/125ml/½cup yoghurt and mix well with a wooden spoon. You should have a thick but 'droppable' paste. If necessary, add another 1tsp/5ml of yoghurt. Continue to beat the paste vigorously with the wooden spoon for about 10 minutes or until it becomes light and airy.

Pour vegetable oil into a large frying pan to a depth of ¾in/2cm. Heat the oil over a medium flame. When hot, lift up a blob of paste, about ¾in/2cm in diameter, on the tip of a teaspoon. Release it into the oil with the help of a second teaspoon. Make all the dumplings this way, dropping them into the oil in quick succession. Turn the dumplings around and fry them slowly until they are reddish in colour and cooked through. Remove the dumplings with a slotted spoon and place on a plate lined with absorbent kitchen paper (paper towels). Let them cool slightly and then cover tightly.

Ten minutes before you sit down to eat, heat the *karhi* over a medium flame. When hot, put in all the dumplings. Cover and continue to simmer over a low flame for another 10 minutes.

MOONG DAL COOKED WITH RED SPLIT LENTILS
Mili Hui Moong Aur Masoor Dal

In my family, we eat this simple, earthy dish quite frequently, generally with plain Basmati rice, a vegetable, such as spinach and, if we are feeling like meat, then Moghlai Chicken braised with Almonds and Raisins goes well with it.

Serves 4

3oz/75g/½ cup skinned *moong dal* (page 200)
2½oz/65g/½ cup skinned, red split lentils – *masoor dal* – (page 200)
½tsp/2.5ml ground turmeric
¾tsp/4ml salt
3tbs/45ml vegetable oil
a small pinch of ground asafetida (optional)
½tsp/2.5ml whole cumin seeds
2 cloves garlic, peeled and finely chopped
1oz/25g, 1 small onion, peeled, cut into half lengthwise and then cut crosswise into fine half rings
3oz/75g, 1 small tomato, chopped
½tsp/2.5ml ground coriander seeds
½tsp/2.5ml ground cumin seeds
¼tsp (or to taste) red chilli powder (cayenne pepper)

Pick over the *moong dal* and the red split lentils. Put them in a bowl and wash them in several changes of water. Drain and put in a small, heavy pan with 1½pints/900ml/4 cups of water and the turmeric. Bring to a boil. Cover partially, turn the heat to low and simmer gently for 1 hour or longer until soft. Add the salt and stir it in.

Heat the oil in a small frying pan over a medium flame. When hot, put in the asafetida. A few seconds later, put in the whole cumin seeds. A few seconds after that, put in the garlic and onion. Stir and fry until the onion is browned. Now put in the tomato. Stir and cook until the tomato is soft. Put in the ground coriander, ground cumin and red chilli powder (cayenne pepper). Stir once and add the contents of the frying pan to the cooked *dal*. Stir to mix. This *dal* can be reheated easily over a lowish flame.

JUJI'S
PUNJABI BLACK-EYED BEANS/ BLACK-EYED PEAS
Punjabi Lobhia

A hearty lunch-time favourite in the Punjab, this is generally served with a bread – such as *parathas*. Yoghurt, another vegetable dish such as cauliflower, meats and relishes may also be served at the same meal.

Serves 6
½ lb/225 g/1½ cups dried black-eyed beans (black-eyed peas) picked over and washed
2 × 1-in/2.5-cm cubes of fresh ginger, peeled and coarsely chopped
6–7 cloves garlic, peeled and coarsely chopped
5 tbs/75 ml vegetable oil or *ghee* (page 201)
6½ oz/190 g, 2 medium-sized onions, peeled and finely chopped
2 tsp/10 ml ground coriander seeds
1 tsp/5 ml ground cumin seeds
4 oz/100 g, 1 large tomato, chopped

4 tbs/60 ml/⅓ cup plain yoghurt
¼–1 tsp red chilli powder (cayenne pepper)
1¼ tsp/6 ml salt
2 tbs/30 ml finely chopped fresh green coriander (Chinese parsley)

Drain the beans. Put them in a pan with 2 pints/1.1 litres/5 cups of water and bring to a boil. Cover, lower the heat and simmer gently for 2 minutes. Turn off the flame. Let the pan sit, covered and undisturbed for 1 hour.

Put the ginger and garlic, along with 4 tbs/60 ml/⅓ cup of water, into the container of a food processor or electric blender. Blend until you have a paste.

Heat the oil in a heavy pan over a medium-high flame. When hot, put in the onions. Stir and fry until the onions are a medium-brown colour. Add the ginger-garlic paste. Stir and fry for 1 minute. Now put in the ground coriander and cumin. Stir for another minute. Put in the tomato. Stir and fry until the tomato is soft. Turn heat to medium. Continue to stir and fry for 2 minutes. Add 1 tbs/15 ml of the yoghurt. Stir and fry until the yoghurt is incorporated into the sauce. Add all the yoghurt this way, 1 tbs/15 ml at a time, until it is all incorporated. Continue to stir and fry for 2–3 minutes. Now add the beans and their liquid, the red chilli powder (cayenne pepper) and salt. Stir to mix and bring to a simmer. Cover, turn the heat to low and simmer gently for about 40 minutes or until the beans are tender. If there is a lot of liquid, turn up the flame a bit, remove the cover and cook for another 10 minutes or until the liquid is reduced. The beans should look fairly thick.

Sprinkle the fresh green coriander (Chinese parsley) over the top when serving.

RICE COOKED IN AN AROMATIC BROTH
Yakhni Pullao

This is a simplified version of the more classic meat *pullaos*. It requires a rich stock made either with lamb (bones are good for this) or with chicken or a combination of the two.

You could serve this mild *pullao* with most Indian and Western meals.

Serves 6
Basmati or any other long-grain rice, measured to the 15 fl oz/425 ml/2 cup level in a glass measuring jug
1½ pints/900 ml/4 cups lamb or chicken stock or a combination of the two
2 medium-sized onions, peeled, cut one of the onions in half lengthwise and then cut crosswise into fine half rings
2 cloves garlic, peeled
1-in/2.5-cm cube fresh ginger, peeled
1 tsp/5 ml whole black peppercorns
8 whole cardamom pods
1 tsp/5 ml whole cumin seeds
2 tsp/10 ml whole coriander seeds
1 tsp/5 ml whole fennel seeds
1-in/2.5-cm cinnamon stick
2 bay leaves
1 tsp/5 ml salt
4 tbs/60 ml vegetable oil

Wash the rice in several changes of water. Drain and put in a bowl. Add about 2 pints/1.1 litres/5 cups of water and leave to soak for 30 minutes. Drain the rice and leave in a strainer for 20 minutes.

Meanwhile, put the stock, the whole onion, garlic, ginger, peppercorns, cardamom pods, cumin seeds, coriander seeds, fennel seeds, cinnamon and bay leaves into a pan and bring to a simmer. Cover, lower the heat and simmer for 30 minutes. Strain, squeezing out as much liquid as possible. You should end up with 1 pint/600 ml/2½ cups of liquid. If you have more just boil it down to get the exact amount.

Heat the oil in a heavy-based pan over a medium flame. When hot, put in the sliced onion. Stir and fry until the onions brown nicely. Add the rice and the salt. Stir and sauté the rice gently without breaking any grains for 2–3 minutes. Turn the heat down if the rice begins to catch. Now add the flavoured stock and bring to a boil. Cover tightly (use a sheet of foil between the pan and the lid, if necessary), turn the heat to very low and cook for 25 minutes.

TOMATO, ONION AND CUCUMBER RELISH
Laccha

This is a very simple, everyday relish – you could almost call it a salad – that is served with most meals in Delhi.

Serves 6
3 oz/75 g, 1 medium-sized onion
4 oz/100 g, 1 medium-sized tomato, cut into thinnish slices
10 oz/275 g, 2 medium-sized

cucumbers, peeled and cut into thin
slices
2 tbs/30 ml lemon juice
½–¾ tsp/2.5–4 ml salt
¼–½ tsp red chilli powder (cayenne
pepper)
freshly ground black pepper
½ tsp/2.5 ml ground roasted cumin
seeds (page 199)

Peel the onion and cut into paper-thin
rounds. Soak in a bowl of icy water for
30 minutes. Drain and pat dry. Separate the rounds into rings.

In a serving plate, arrange the
tomato slices in a single or slightly
overlapping layer. Arrange the
cucumber slices similarly on top of the
tomatoes. Scatter the onion rings over
the cucumbers. Sprinkle the lemon
juice, salt, chilli powder (cayenne pepper), black pepper and cumin over
everything. Toss just the onion rings,
leaving the bottom layers undisturbed.

UTTAR PRADESH

WITH

RAJASTHAN AND MADHYA PRADESH

I t is a few days before Divali, the Festival of Lights, in the city of Benares and the silk merchants have just finished taking stock. It has been another bumper year.

In celebration of the festival, which is after all dedicated to Laxshmi, the goddess of wealth, and in order to keep the wheels of the silk business lubricated, sweets are being delivered to all the dealers that matter. On their heads, coolies carry trays piled high with stacks of cardboard boxes, each neatly tied with a slim ribbon. They manoeuvre their way deftly through the narrow cobbled lanes of seventeenth-century Kunj Gulley, the picturesque heart of the wholesale silk industry. Ensconced in the boxes could be *malai gujiyas*, sheets of reduced milk folded over mounds of sweetened nuts, or *lal peras*, deep red, caramelized sweetmeats, or the last of the seasonal *malpuas*, sweet pancakes of ancient origin, or perhaps *gari ka cheewra*, octagonal, wafer-thin coconut flakes that, rather like snowflakes, disappear upon entering the mouth, leaving mere hints of the coconut they came from and the powdered sugar with which they were sweetened.

The merchants, clad in fresh white *kurtas*, carry on their business from deceptively humble shops, freshly painted aqua, peach, mauve or green for Divali. The shops seem unfurnished. There is a busy black telephone on the cushioned floor, however, and large wads of money appear and disappear. Now and then, a small radio is turned on for the cricket commentary. When business gets taxing, a *lassi* is sent for from the local sweet shop. *Lassis*, yoghurt drinks, are quite superb in Benares. They come in clay cups, *purvas*, and are thick and sweet, topped with chunky squares of yoghurt cream.

Business at the retail end, in saree shops, is equally frenzied. There are Divali gifts to be given and the winter wedding season, when no respectable bride's trousseau will be considered complete without at least a few Benaresi sarees in it, is just about to begin.

Families amble into a shop, kicking off their shoes at the door, and make themselves comfortable on the mattressed floor. What kind of saree would they like to see? A brocaded *tanchoi*, a shimmering, gauze-like 'tissue' with threads of pure gold, or a self-patterned satin silk? Once that question has been settled, the next one comes fast on its heels. Tea, Coffee, a cola or *thandai*? It is best to settle on a *thandai* as it is pure ambrosia. Yellow with saffron, it consists of icy cold milk blended, in the Divali season, with almonds, pistachois, cardamom, black pepper (yes, black pepper) and sugar. It helps make shopping extremely pleasurable.

Benares, thought to be one of the world's oldest living cities (it has been bustling for at least three thousand years), is also one of Hindu India's holiest. Pilgrims from the entire nation congregate here, making religion an even bigger business – if one can call it that – than silk. The focus for the pilgrims is the River Ganges, whose holy waters here, it is believed, can wash away a lifetime of sins.

The days begin well before dawn as thousands of bathers descend the steps that line the west side of the river. They face the slowly brightening east, bathing and praying in one combined ritual. As they leave, they carry small vessels with them, filled with Ganges water. Some will use drops of it sparingly for sacred ceremonies. Others will cook every single meal with it, even boiling it to brew their tea.

There will follow a trip to a temple, with an offering of flowers and sweets, and then on to breakfast, perhaps in Kachori Gulley, or the Lane of Fried Breads. Here anyone willing to sit on a rough bench can, for small change, feast on *pooris*, deep-fried, wholewheat breads that puff up like balloons, or *kachoris*, the same bread stuffed with split peas or corn or fenugreek greens, all fresh from hot *karhais* (woks). They are eaten off leaf-plates with *ghugni*, small black chickpeas stewed with mustard and cumin seeds, or *aloo bhaji*, potatoes spiced with ginger, cumin seeds and dried mango powder, or else *aloo koda*, a delightful combination of potatoes and pumpkin. People staying in five-star hotels, such as the Taj Ganges, may order similar breakfasts, and have them on proper china, with knives and forks!

It takes years of practice to make really fine, soft *pooris*. It is said in Benares that if twenty-five pooris were stacked on a plate and a coin dropped on top of the lot, the sound of the coin hitting the plate should be heard with clarity. Each area in India is prone to its own exaggerations and this is a Benaresi version. But I did meet a lady in Benares whose *pooris* come close. This lady's *pooris* are so much in demand amongst her relatives and friends that whenever she travels, she carries her favourite and trusted rolling pin with her, just as a French chef might carry his knives.

Even though Benares, like any large Indian city, has most religions represented in it, it is, by long tradition, quite Hindu in its basic character. It was for this reason that I decided, quite arbitrarily, to concentrate here on vegetarian foods and to visit several Marwari families who specialize in them.

Marwaris, originally from Rajasthan, are from the *bania* or business community. They have settled all over the North, wherever commerce has taken them. Their food, often suggesting the austerity of their desert motherland, specially in its ingredients, is quite superb — and they are strictly vegetarian, even to the point of refraining from the use of onions and garlic.

Marwari kitchens are hallowed territory. No one may enter except professional Brahmin cooks called 'maharaj', if male, and 'maharajan', if female. Their high caste is not enough. The cooks must bathe before they enter the kitchen, wearing special, freshly washed clothing. They must see to it that no person other than themselves gets to touch a pot, or ladle. The purity of the kitchen must pass directly to the diner. It is for this reason that serving dishes are never used. Instead, the food — every dish, from vegetables to sweets — is served directly from the cooking pots on to individual metal plates, *thalis*. There was a time when orthodox Marwaris did not eat a single morsel outside their own homes. This seems to be changing now, specially with the younger generation.

At one of my lunches with a traditional Marwari family, my fully served *thali* was put before me by the cook. Arranged on it, from right to left inside the rim, was a perky salad of shredded fresh ginger, white radish and green chillies; an aubergine (egg-plant) *kalonji*, where the vegetable had been stir-fried in a *karhai* with fennel, fenugreek, coriander and red chillies until it was almost black; scrumptious potatoes and cauliflower cooked together with cumin seeds and fresh ginger; earthy *toovar dal* flavoured with *ghee*, asafetida, cumin and fenugreek seeds; a chickpea flour and yoghurt *karhi* (a soupy dish) filled with bobbing dumplings; *rasgullas* (fresh cheese balls in syrup), and yoghurt. In the centre of the *thali* were *kachoris* and *rotis* (wholewheat griddle breads). Finally, *papadums* were served, signifying that the meal had ended.

If Benares is a Hindu city, then Lucknow, also in Uttar Pradesh, is a Muslim one, and a charmingly old-fashioned one at that. There is a halva recipe in Lucknow that goes like this: take the yolks of a hundred eggs. Add equal quantities – in weight – of *ghee* (clarified butter), milk and sugar. Stir and cook gently until the halva becomes grainy like semolina. Add fine shavings of almonds and pistachios and spread out in a tray. Cool a bit and cut into squares or diamonds.

This is Lucknow, once the capital of the independent Muslim kingdom of Oudh, and the best foods here are rich. The city itself rose to greatness in the late eighteenth century when the Moghul empire was collapsing. Before the British finally subjugated it – and it took some doing – Lucknow had a brief moment in the sun.

Cooks here took special pride not only in the taste and texture of their creations but in their ability to astound and amaze their patrons. A 'pearl' pilaf, for example, might appear on the royal *dastarkhan* (floor eating arrangement). To all appearances, it would look like rice grains intermixed with pearls. But the pearls would turn out to be edible, laboriously made by mixing egg yolks with real gold and silver tissues, stuffing the mixture in the esophagus of a chicken, tying the esophagus at regular intervals with thread, boiling it, and then cutting it open to reveal the 'pearls'!

Even though the extravagances of the old court have gone the way of the court itself, the spirit of that extravagance, the civility, graciousness and flowery language have all remained, especially amongst the gentry. During the mango season, large picnics are arranged. Mangoes, it is felt, are best eaten in mango orchards, soon after they have been plucked from the tree, allowing just a brief period for cooling them down in buckets of ice. Lucknow produces many varieties of mangoes, including my childhood favourite, the Dussheri. Elongated and with a slim, flat stone, Dussheri has the sweetest orange flesh imaginable. Eaten straight off a tree, it is pure nectar.

I have been in drawing-rooms in Lucknow when the impulsive suggestion was made, 'Why do we not all go to Tunda's for kebabs?' Tunda, a Lucknow landmark, is the name of a kebab shop in the heart of the city. We then all piled into cars, the men in crisp, embroidered *kurtas*, and the women in pale summer voiles, and off we went. Since the shop is hardly the place where one can sit down and relax – it is just a simple stall – we took the kebabs away and had an elegant dinner party sitting in the cars. Tunda's kebabs are cooked in enormous cast-iron trays. They are shaped like hamburgers and are made of very finely minced (ground) meat mixed with dozens of spices, nuts and seeds including nutmeg, mace, cardamom, saffron, coconut, fennel seeds and peanuts. The kebabs, crumbly and soft, are browned on both sides and then wrapped up in a lightly leavened *paratha* or flaky griddle bread.

Kakori kababs are another Lucknow speciality. A voice on the telephone might drawl, 'I am arranging for the Kakori man tomorrow. Do come. And, please, bring the whole family.' A man from the small town of Kakori, very near Lucknow, will show up hours in advance, probably with assistants, meat, spices, charcoal and skewers, and begin working on the kebabs that have made his town famous. He will pound meat and fat for hours on end, until it is a paste. To this he will add ground spices such as poppy seeds and cloves and continue pounding with sprinklings of water until the meat paste turns almost gluey. This he will somehow wrap around skewers in cigar shapes and grill them quickly over live charcoal before they can fall off. The resulting kebabs will be slightly crisp on the outside and soft as silk on the inside. It is quite a feat to make *Kakori kababs*. It is easy to eat them.

Breakfasts in Lucknow, leisurely affairs, could consist of *kulchas*, flat, sour-dough breads eaten with *nahari,* a slow-simmered shank stew, or *roghni roti,* rich, wholewheat breads eaten with spicily fried liver. For lunch, there would be more meat – a *korma*, meat cooked with browned onions, cardamom, ginger and garlic, *toovar dal*, flavoured with garlic, carrots perhaps, flavoured with fresh dill and, in the winter, white radishes cooked with their greens.

At formal banquets, tables literally groan with food – whole marinated legs of lamb, *raan*, cooked with almonds and poppy seeds, *pasanda kababs*, 'scallopini' cut from leg of lamb, cooked with black cumin, fennel and cardamom and smoked before being served, whole chickens stuffed with quails, rice and meat cooked together in an aromatic broth, sweet pilafs, sweet-and-sour pilaf (*mutanjan*), *shirmals*, flaky oven breads flavoured with saffron, yoghurts, chutneys, to say nothing of the famous egg halva.

Betel leaves appear next, in small round silver trays with domed covers. Well-fed guests stuff them into their cheeks and keep them there, allowing the sweet, clean flavour to linger. Cheeks still bulging, they leave saying, 'What a meal . . . a meal without an equal . . . the *raan* . . . so tender, the meat was falling off the bone . . . you outdid yourself . . . truly, an incomparable meal . . .'

To the west of Uttar Pradesh, stretches the desert of Rajasthan – lots of kingdoms of Rajput warriors, now knit together into one state. Royalty here, even though Hindu, generally served the Moghuls well, marrying off their princesses to the emperors and often leading their armies into battle to fight for the consolidation of the Moghul empire. They adopted the purdah system of the Delhi court, keeping their women behind lace-like walls of filigreed stone – described as the 'millinery of masonry' – and cooked many meat and rice dishes just like their Muslim overlords. With one major difference. The Rajputs hunted and ate wild boar. In this area, as well as in Madhya Pradesh, the fat and the skin of the animal may be cooked with fried onions, coriander, cumin, garlic and ginger, and it can be used to flavour a spicy dish of *moong dal* and millet. Wild boar is also used to make an amazingly good pickle.

There are many dishes that must have been developed by Rajput warriors while on the run – or at hunting parties. Meats, including poultry, game and fish, are marinated, skewered and grilled over live fires to make *soola kababs*. On occasion, large pits are dug in the earth and lined with well-lit dried cow dung, a very common fuel in the countryside. On this is placed a large pot which, in turn, is lined with cinnamon sticks. Next a chicken, well marinated with a paste of ginger, saffron, cloves, cardamom, mace and coriander seeds, and stuffed with seasoned minced (ground) meat, is carefully placed over the cinnamon sticks so as not to touch the sides or bottom of the pot. The pot is then covered and sealed shut with dough. More lit cow dung is placed over the top and levelled off with the ground. The chicken bakes very slowly. When the pot is first opened, the aroma is quite breathtaking.

The common drink at most gatherings of old feudal families used to be *asha*, an alcoholic beverage, based on jaggery (raw sugar), that mellowed the mind with great speed. It used to be privately distilled, the clear gin-like liquid flavoured at times with saffron or fennel and drunk by men sitting in a circle, passing beakers shaped like birds and animals. Alas, private distillation is now banned, and afficionados of *asha*, complaining of quality, have turned to the more prosaic whisky and gin.

South of Uttar Pradesh lies the central Indian state of Madhya Pradesh, with its capital in Bhopal. Though the state today is made up of rather disparate elements, Bhopal city, once the capital of a large kingdom of the same name, has been Muslim, rather like Lucknow, since it was taken over by an Afghan at the beginning of the eighteenth century.

I last visited Bhopal just a month before the tragic industrial disaster and found a gracious and old-fashioned city sprawling on the banks of two large lakes. (I am told that the city is bouncing back with an immense show of courage.) The foods I was served on that trip were Muslim in character, but perfumed generously, in a very Bhopali manner.

Take the *korma* I was offered one day for lunch. Cubes of lamb had first been marinated in a mixture of ginger, garlic and salt and then fried along with black cardamom pods, bay leaves, cinnamon sticks, black cumin seeds and onions. Then beaten yoghurt, coriander and red chillies were added and the meat was allowed to braise until it was almost done. The next step was unusual. Generous amounts of whole spices – nutmeg, mace, cardamom, cloves and star anise – along with crisply browned onion slices, were thrown on a grinding stone and ground to a fine paste with sprinklings of *kewra*, a highly perfumed attar made from the pandanus flower. This paste was spread over the meat and the lid sealed with dough. The pot was then placed over gently glowing coals. More coals were spread over the lid and the meat was allowed to 'bake' in this fashion until it was perfumed all the way down to the bone. What a superb dish it was!

With the *korma* we were served *baghare chaval*, rice – also very aromatic – flavoured with lots of fresh ginger and garlic, a simple dish of spinach where the chopped up leaves were cooked quickly with fried onions and fresh red chillies (a wonderful contrast of colours), and *baigan ki boorani*, an Afghan dish, I am told, in which fried slices of aubergine (eggplant) are served with dollops of garlic-flavoured yoghurt. It was easily one of the most satisfying meals I have ever eaten.

Fish from Bhopal's lakes is also very popular. In the evenings, when the sun's glow transforms the still expanse of water into a sheet of gold, fishermen gather by the hundreds to catch excellent white-fleshed fish such as *sanwal*. This is rushed (often on bicycle) to homes tucked inside narrow lanes, some with the most charming walled courtyards sprouting guava trees and vines of cascading Bougainvillaea. It is cut, dipped first in seasoned yoghurt and then in a paste of green coriander (Chinese parsley), green chillies and garlic, and deep-fried. It is best devoured as soon as it is made, but may be served as part of a dinner that includes *achar gosht*, meat braised with green chillies and pickling spices, *murghi rizala*, chicken cooked with yoghurt and green coriander (or, as an alternative, chicken cooked in fresh pomegranate juice), *muzafir*, a sweet 'pilaf' made with fine vermicelli and nuts, and *salim gobi*, a whole head of cauliflower, cooked with ginger, red chillies and garlic.

The meal ends with betel leaves, usually prepared by the eldest lady of the house and served by one of the younger ones. Betel leaves, and all the paraphernalia that is attached to them, figure quite prominently in a Bhopali's life. In the old days, when a young bride came into her new home, by pre-nuptial arrangement her husband gave her an allowance which was euphemistically called 'expenses for the betel-box'. Even today, a true Bhopali is known as a 'quicklime licking Bhopali', quicklime being one of the ingredients used in preparing betel leaves, an ingredient for which Bhopalis seem to have a great fondness.

In Bhopal, it is not at all unusual to see a gentleman with a briefcase suddenly stop and take from it several items. First a silver box with a wet lining of red cloth. This contains crisp, green betel leaves smeared with a little katechu paste. The gentleman will pop two such leaves into his mouth. Then he will pull out a small cloth pouch, hand sewn and embroidered with beads. It has four strings, two to open it, and two to close it. Inside are three compartments, one for neatly cut pieces of betel nut, one for whole cardamom pods and cloves and the last for tobacco. The gentleman will open the pouch, take a little bit from each compartment and pop them into his mouth as well. He will then close the pouch. He is not done yet. Attached to the ends of the four strings are the following: a small phial filled with quicklime, a tiny spoon to remove the quicklime, a toothpick and an earpick – all made of silver. The gentleman will open the phial, remove some quicklime and put it into his mouth. Then he will start to clean his ears.

RECIPES FROM UTTAR PRADESH
WITH RAJASTHAN AND MADHYA PRADESH

CARROTS WITH DILL
Gaajar Aur Sooay Ki Bhaji

A quick and easy dish that may be served both with Indian and Western meals. It goes particularly well with Skewered Lamb Kebabs made with Cooked Meat or Quick Kebabs and Flaky Pan Bread.

Serves 4
1 lb/450 g carrots, peeled
¼-in/0.5-cm cube ginger, peeled
4 tbs/60 ml vegetable oil
½ tsp/2.5 ml whole cumin seeds
⅛ tsp ground asafetida (optional)
1–2 fresh hot, green chillies, finely
   chopped
1 tsp/5 ml ground coriander seeds
¼ tsp ground turmeric
1 oz/25 g/⅔ cup cleaned and chopped
   fresh dill
½ tsp/2.5 ml salt.

Cut the carrots, crosswise, in ⅛-in/0.25-cm thick slices.

Cut the ginger, crosswise, into very thin slices. Stacking the slices over each other, cut them, first into very thin strips and then cut the strips into minute dice.

Heat the oil in a frying pan, wok or *karhai* over a medium flame. When hot, put in the cumin seeds. A few seconds later, put in the asafetida. A second later, put in the ginger and green chillies. When the ginger starts to brown, put in the carrots, coriander and turmeric. Stir for 2 minutes. Add the dill and the salt. Stir. Cover, lower the heat and simmer for 1–2 minutes or until the carrots are just done. Lift the carrots out of the pan with a slotted spoon, leaving as much oil behind as possible.

RADISHES COOKED WITH THEIR LEAVES
Mooli Ka Saag

A simple dish, enjoyed equally by peasants and jetsetters in Uttar Pradesh, this may be served with almost all Indian meals. It has a slightly bitter taste that I happen to adore. I love it best with a sauced meat or chicken dish, some plain yoghurt, an Indian bread and some nice, hot pickle. Oh yes, some relish with onions to give the meal a little crunch!

Normally, long white radishes (*mooli*) are used in India. They are not always easy to find in the West. When I do find them, I find them minus their precious green leaves. In desperation, I decided one day to substitute radishes. They did, naturally, lose their colour during the cooking, but they were delicious.

Serves 4
about 1½ lb/700 g, 2 large bunches
     white radish (*mooli*) or red radishes
     with green leaves
1-in/2.5-cm cube fresh ginger, peeled
3–5 fresh, hot green chillies
5 tbs/75 ml vegetable oil
about ½ tsp/2.5 ml salt
2 tsp/10 ml ground coriander seeds
1 tsp/5 ml ground cumin seeds
¼ tsp ground turmeric

Break off and separate the radish
leaves. Wash well to remove all grit.
Holding a handful of greens at a time,
cut crosswise at ¼-in/0.5-cm intervals,
chopping up both the leaves and the
stems. Put in a bowl.

Wash the radishes and discard their
tails. Cut them into ¼-in/0.5-cm dice.

Cut the ginger, crosswise, into very
fine slices. Stacking several slices over
each other at a time, cut them first into
very thin strips and then cut the strips,
crosswise, into minute dice. Cut the
green chillies, crosswise, into very thin
slices.

Heat the oil in a large, non-stick
frying pan, wok or *karhai* over a
medium-high flame. When hot, put in
the ginger and the green chillies. Stir
and fry until the ginger starts to
brown. Now put in the chopped radish
leaves, the chopped radishes, salt, coriander, cumin and turmeric. Stir.
Cover and cook on a medium-low heat
for about 15 minutes or until the
greens are tender. Remove the cover,
turn the heat up and boil away any
liquid that may have formed.

**STIR-FRIED AUBERGINE/
EGGPLANT**
Baigan Ki Kalonji

Although this recipe comes from a
maharaj – professional Brahmin cook,
working for a Benares family – the
seasonings in it have very Bengali
overtones. It is interesting to speculate
on the reasons. First of all, Bengal is
not very far from Benares – and its
influence extends well beyond its bor-
ders. Secondly, *maharajs* work for a
successful business community of *Banias* and *Marwaris* that have settled over
much of the northern half of India.
Many live in Calcutta, Bengal's capital,
and this could account for some of the
cook's leanings.

This dish should be made, ideally, in
a heavy wok or *karhai*, though I have
cooked it, quite successfully, in a
frying pan as well. You could serve it
with Chicken with Apricots and Potato
Straws, Plain Rice and Tomato and
Onion with Yoghurt.

Serves 4
5 tbs/75 ml/6 tablespoons mustard oil
     or vegetable oil
1 tsp/5 ml *panchphoran* (page 202)
⅛ tsp ground asafetida (optional)
1 lb 2 oz/500 g, 1 medium-sized
     aubergine (eggplant), cut, with skin,
     into 1-in/2.5-cm cubes
2 tsp/10 ml ground coriander seeds
about ¼ tsp red chilli powder (cayenne
     pepper)
¼ tsp ground turmeric
½ tsp/2.5 ml salt
½ tsp/2.5 ml ground *amchoor* (page
     196) or about 1 tsp/5 ml lemon juice

Heat the oil in wok, *karhai* or frying pan over a medium-high flame. If you are using mustard oil, let it get very hot and smoke for a few seconds to release it pungency. However, if you are using a different type of oil do not let it get smokingly hot. Put in the *panchphoran* and asafetida. A second or two later, put in the aubergine (eggplant). Stir for 1 minute and turn the heat down to medium. Put in the coriander, chilli powder (cayenne pepper), turmeric and salt. Now keep stirring and frying for 15–20 minutes, adding 1 tbs/15 ml of water every minute or so, until the vegetable is cooked. It will brown during this period. Sprinkle the *amchoor* over the top and stir again.

NAHEED ANEES'

AUBERGINE/EGGPLANT WITH A YOGHURT SAUCE

Baigan Ki Boorani

Here is a dish eaten by the aristocratic Muslim families of Bhopal. It combines three things that I love – aubergine (eggplant), garlic – lots of it, and yoghurt. It shows its Afghan/Persian ancestry by not being the slightest bit hot.

You may serve it with almost any Indian meal. I find that it goes particularly well at a festive meal with Lucknow's Whole Leg of Lamb and Hyderabadi Pilaf of Rice and Split Peas. You should serve some crunchy relish on the side as well, even if it is just slices of cucumbers seasoned with salt, pepper and lemon juice.

Serves 3–4

about 1 lb/450 g, 1 large aubergine (eggplant)
2 tablespoons/30 ml/ground coriander seeds
1½ tsp/7.5 ml ground turmeric
9 cloves garlic, peeled and mashed to a pulp – keep one of the mashed garlic cloves separated from the rest
salt
about 9 tbs/135 ml/¾ cup vegetable oil
6 oz/175 g, 2 medium-sized onions, peeled, cut in half lengthwise and then cut crosswise into very fine, even, half rings
8 fl oz/250 ml/1 cup plain yoghurt

Cut the aubergine (eggplant), crosswise into ½-in/1-cm thick rounds.

Put the coriander seeds, turmeric and 8 of the mashed garlic cloves into a small bowl. Add ¼ tsp of salt and 4 tbs/60 ml/⅓ cup of water. Mix.

Line 2 dinner plates with absorbent kitchen paper (paper towels) and set aside.

Heat 5 tbs/75 ml/½ cup of the oil in a frying pan, preferably a non-stick one, over a medium-high flame. When hot, put in the onions. Stir and fry until the onions have turned dark brown and crisp. Remove with a slotted spoon and spread out on one of the plates lined with absorbent kitchen paper (paper towels).

Turn the heat down to medium and put in as many aubergine (eggplant) slices as the pan will hold in a single layer. They will suck up the oil. Let one side brown lightly and then turn the slices over. Add another 2 tbs/30 ml/3 tablespoons of oil, dribbling it along the sides of the pan. Brown the second side. Turn the slices over once more, browning the first side more thoroughly. Remove the slices with a slotted spoon and put on the second dinner plate lined with absorbent kitchen paper (paper towels). Put in a second, and, if needed, a third batch of aubergine (eggplant) slices and cook the same way, adding 2 tbs/30 ml/3 tablespoons of oil after turning the aubergine (eggplant) slices over.

Put the coriander seed, turmeric and garlic mixture into the oil. Stir and fry it for 2 minutes or so. The paste should dry up and the garlic should get properly fried. Now add 2 tbs/30 ml/¼ cup of water. Stir once and turn off the heat.

Put the yoghurt in a bowl. Add the 1 remaining mashed garlic clove and ¼ tsp of salt to it. Stir to mix.

When you get ready to eat, sprinkle the aubergine (eggplant) slices with about ¼ tsp of salt and arrange them, in a single layer, in a large serving plate. Spoon some of the coriander spice mixture over each slice, spreading it over the top. Now cover the slices with large dollops of the yoghurt. Crumble the browned onions and scatter them over the yoghurt. Serve at room temperature.

MRS CHHABI RAMAN'S
DRY CAULIFLOWER
Sookhi Gobi

It is important for many of India's cauliflower dishes that the vegetable be cut quite small while preserving the shape of the flowerets. To do this, break off a large floweret. Now try breaking or cutting it into small flowerets, bearing in mind that each floweret should have a proportionate stem. You should end up with a floweret no wider or longer than 1 in/ 2.5 cm. Long stems should be cut crosswise into ¼-in/0.5-cm slices and added to the dish.

This lightly spiced vegetable can be served with all Indian meals. I find it also goes quite well with meals of roasted and grilled (broiled) meats. My children love to add it, cold, to a dressed green salad – a final toss and it is ready to be eaten with cold meats or other salads.

Serves 6
2-in/5-cm cube fresh ginger, peeled
6 tbs/90 ml/½ cup vegetable oil
⅛ tsp ground asafetida
⅛ tsp whole cumin seeds
¼–½ tsp red chilli powder (cayenne pepper)
4 tsp/20 ml ground coriander seeds
1 tsp/5 ml ground turmeric
2 lb/900 g head of cauliflower, cut into 1-in/2.5-cm flowerets (see above)
1½ tsp/7½ ml salt
½ tsp/2.5 ml *garam masala* (page 200)
1 tsp/5 ml ground *amchoor* (page 196) or 2 tsp/10 ml lemon juice (more may be added, if desired)

Cut the ginger, crosswise, into very thin slices. Stacking several of the slices over each other at a time, cut them first into very thin strips and then cut the strips crosswise into minute dice.

Heat the oil in a very large frying pan, wok, *karhai* or other wide utensil over a medium-high flame. When hot, put in the asafetida and, a second later, the cumin seeds. As soon as the cumin seeds begin to sizzle, put in the ginger. Stir the ginger around for a few seconds until it just starts to brown. Now put in the red chilli powder (cayenne pepper), coriander and turmeric. Stir once and quickly put in the cut cauliflower and salt. Stir the cauliflower around for 1 minute. Add 4 tbs/60 ml of water and cover the pan immediately. Turn heat to low and cook for 5–10 minutes or until the cauliflower is just done. Stir once or twice during this period. (Add 1 tbs/15 ml more water if it seems to dry out.)

When the cauliflower is just done, remove the lid. If there is any liquid in the pan, dry it off by turning up the heat a bit. Sprinkle the *garam masala* and *amchoor* over the top and stir to mix.

SHRIMATI BINA DEVI BURMAN'S
SPICY POTATOES
Aloo Bhaji

The lady whose name appears above this recipe is a superb cook. She is not a professional – just one of those many wives and mothers in India who can, without any fanfare, turn out three outstanding meals every day.

I had this exquisite potato dish for breakfast in the bazaars of the old city of Benares, where it was served with *kachoris*, stuffed fried breads, and pickles. The cook there had casually tossed off the recipe to me as he stirred the contents of his enormous *karhai*. As often happens in these cases, the recipe was incomplete and I found

myself turning to the delightful and knowledgeable matriarch of the Burman household for help. Here is her recipe. The potatoes are never cut with a knife. They are just boiled and peeled and then broken by hand into small pieces. They are best eaten with Pooris.

Serves 4

1½ lb/700 g, 5 medium-sized firm, waxy potatoes, preferably new or red
¾-in/2-cm cube fresh ginger, peeled
5 tbs/75 ml vegetable oil
1 tsp/5 ml whole black mustard seeds
½ tsp/2.5 ml whole cumin seeds
pinch ground asafetida
1–2 fresh, hot green chillies, very finely chopped
1½ tsp/7.5 ml ground coriander seeds
¼ tsp ground turmeric
½ tsp/2.5 ml red chilli (cayenne pepper)
1–1½ tsp/7.5 ml ground *amchoor* (page 196) or lemon juice
1–1½ tsp/5–7.5 ml salt
¾ tsp/4 ml *garam masala* (page 200)

Boil the potatoes. Allow them to cool a bit and peel. Break them by hand so that no piece is larger than ½ in/1 cm on any of its sides. There will be some very small pieces but that is as it should be.

Cut the ginger crosswise into very thin slices. Stacking several slices over each other, cut them first into very thin strips and then cut the strips, crosswise, into minute dice.

Heat the oil in a wok, *karhai* or a non-stick frying pan over a medium flame. When hot, put in the mustard seeds. As soon as the seeds begin to pop, put in first the cumin seeds and, a second later, the asafetida. Now put in the ginger and green chillies. Stir for a few seconds until the ginger gets lightly browned. Now put in the coriander, turmeric and red chilli powder (cayenne pepper). Stir once and put in all the broken potatoes. Stir and fry for 1 minute. Now put in about 4 fl oz/ 125 ml/½ cup of water. Lower the heat and mix gently for ½ minute. Add the *amchoor*, salt and *garam masala*. Stir gently to mix and cook for another minute.

MRS PRABHA GUPTA'S
POTATOES AND PEAS IN A YOGHURT SAUCE
Aloo Matar Ki Karhi

Throughout India, yoghurt is eaten in many forms, including those that require that it be heated. As yoghurt curdles when boiled, it is first stabilized with chickpea flour. The pulse (legume) flour adds extra nutrition to the dish – a very important consideration for India's numerous vegetarians. This recipe comes from one such Benares family of *Banias* or businessmen. *Karhis*, eaten all over India, have endless regional variations and may be served with Plain Rice or with Indian breads. Other meats and vegetables can also be served at the same meal.

Serves 4
1-in/2.5-cm fresh ginger, peeled
3 tbs/45 ml vegetable oil
½ tsp/2.5 ml whole black mustard seeds
½ tsp/2.5 ml whole cumin seeds
1–2 fresh, hot, green chillies, very finely chopped
12 oz/350 g, 3 medium-sized potatoes, peeled and cut into 1-in/2.5-cm dice
⅛ tsp ground turmeric
½ pint/300 ml/1¼ cups plain yoghurt
1 oz/25 g/2 tablespoons + 1 teaspoon chickpea flour (gram flour/*besan*)
1 tsp/5 ml salt
¼ tsp sugar
5 oz/150 g/1 cup fresh or frozen, shelled peas (if frozen, defrost enough to separate)

Cut the ginger, crosswise, into very thin slices. Stacking a few of the slices on top of each other at a time, cut them first into very thin strips and then cut the strips crosswise into minute dice.

Heat the oil in a wide, heavy-based pan over a medium-high flame. When hot, put in the mustard seeds. As soon as the seeds begin to pop (this takes just a few seconds), put in the cumin seeds. A few seconds later, put in the ginger and the green chillies. Stir for ½ minute and put in the potatoes and the turmeric. Stir the potatoes once or twice to mix, and then put in ¼ pint/ 150 ml/⅔ cup of water. Cover, turn the heat to low and simmer gently for 6–8 minutes or until the potatoes are just tender.

While the potatoes are cooking, put the yoghurt in a bowl. Beat lightly with a fork or whisk until smooth and creamy. Add ½ pint/300 ml/1¼ cups of water and mix again. Put the chickpea flour in another bowl. Slowly add the yoghurt mixture, mixing all the time to avoid lumps. (If there are any lumps, strain the mixture through a sieve.) Add just ½tsp/2.5ml of the salt and all the sugar to the yoghurt-chickpea flour mixture and stir.

When the potatoes are just tender, add the peas and the remaining ½tsp/2.5ml of salt. Mix. Cover and continue to cook for 2–3 minutes or until the peas are tender. Now pour in the yoghurt-chickpea flour mixture. Stir as you bring it to a simmer over a medium flame. Lower the flame again and simmer gently for 2 minutes.

NAHEED ANEES'
BHOPALI FISH WITH GREEN SEASONINGS
Bhopali Hare Masale Ki Macchli

Fish abound in Bhopal's lakes and anglers line the shores on most weekends and holidays. Here is one simple but tasty way in which the freshly-caught fish is cooked. You may deep-fry it in a wok or *karhai*, or else shallow fry it in a frying pan, making sure the oil comes at least halfway up the pieces of fish.

This dish may be served with Bhopali Pilaf with Peas and Carrots, and Aubergine/Eggplant with a Yoghurt Sauce – or, if you like, with boiled potatoes and a green salad.

Serves 4
1½lb/700g thick-cut fillets of any firm, white-fleshed fish such as cod, halibut, haddock, scrod or red snapper, or 1¾lb/800g of 'steaks' with bone
salt
2tbs/30ml lemon juice
3oz/75g, about 1¼ cups, well packed

fresh green coriander (Chinese parsley)
6 fresh hot green chillies
4–6 cloves garlic, peeled
6floz/175ml/¾cup plain yoghurt
vegetable oil for deep or shallow frying (see note above)

If you have a large fillet, cut it into pieces that are about 2–2½in/5–6.5cm long and 1½in/4cm wide. Spread the pieces out in a single layer in a large plate and sprinkle with about ⅓tsp of salt and 1tbs/15ml of lemon juice. Turn the pieces over and repeat with another ⅓tsp of salt and 1tbs/15ml of lemon juice. Set the plate at a tilt and leave it tilted for 2–3 hours. As water accumulates at one end, discard it.

Put the green coriander (Chinese parsley), green chillies, garlic, ¼tsp of salt and 2tbs/30ml of water into the container of a food processor or blender. Blend until you have a paste. Empty the paste into a deep dish or shallow bowl. Put the yoghurt into another deep dish or shallow bowl. Add ¼tsp of salt to the yoghurt and mix it in.

Set the oil to heat in a wok, *karhai* or frying pan over a medium flame. When very hot, dip 2 or 3 pieces of fish, first in the yoghurt and then in the green paste to cover thoroughly and then put them in the hot oil. Fry for about 5 minutes, turning the pieces over once, until the fish is cooked through. Remove with a slotted spoon. Fry all the pieces of fish this way and serve hot.

RAJASTHANI GRILLED (BROILED) OR BAKED CHICKEN
Rajasthani Murgh Ka Soola

In Rajasthan, the men – who have traditionally been warriors – do a great deal of outdoor cooking, generally of meats which are skewered and cooked over an open fire. There are many variations of this particular dish. The one here happens to be the simplest. I have adapted it so the cooking can be done without skewers over a charcoal grill or indoors in an oven.

Ideally, the chicken should be marinated overnight though, at a pinch, 4 hours will do.

You could serve this with Aubergine/Eggplant with a Yoghurt Sauce and Bhopali Pilaf with Peas and Carrots. I sometimes serve it with a plain green salad.

Serves 4

2 lb/900 g chicken, cut into serving pieces (whole legs cut into 2 and whole breasts into 4)
salt
2 tbs/30 ml lemon juice
5 tbs/75 ml vegetable oil
4 oz/100 g, 1 large onion, peeled, cut in half lengthwise and then cut crosswise into fine half rings
8 large cloves garlic, peeled and sliced crosswise
3 tbs/45 ml/¼ cup slivered, blanched almonds
2 × 1-in/2.5-cm cubes of fresh ginger, peeled and coarsely chopped
1½ tsp/7.5 ml *garam masala* (page 200)
4 tsp/60 ml/⅓ cup plain yoghurt
½–¾ tsp/2.5–4 ml red chilli powder (cayenne pepper)

Skin the chicken pieces and spread them out in a large plate in a single layer. Prick them thoroughly with a tip of a sharp knife and then sprinkle ¼ tsp of salt and 1 tbs/15 ml of lemon juice over them. Turn the pieces over and prick them again with the knife and sprinkle another ¼ tsp of salt and 1 tbs/15 ml of lemon juice over this second side. Rub the salt and lemon juice into the flesh. Put the chicken pieces in a bowl and set aside for 1 hour or more. Turn the chicken pieces over a few times during this period.

Meanwhile, prepare the second marinade: heat the oil in a frying pan over a medium-high flame. When hot, put in the onion and garlic. Stir and fry until the onion turns reddish-brown in colour. Turn heat to low as you remove the onion and garlic with a slotted spoon and place in a bowl. Put the almonds into the same hot oil. Stir and fry for a few seconds until they turn golden brown. Remove with a slotted spoon and put with the onion and garlic. Turn off the heat and save the oil in the pan.

Put the fried onion, garlic and almonds, as well as the ginger and 5 tbs/75 ml/6 tablespoons of water, into the container of a food processor or blender. Blend until you have a smooth paste. Empty into a bowl. Add the *garam masala*, yoghurt, red chilli powder (cayenne pepper) and ½ tsp/2.5 ml of salt. Mix. Pour this marinade over the chicken and mix well. Prick the chicken pieces again with the point of a sharp knife, again pushing as much of the marinade into the flesh as possible. Cover the chicken and refrigerate overnight.

49

To grill (broil) outdoors over charcoal: light the charcoal and let it get ashen-white. Make sure that the grill (broiler) is placed so it is at least 5 in/12.5 cm away from the source of heat. Spread the chicken pieces out on the grill (broiler). Extra marinade should be put on top of the pieces. The chicken should cook slowly. Turn the pieces from time to time and cook for about 40 minutes in all. If your grill (broiler) is the type with a cover, you could use it after you have browned the chicken on both sides. Baste the chicken frequently with the oil left over from frying the onion, garlic and almonds.

To bake the chicken in an oven: preheat the oven to 400°F/200°C/gas mark 6. Spread the chicken pieces out in a shallow baking tray in a single layer. Extra marinade can be put on top of the pieces. Dribble half of the oil left over from frying the onion, garlic and almonds over the chicken and put the baking tray in the oven. Bake for 20 minutes. Turn the chicken pieces over. Dribble the remaining oil over the chicken and return it to the oven. Bake for another 20–25 minutes, basting it once or twice with the juices.

QUDSIA'S
LAMB COOKED WITH PICKLING SPICES
Achar Gosht

A recipe from Bhopal, this is a tart, spicy dish that tastes as good with Indian breads – such as *parathas* – as with any rice dish. Any vegetable dish from Delhi or Uttar Pradesh may be served with it as well.

Serves 6
3×1-in/2.5-cm cubes of fresh ginger, peeled and coarsely chopped
6–8 cloves garlic, peeled and coarsely chopped
5 oz/150 g, 2 smallish onions, peeled, one coarsely chopped, the other cut in half lengthwise and then cut crosswise into fine half rings
1 bay leaf, crumbled
2 large black cardamom pods
1-in/2.5-cm cinnamon stick
5 whole cloves
½ tsp/2.5 ml whole cumin seeds
½ tsp/2.5 ml whole black peppercorns
7 whole fresh green chillies
½ tsp/2.5 ml whole black mustard seeds
⅛ tsp whole fenugreek seeds
⅛ tsp whole nigella seeds (*kalonji*)
5 tbs/75 ml/½ cup vegetable oil
2 lb/900 g boneless meat from lamb shoulders, cut into 1½-in/4-cm cubes
2 tbs/30 ml ground coriander seeds
½ tsp/2.5 ml red chilli powder (cayenne pepper)
¼ tsp turmeric
¼ tsp salt
3 tbs/45 ml lemon juice

Put the ginger, garlic, and the chopped onion into the container of a food processor or blender. Blend, adding about 2 tb/30 ml of water or just enough to make a smooth paste.

Put the bay leaf, black cardamom pods, cinnamon, cloves, black cumin seeds and peppercorns into a mortar and crush very lightly. The spices should just break up slightly.

Cut long slits in the green chillies, staying away from the top and bottom end. Mix the whole cumin seeds, mustard seeds, fenugreek and nigella seeds and carefully stuff the green chillies with this mixture. (As green chillies vary in size, you may have some mixture left over. Save it for another day.)

Heat the oil in a wide, heavy pan over a medium flame. When hot, put in the lightly crushed spices from the mortar. Stir once or twice. Now put in the sliced onion. Stir and fry for 10–12 minutes or until they brown a bit on all sides. Add the meat. Stir and brown for 7–8 minutes. Add the ginger-garlic-onion paste. Stir and fry for another 10 minutes or until the paste has browned. If it sticks to the pan, just sprinkle in some water and keep stirring. Put in the coriander, red chilli powder (cayenne pepper) and turmeric. Stir. Cover tightly, first with foil and then a lid, turn the heat to low and simmer gently for 20 minutes. Remove the lid and foil. Put in the stuffed green chillies and the lemon juice. Stir. Cover again with the foil and the lid and cook on a very low heat for another 25–30 minutes or until the meat is quite tender.

RASHID'S COOK, NASEEM, MAKES
LUCKNOW'S WHOLE LEG OF LAMB
Lucknavi Raan

Many of the meats in North India are tenderized with green papaya before they are cooked. This gives them a soft and uniquely Indian texture. In my effort to try and get the same texture, I discovered that an 'all natural' meat tenderizer found in US supermarkets contains papain from the papaya fruit. It contains salt as well, which works quite well for this recipe as the meat is supposed to be rubbed with both green papaya and salt at the same time.

If you happen to have a papaya tree and want to use its fruit for this recipe, pick a small 3–4-in/7.5–10-cm long, *unripe*, hard green fruit and use about half of it, skin and all, ground up first in a blender or food processor.

Rather like a pot roast, this leg may be served with rice, potatoes and vegetables, or with Flaky Oven Bread, vegetables and relishes.

Serves 4–6
5-lb/2.3-kg leg of lamb with the H-bone removed or 5-lb/2.3-kg from the slimmer half of a very large 8–9-lb/3.6–4-kg leg of lamb
2 tsp/10 ml meat tenderizer mixed with 4 tbs/60 ml/¼ cup plain yoghurt
2 tbs/30 ml whole cumin seeds
2 tbs/30 ml whole white poppy seeds or blanched, slivered almonds
1 oz/25 g/3 tablespoons chickpea flour (gram flour/*besan*)
1 whole nutmeg, lightly crushed
2-in/5-cm cinnamon stick, broken up
9 whole cardamom pods
1 tbs/15 ml black peppercorns
1½ tsp/7.5 ml whole cloves
1½ tsp/7.5 ml whole mace
4–5 whole, large black cardamom pods (omit if unavailable)
5–6 whole dried hot red chillies (use more or less, as desired)
¾ pint/450 ml/2 cups plain yoghurt
1 tbs/15 ml bright red paprika
good ¼ pint/good 150 ml/good ⅔ cup vegetable oil
8 oz/225 g, 2 large onions, peeled,

halved lengthwise and cut into very fine half rings

Trim off all the outside fat from the leg and cut or pull off the parchment-like fell that covers some of it. Cut many deep gashes in the meat – about ½-in/1-cm apart – with the point of a sharp knife, and then push the meat tenderizer-yoghurt mixture deep into these gashes. Cover the leg with the same mixture and set aside for 30 minutes to 1 hour.

Meanwhile, put the cumin seeds into a small, cast-iron frying pan over a medium flame. Stir and roast the seeds until they are a shade darker and give off a lovely, roasted aroma. Put the seeds into the container of a clean coffee grinder or other spice grinder and grind as finely as possible. Empty into a large bowl.

Put the poppy seeds into the same frying pan and roast in the same way as the cumin seeds. Grind also and put with the ground cumin seeds.

Put the chickpea flour into the same frying pan. Stir and roast over a medium-low flame until pale brown in colour. Put with the ground seeds.

Now put the nutmeg, cinnamon, cardamom pods, black peppercorns, cloves, mace, large black cardamom pods and red chillies into the coffee grinder or other spice grinder. Grind as finely as possible. Empty into the bowl with the other seasonings. Add the yoghurt and the paprika to the spices as well and mix. Rest the leg of lamb in the bowl and stuff as much of the spice mixture as is possible into the gashes. Cover the leg with the remaining spice mixture and set aside, covered, for 3–4 hours.

Heat the oil in a heavy-based pan (that is large enough to hold the meat) over a medium flame. When hot, put in the onions. Stir and fry until brown. Then put in the leg and all the spice mixture. Let the leg brown lightly on one side. Then turn it over using two kitchen spoons and brown the second side. The sauce will stick to the bottom of the pan. There is no avoiding this. Patiently scrape it off with a spatula and keep frying. When the oil separates from the spices and the leg is lightly browned, add 12 fl oz/350 ml/ 1½ cups of water and bring to a simmer. Scrape loose whatever is stuck to the bottom of the pan and mix it in. Cover tightly and cook for about 50 minutes, turning the leg over a few times during this cooking period.

The meat should be quite tender by now. Remove the cover and, over the next 10–15 minutes, boil away enough of the liquid to leave you with a thick sauce.

When you get ready to serve, lift the leg out of the sauce and place it in the centre of a platter. Spoon the sauce over the meat, leaving all the oil behind.

NAHEED ANEES'
BHOPALI PILAF WITH PEAS AND CARROTS
Bhopali Matar Gajar Pullao

There are many versions of this delicious pilaf in Bhopal. Naheed, a very elegant, aristocratic Muslim lady, makes a simpler pilaf for her everyday cooking. She just leaves out the peas and carrots and calls her dish, *Baghare*

Chaval (Flavoured Rice). It, too, is superb. You may serve either version with a meat, such as Lamb Cooked with Pickling Spices, and a yoghurt relish.

Serves 6

Basmati or other long-grain rice measured to the 15 fl oz/450 ml/2 cup mark in a glass measuring jug
1½-in/4-cm cube of fresh ginger, peeled and coarsely chopped
6–8 large cloves garlic, peeled and coarsely chopped
4 tbs/60 ml/⅓ cup vegetable oil or *ghee* (see page 201)
4 whole cloves
1 large, whole black cardamom pod or 3 green or white cardamom pods
1-in/2.5-cm cinnamon stick
2 bay leaves
¼ tsp whole black cumin seeds
½-in/1-cm, small piece of whole mace
3½ oz/8.5 cm, medium-sized onion, peeled cut in half lengthwise and then cut crosswise into very fine half rings
2½ oz/65 g, 2 small carrots, peeled and cut roughly into the same size as the peas
4½ oz/115 g/1 cup shelled peas, fresh or frozen ones that have been defrosted
1 tsp/5 ml salt

Pick over the rice and wash it in several changes of water. Drain. Put the rice in a bowl and cover with 2 pints/1.15 litres/5 cups of water. Leave to soak for 30 minutes. Drain thoroughly.

Put the ginger, garlic and 1 tbs/15 ml of water into the container of a food processor or blender. Blend until you have a paste.

Heat the oil in a heavy pan over a medium-high flame. When very hot, put in the cloves, black cardamom, cinnamon, bay leaves, black cumin seeds and mace. Stir once and put in the onion slices. Stir and fry until the onion slices turn reddish-brown. Now put in the ginger-garlic paste. Fry for 2 minutes. Put in the carrots and peas. Stir and fry for 1 minute. Now put in the drained rice and the salt. Lower the flame a bit. Stir and fry the rice for 2–3 minutes. Now put in 1 pint/600 ml/2½ cups of water and bring to a boil. Cover very tightly, turn the heat to very low and cook gently for 25 minutes.

FROM THE CHOWK IN LUCKNOW
FLAKY OVEN BREAD
Shirmal

Versions of this unleavened bread are made throughout Muslim India. In the bazaars of Lucknow, the bread bakes in a *tandoor*-like oven, stuck to its very hot, cast-iron walls. When it is done, it is sprinkled lightly with saffron milk to keep it moist. These days, what with saffron being so expensive, food colouring is used and the *shirmals* wind up looking the same colour as *tandoori* chicken – an unnatural orange-red! I think it is best to use very little saffron – or none at all, rather than food colouring. You could smear some melted *ghee* on the *shirmals* instead of sprinkling them with saffron water, if you prefer, or you could do both, as I have done. *Shirmals* may be served with most Indian meals and go particularly well with meat dishes such as Quick Kebabs, Minced/Ground Lamb Patties, Skewered Lamb Kebabs made with Cooked Meat or Lucknow's Whole Leg of Lamb, as well as vegetables, *dals* and relishes. I have even been known to eat left-over *shirmals* for breakfast with cheese or with butter and jam!

Makes 8 breads and serves 8
1 lb/450 g/3¾ cup plain white flour
1 tsp/5 ml salt
2 tsp/10 ml sugar
3½ oz/90 g/7 tablespoons *ghee* or
    clarified butter
½ pint/300 ml/1¼ cup milk
flour, for dusting
an extra ¼ pint/150 ml/⅔ cup milk
    with a few strands of saffron soaked
    in it for 1–2 hours
8 tsp/40 ml extra *ghee* or clarified butter

Put the flour, salt and sugar into a large bowl. Add the *ghee* and rub it into the flour with your fingers. Now begin to add the milk slowly. Try to form a ball. Keep adding the milk until you can form a ball. Start kneading, adding a little more milk as you do so. Keep kneading as you incorporate all the milk (*not* the saffron milk). Knead until the dough is soft and very smooth. Put the dough in a clean bowl. Cover and set aside for 2 hours. Knead again and set aside for another hour.

Heat the oven to 500°F/240°C/gas mark 9 and put a large, cast-iron frying pan on a shelf set in the middle of the oven to heat as well. Heat your grill (broiler) also.

Knead the dough again and divide into 8 equal balls. Flatten the balls into smooth patties and set aside. Keep seven covered as you work on the eighth.

Dust your work surface with a little flour and put the patty on it. Dust its top with flour. Now roll it out until it is about 6-in/15-cm in diameter and about ¼-in/0.5-cm thick. Prick the *shirmal* all over with a fork or with the tip of a knife.

Lift the *shirmal* carefully onto the spread palm of your hand. Open the oven and slap the bread into the heated frying pan. Bake for about 2 minutes. Now dip the tips of your fingers in the saffron milk, open the oven door, and sprinkle just what clings to your fingertips on to the *shirmal*. Do this by flicking your fingers. Do this one more time and close the oven door. Cook the *shirmal* for a total of about 5 minutes. It should develop a few brown spots on top and brown a bit underneath. Take it out and put it under your grill (broiler) for about 10 seconds.

Now flick a few more drops of saffron milk on it and, if you like, smear about ½ tsp/2.5 ml of *ghee* over it. Wrap immediately in aluminium foil or in a very lightly dampened tea towel (dish towel). Make all the *shirmals* this way.

MRS CHHABI RAMAN'S
YOGHURT WITH APPLE
Sev Ka Raita

If you are looking for a cooling relish to serve with spicy Indian dishes, this is it. In the vegetarian households that traditionally serve it, it has a double function – it acts as a refresher and a digestive, both at the same time.

The yoghurt may be mixed with its

Chicken with Apricots and Potato Straws.

Batloo, millet bread, its pressed decoration suggesting that it could have emerged from a potter's kiln.

Diced potatoes with Turmeric and Cumin, Puréed Vegetables, *Papadum*, Corn cooked with Milk.

A deft-fingered Gujarati woman making *chapatis*, wholewheat griddle breads.

Rice with Tomatoes and Spinach, Prawns cooked in the Maharashtrian manner.

A favourite sweet – luscious syrup-
filled *jalebis*.

Cucumbers with Fresh Coconut, Lamb
cooked in the Kolhapuri style.

Red Kidney Beans cooked with Turnips, Aubergines with Apple.

seasonings well in advance, but the apple should be grated into it just before serving.

Serves 4
½ pint/300 ml/1¼ cups plain yoghurt
½ tsp/2.5 ml roasted and ground cumin seeds (page 199)
⅛ tsp red chilli powder (cayenne pepper)
¼ tsp finely grated, peeled fresh ginger
⅓–½ tsp/1–2.5 ml salt

about half a big, hard, somewhat tart apple, such as a Granny Smith

Put the yoghurt in a bowl. Beat lightly with a fork or a whisk until smooth and creamy. Add the cumin, red chilli powder (cayenne pepper), ginger and salt. Mix. Cover and refrigerate.

Just before serving, peel the apple and core it. Grate it very coarsely, using the largest holes in the grater and mix in with the yoghurt.

GUJARAT

As the steam train slowly puffs its way towards Dakor in Gujarat, a compartment filled with pilgrims settles down to eat. A slightly sooty seat is dusted off and covered with a tablecloth. Glass bangles jingle as triple-knotted bundles are untied, bottles unscrewed and hands delve deep into polythene bags.

These pilgrims seeking Lord Krishna's blessings happen to be Gujarati vegetarians. Much of their food is based on grains, beans, roots and vegetables grown on their family farms. Millet is a staple here, a grain they say that has more protein, Vitamin E and iron than wheat, and less carbohydrate and fat. It has been ground at home on a grinding wheel, mixed with spinach and green chillies to make a dough, and then formed into breads – *dhebras* – on a cast-iron griddle. These breads are to be eaten with *chhundo*, a marvellous sweet chutney made with green mangoes, cardamom and cloves, and some plain yoghurt. There is some *batata shaak* as well, diced potatoes sautéed with mustard and cumin seeds; and one of Gujarat's glories, *dhoklas*, delightfully spongy, savoury, steamed 'cakes' made from a split pea batter.

The modern state of Gujarat, perched at the top of India's western coastline, was formed only in 1960 by an independent India anxious to preserve cultural differences within the nation by organizing states on a linguistic basis. It was not always easy to make neat divisions. Under the British, Gujarat had been part of the Bombay Presidency, with the city of Bombay as its capital. When state lines were redrawn, Bombay found itself the capital of Maharashtra! Today, it would be fair to say that Gujarati food belongs to all Gujarati-speaking people, whether they happen to be in Ahmedabad, the state capital, in Saurashtra, the western portion of the state, in cosmopolitan Bombay, which is not in the state at all, or, for that matter, in one of thousands of villages that stand guard over ancient fields.

In Saurashtra, vast stretches of the earth are dry, caked and cracked. One wonders how any tender green thing could summon up the strength to break the hard crust and sprout at all – but sprout it does. In fields separated by cactus, there are peanuts, stalks of millet and wheat, sesame seeds, and lots of tall sugar-cane, its plume-like tops waving defiantly in the breeze. These dusty fields have nourished beloved old gods like Lord Krishna, who established a kingdom on this coast, and ascetic new ones, like Mahatma Gandhi, who was born not too far from Dwarka, the capital of that kingdom.

Grateful villagers celebrate the emergence of new crops by eating *paunk*, the fresh kernels of wheat or millet with sugarballs. And when the season's first sugar-cane is pressed to make jaggery (*gur*), raw, unprocessed lump sugar, the entire village is in joyful attendance. Wood fires are lit under enormous cast-iron trays. Two or three pairs of hands are needed to stir the steadily thickening juice. They stir for hours – until it reaches the stage when it can be poured into another batch of trays to set. Somewhat like fudge when it is done, it is devoured while it is still hot.

Most of the jaggery will be made into large, loaf-like lumps. Some will be sold commercially, some kept by the villagers for their own consumption. Gujaratis often like to sweeten their split peas and vegetables just a little bit. Jaggery is perfect for that. It is also a perfect accompaniment for *ghee*-smeared millet breads. The best of the jaggery will be packed in boxes and offered to friends as one might the very best of chocolates.

Surrounded by both barren land and blooming fields is the ancient feudal town – once a royal principality – of Jasdan. Huge hills of dry red chillies are piled up in the market, not far from the palace gate. It is the season for them, as it is for cumin, coriander, garlic, turmeric and fennel. All will be sunned carefully and stored for the year. The red chillies will be pounded in mortars and stored in tins with a small lump of asafetida. The asafetida will keep the bugs at bay. Some of the red chillies will be used to make one of Saurashtra's all-important spice mixtures – *lehson masala* or garlic spice mixture.

Just as a *rouille* enlivens a fish soup in the south of France, Saurashtra's garlic spice mixture – a combination of garlic, red chillies and salt pounded together, adds extra pep to a lot of its foods. I have seen Saurashtrans make a large ball of it, rub it with oil and then take it with them on month-long treks. In one small village just outside Bhavnagar, I watched farm hands at work on a humble but classic preparation. Some thorny twigs, the only fuel available, were set alight. An aubergine (eggplant) was placed over them and covered with more burning twigs. When its skin was scorched and the vegetable roasted, it was removed, peeled and mashed. The garlic spice mixture was beaten in. A depression was then made in the centre of the mashed vegetable and some *ghee* poured into it. Meanwhile, a piece of terracotta, probably broken off some water vessel, was heated over the twigs and dropped into the *ghee*. The vegetable dish was covered immediately so the rising smoke could flavour the aubergine. The dish was simple – and spectacular.

Inside the palace in Jasdan, slatted shades are drawn against the intense heat. In the dark, cool verandahs, women move around with grace and efficiency – the beautiful Queen Mother in white, her waiting-women in black, all prettily tattooed on their fingers, arms and throat. The royal family here is from the Kathi clan, known for its generous hospitality. 'When we pour tea,' the Queen Mother says, 'we must never look as if we are stinting. So we pour and pour until the tea overflows from the cup into the saucer. First we drink from the saucer, then from the cup. That is our custom.'

Lunch gives ample evidence of both the family's generosity and taste. The meal, laid out on individual silver *thalis* (plates), is all vegetarian. This is the Queen Mother's choice, as the clan normally eats meat freely. The dishes are unique to this area and each one is superb. Among the foods I eat is *moongphuli nu shaak*. It looks like a meat dish but is not. A paste of roasted peanuts and chickpea flour has been steamed and cut into cubes. It is then cooked with whole cumin, mustard and fenugreek seeds as well as a sauce that has onions, garlic, yoghurt and tomatoes in it. I also find myself devouring *hariso*, a delicately sweetened rice flour custard, flavoured with cardamom and nutmeg, and then cut into shivering, cooling diamonds. The bread is *batloo*, a flat griddle bread of millet flour which, pocked with tiny depressions made by the cook's fingers, looks like the cracked earth of the surrounding countryside.

Wankaner lies farther to the north, another former royal kingdom whose massive palace sits perched on a lonely brown hilltop. In the sprawling town below, a jeweller's wife cooks a simple lunch for her family – and for me. There are no counters in her spotless kitchen. Two kerosene stoves sit on the floor, as do the jeweller's wife and her daughter-in-law. Plain rice is to be eaten with *toovar dal*. The *dal* will be sweet and sour. The sweet will come from jaggery and the sour from *kokum*, the sour rind of a mangosteen-like fruit. Two vegetables are made with great speed. For the *palag bhaji*, or spinach, the leaves are cut up and stirred around with cumin seeds and asafetida until they wilt. Then some coriander, ground cumin, red chillies and turmeric are added. A few minutes later, some chopped tomatoes are thrown in. That is all there is to it. For the *sambhara*, shredded cabbage and carrots are stir-fried with mustard and fenugreek seeds. The dish cooks in five minutes. There is yoghurt, of course, and a seasonal relish, *kachi kedi nu athanu*, made by combining chopped up sour, green mango with split and skinned mustard seeds, oil, red chillies and salt. Lunch is ready.

In the capital city of Ahmedabad, some of India's richest industrialist families manage to combine a sophisticated, jet-set existence with strict vegetarian diets and kitchens presided over by traditional, orthodox chefs. They might live in a home designed by Le Corbusier, but shoes must be removed before entering the kitchen. Some of these families are great collectors of art and patrons of artists. It is not surprising that they should also serve some of the most elegant Gujarati vegetarian food in the country. I have gone to bed in one such home with a mound of highly scented jasmines carefully placed next to my pillow and woken up to a breakfast, sent up to me in my room, consisting of the most delicate rice flour pancakes. To make them, a batter of rice flour and buttermilk had been spread on a large leaf and then topped with another leaf. The pancake, thus ensconced, was baked on a griddle. To eat it, one first discarded the top leaf. Then one proceeded to peel off and devour the pancake. And the best place to do this was the *hindola*, a beautifully carved wooded bench-swing, so typical of Gujarat, that was suspended from the ceiling of my room.

Ahmedabad has one distinction that sets it apart from other provincial capitals. At the moment it is the only city in India where the best of regional fare may be sampled in a fine restaurant. This vegetarian restaurant, Vishala, is set up like a village, with thatched roof pavilions for banquet-style dining.

Everyone sits on the floor in rows, as they might at a wedding, and the food is doled out on disposable plates made out of semi-dried leaves 'stitched' together with twigs. *Handvas* are served here, savoury split pea 'cakes', encrusted with sesame seeds, as well as rice steamed with tiny stuffed aubergines. I have had wonderful dishes of corn cooked with 'drumsticks', a long bean-like vegetable, and *khandvi*, perhaps the best of all Gujarati creations, which resembles tiny, rolled-up crepes.

Not all Gujarati-speaking people are vegetarians. Some are not even Hindus. One of the oldest Muslim communities in Gujarat is that of the Bohris, disciples of the eleventh-century missionary, Abdullah, and converts from Hinduism. They are known for their works of charity, their social awareness, their shrewdness and their soups. They are among the very few communities in the country with a passion for serving hot soups, cold soups, breakfast soups, soups with ground cashew nuts and soups made out of lamb trotters. My absolute favourite is *sarki*, a gazpacho-like cold summer dish that uses *toovar dal* for the basic stock and then adds wonderfully crunchy bits of diced cucumbers, tomatoes and spring onions (scallions) to it. As a final flourish, dollops of yoghurt are added just before serving.

Bohris do more than serve good soups. They set a superb table. Except, their 'table' is not a table at all but a very large metal plate, a *thal*, set on a stool, designed to have eight to ten people sitting around it on the floor. All dishes are set down in the centre of the *thal* and are communal. At a large banquet, several *thals* are set out in a room or rooms, each seating about eight to ten people. (When you ask a Bohri the size of a particular room in his house, he might well answer, 'Quite large. About a ten-*thal* room.')

In a style of eating that is totally unique to them, Bohris alternate salty dishes with sweet ones for the first half of the meal. At a recent Bohri banquet, after Allah had been praised and we had eaten a pinch of salt, as required by custom, our first course was *malai na khajla*. Still warm rounds of lightly swee-tened flaky pastry had been stuffed with clotted cream. They disappeared almost as soon as they had been set down. I was told that this sweet is very hard to make. Some who have mastered it – and sold the product – have made enough money to educate their children and take off for greener pastures in the Middle East. Another sweet, quite the equal of this one, is *sagla bagla*. It is only available in the Bohri ancestral town of Surat. Only one man can make it and he refuses to part with the recipe. It has to be ordered in advance. What comes after the special order is ready is a box of white flakes that tend to fly away when ceiling fans are turned on! Imbedded in the flakes is a thick layer of sweetened nuts. Among the other stunning Bohri dishes are *lagania sheek*, a very fine paste of seasoned minced (ground) meat topped with beaten egg and baked, and *kuddal palida*, a tart and hot split pea broth served with a special pilaf that combines meat, rice and split peas.

Parsis are another Gujarati-speaking minority. They are Zoroastrians who fled Iran in the eighth century owing to religious persecution and headed east, landing just north of Bombay. When the British set up their first trading post in the port city of Surat, and later, when Bombay came under British rule, Parsi fortunes began to boom. The Parsis had already mastered Gujarati. With a haste born of natural shrewdness, they mastered English as well and soon became very successful merchants. Some went into shipping, making fortunes from the China trade. Others used their knowledge of English to become butlers in English households. Yet others opened provision stores, selling everything from Cheddar cheese to tinned sar-dines. Many Parsi homes boasted of having three cooks, one for English food (usually a Goan who had been sent to England for training), one for Indian food and a third for Parsi food.

Parsi food is a delicious blend of Western influences, a Gujar-ati love of sweet-and-sour mixtures, and the Persian genius for combining meat with dried fruit such as apricots.

To enjoy the flamboyance of Parsi meals, it is best to attend a *lagan nu bhonu* or wedding-style banquet. No cooking for this is done at home. The entire affair is placed in the trusted hands of a capable caterer.

Drinks are served first. Men tend to drink whisky. Women decked out in diamonds and pearls, tend to stay with wine and soft drinks. The talk turns on the difficulty of getting pianos tuned, the problems of holding on to good cooks and, inevitably, the latest exploits of 'our very own' Zubin Mehta.

Long tables have already been set and covered with tablecloths. The first shift moves in. Twenty-five people sit at each table, all on one side. Waiters begin to fly by with jet speed, laying banana leaves in front of each person. Aerated water of different hues and flavours is offered. Pineapple? Raspberry? Ginger? Lemon? Parsis do not seem to believe in drinking water at such a festive time. The first food is now placed on the leaf-plates. It is *meva nu achar*, a sweet chutney made with carrots and dried fruit. At this point, a breathless waiter asks, 'Who wants cutlery?' Those who want it are given a fork and a spoon. Now ice comes around, usually in a plastic basin, for those who want to plop it into their drinks. Wafers, made of potatoes and sago, come next, followed by wholewheat griddle breads, *chapatis*. 'How many chapatis?' the waiter wants to know. 'Three, five, six?' He leaves stacks for each person.

Then comes the fish course. This could well be *patra ni macchi*, pieces of Arabian Sea pomfret, smothered in a fresh coriander chutney, wrapped in banana leaves and steamed. It is soon time for the chicken and meat courses. *Sali jardaloo murgi* is a sweet-and-sour Persian-style dish of chicken and dried apricots. It is served with crunchy potato straws. *Kid gos* consists of large chunks of very young lamb, stewed with ground cashews and coconut milk.

The Parsis are not anywhere near finished. There is still the egg course, which consists of beaten eggs poured over sautéed onions and baked, and there is the sweet, *lagan nu castar*, a rich custard made with boiled down milk and nuts.

As if this were not enough, the entire meal is then repeated. The guests groan with pleasure and keep eating. A clear sign that the meal has begun to wind down is the appearance of the pilaf, rice studded with meat and potatoes, which is to be eaten with a well-spiced *toovar dal*. Ice cream, chocolates, betel leaves and fennel seeds follow. Fennel seeds are a much needed digestive.

Meanwhile, the poor caterer runs back and forth, counting

heads. Anyone whose feet do not touch the ground is considered a child. One shift has finished eating. But the second
shift is waiting. And the whole dinner starts all over again.

NOTE: The state of Sindh, part of the Bombay Presidency under
the British, became a part of Pakistan when India was parti-
tioned. The state may have been lost to India but many of its
exquisite dishes have remained with us, still cooked by members
of the Sindhi community scattered across the land. I have
included one superb Sindhi dish in the recipe section of this
chapter.

RECIPES FROM GUJARAT

FAIJI FATTEH'S
COLD SUMMER SOUP WITH CUCUMBERS AND TOMATO
Sarki

The Bohris, Muslims from Gujarat, drink a lot of soups which they serve in Chinese bowls acquired through India's ancient trade with China. These soups are geared to the seasons. The base for two of them, *sarki*, a summer soup and *sarka*, its winter counterpart, is a split pea – *toovar dal* – that has an ochre colour and an earthy taste. This pulse (legume) is boiled in lots of water. Then, just the water that rises to the top is poured off – as if it were a stock made with bones and meat. It is this split pea stock (broth) that is used. In the summer, cooling vegetables, such as chopped cucumbers and tomatoes are added to it and in the winter, an extraction from ground nuts and seeds, as well as coconut milk.

Here is the summer soup, *sarki*. It is not unlike the Spanish *gazpacho*, only much more interesting, I think. You may serve it with any Indian or Western meal as a first course.

If you cannot get *toovar dal*, use yellow split peas. The broth will have a much sweeter flavour but it will still make a good soup.

Serves 5–6
13 oz/375 g/2 cups skinned *toovar dal* or yellow split peas, picked over, washed and drained (page 200)
½ tsp/2.5 ml ground turmeric
½ tsp/2.5 ml ground roasted cumin seeds (page 199)
2 tbs/30 ml lemon juice or a bit more, as desired
1¼–1½ tsp/about 6–7 ml salt
freshly ground black pepper
1 fresh hot green chilli, *very* finely chopped
2 spring onions (scallions)
8 oz/225 g, 1 large tomato
2 small pickling cucumbers or 7 oz/200 g cucumber with not very mature seeds
2 tbs/30 ml chopped fresh green coriander (Chinese parsley)
about 6 tbs/90 ml plain yoghurt

Put the *dal* or yellow split peas in a pan, along with 3¼ pints/2 litres/8 cups of water and the turmeric. Bring to a boil. Turn heat to low, cover partially and cook for 1½ hours or until the *dal* is quite tender. Turn off the heat and let the pan just sit for 5 minutes.

With a ladle, take out all the thin liquid on top of the *dal*. Add enough of the remaining thicker *dal* to make up 2 pints 2 fl oz/1.25 litres/5¼ cups. Put in a blender – you may have to do this in two batches – along with the roasted cumin, lemon juice, salt, black pepper and green chilli. Blend. Taste for seasoning.

Chill for a few hours in the refrigerator. (If allowed to get too cold, the soup tends to thicken and jell somewhat. If that happens, stir well before going on with the next step.)

Meanwhile, cut the spring onions (scallions) into 2-in/5-cm lengths. Holding several together, cut them into paper-thin rounds. Put in a bowl, cover with cold water and refrigerate for a couple of hours. Drain and dry with absorbent kitchen paper (paper towels).

Drop the tomato into boiling water for 15 seconds. Take it out and peel it. Deseed, if liked. Cut into ¼-in/0.5-cm dice as well.

Add the green coriander (Chinese parsley) to the soup and pour into individual bowls. Divide the tomato, cucumbers and spring onions (scallions) among the soup bowls and top with a dollop of yoghurt.

ARJUN SAJNANI'S
PURÉED VEGETABLES
Sai Bhaji

I have had many puréed vegetables – carrots and peas and spinach, even artichoke hearts – some in the finest of French restaurants. None of them have ever been as good as this one from the former Indian state of Sindh (now in Pakistan). It is really a happy medley of vegetables, as it combines spinach, potatoes and tomatoes. Some people like to add sorrel and dill as well. Sindhis eat it with Rice Cooked with Split Peas. I often serve it with

either Lamb with Cardamom or Lamb Cooked in the Kolhapuri Style or with Moghlai Chicken braised with Almonds and Raisins, and rice.

It can be served with most Western meals as it is very delicately spiced.

Serves 6–8
6 oz/175 g/½ cup skinned *chana dal* or
    yellow split peas (page 200)
3 tbs/45 ml vegetable oil
1¼ lb/550 g washed fresh leaf spinach
    or 2 × 10-oz/283-g packets of frozen
    leaf spinach
6–7 oz/175–200 g, 1 large potato,
    peeled and diced
3 oz/75 g, 1 medium-sized onion,
    peeled and coarsely chopped
1¼ lb/550 g, 4 medium-sized tomatoes,
    chopped
5 fresh, hot, green chillies
1 tsp/5 ml salt

Wash the *chana dal* well and leave it to soak, covered by about 1 in/2.5 cm of water, for 1 hour. Drain.

Heat the oil in a large pan over a medium-high flame. When hot, put in all the ingredients as well as 1¼ pints/¾ litre/3 cups of water and bring to a boil. Cover, turn heat to low and boil for 1 hour. Remove the cover, turn the heat up to high and boil rapidly for another 20 minutes or until the liquid is reduced and what remains looks a bit like a thick stew.

Pour this, in two batches, if necessary, into the container of a blender or food processor. Blend. You should end up with a thick purée.

NEVEDITA'S
CORN COOOKED WITH MILK
Makai Nu Shaak

Here is a dish from the western region of Saurashtra. Maize is generally used, but sweetcorn, available more easily in the West, works quite well. I have even used frozen corn quite satisfactorily.

This is a nice dish to serve at a brunch (with toast) or you could also serve it as a vegetable with any Indian meal.

Use a frying pan or a heavy pan that is good for boiling milk.

Serves 4
10 oz/275 g/2½ cups corn, either taken off a cob or frozen corn that has been dropped in boiling water, defrosted and drained
¾ pint/450 ml/2 cups whole milk
1 tbs/15 ml vegetable oil
⅛ tsp whole cumin seeds
½ tsp/2.5 ml very finely grated fresh ginger
1 fresh hot green chilli, very finely chopped
¼ tsp sugar
¼ tsp salt
pinch red chilli powder (cayenne pepper)
2 tbs/30 ml freshly grated coconut (page 197)
1 tbs/15 ml finely chopped fresh green coriander (Chinese parsley)

Put the corn and the milk in a heavy pan. Bring to a simmer, making sure it does not boil over. Keep simmering vigorously, stirring now and then, until there is very little milk left – just enough to keep the corn looking wet – 2 tbs/30 ml.

Heat the oil in a non-stick frying pan or pan over a medium flame. When hot, put in the cumin seeds. A few seconds later, put in the ginger and green chilli. Stir once. Now put in the corn, sugar, salt and red chilli powder (cayenne pepper). Stir to mix. Add the coconut and green coriander (Chinese parsley). Stir to mix again and turn off the heat.

DICED POTATOES WITH TURMERIC AND CUMIN
Batata Nu Shaak

This exceedingly simple dish takes just about 15 minutes to cook and is adored by everyone in our household. It may be served with most Indian meals – at picnics, it goes particularly well with breads, pickles and relishes – and it can also be served with Western meals of roasted and grilled (broiled) meats.

It is best to use unskinned new potatoes for this dish. They would, of course, be scrubbed and wiped dry first. I find that if I cut the potatoes ahead of time and leave them soaking in water, the dish, for some reason, does not turn out as well. So cut the potatoes just before you are ready to cook them. If you have a wok, do use it. It is the ideal utensil for this dish. Otherwise, a frying pan will do.

Serves 6
1½ lb/700 g new potatoes (in US, red potatoes work very well), scrubbed but not peeled
5 tbs/75 g/½ cup vegetable oil
⅛ tsp ground asafetida (optional)

½ tsp/2.5 ml whole black mustard seeds
½ tsp/2.5 ml whole cumin seeds
⅛ tsp ground turmeric
½ tsp/2.5 ml ground coriander seeds
½ tsp/2.5 ml ground cumin seeds
¼ tsp red chilli powder (cayenne pepper)
¾ tsp/4 ml salt

Cut the clean potatoes into ½-in/1-cm dice. Heat the oil in a wok or frying pan over a medium heat. When hot, put in, in quick succession, first the asafetida and, a second later, the mustard seeds and then the cumin seeds. Now put in the potatoes and stir once or .twice. Sprinkle in the turmeric. Continue to stir every now and then and cook for about 15 minutes or until the potatoes are lightly browned and almost done. Sprinkle in the ground coriander, ground cumin, red chilli powder (cayenne pepper) and salt. Stir and cook for another 1–2 minutes.

THE FARIYAS HOTEL'S
FISH IN A PACKET
Patra Ni Macchi

A dish from the Parsi community, served at all their wedding banquets. Fish is smothered in a fresh coconut chutney, wrapped in banana leaves and steamed. Having no easy access to banana leaves, I have used foil.

In India, pomfret is used for this dish. Instead, you may use 1-in/2.5-cm thick steaks of bass, pampano or red snapper – or thick chunks of cod, halibut or haddock. Salmon, however extravagant, works quite superbly. It needs to be cut, crosswise, into steaks.

Serves 4
enough grated fresh coconut to fill a glass measuring jug to the 12 fl oz/ 350 ml/1½ cup mark
2½ oz/60 g/1 well-packed cup fresh green coriander (Chinese parsley), coarsely chopped
4 cloves garlic, peeled
1 tsp/5 ml ground cumin seeds
5 fresh hot green chillies, coarsely chopped
2 tsp/10 ml sugar
2½–3 tbs/37–45 ml lemon juice
1 tsp/5 ml salt
small bundle ½ oz/15 g/¼ cup fresh mint, coarsely chopped
about 1½ lb/700 g, 4 fish steaks, cut about 1 in/2.5 cm thick (see note above)
8 fl oz/250 ml/1 cup distilled white malt vinegar or cider vinegar
1 tbs/15 ml vegetable oil
8–10 curry leaves, fresh or dried

Put the coconut, green coriander (Chinese parsley), garlic, cumin seeds, green chillies, sugar, lemon juice, salt and mint into the container of a food processor or blender. Blend until you have as fine a paste – or chutney – as possible.

Cut four pieces of foil, each 12 in/ 30.5 cm square. Smother a quarter of the chutney on each fish. Fold two opposite ends of the foil over the fish, one after another. Now do the same with the remaining ends.

Prepare a utensil for steaming. I use a large wok, arranging four criss-cross chopsticks at the bottom. You could set a trivet inside a large pan. Now put the vinegar, oil and curry leaves into the pan. This is the liquid that is going to be used for steaming and it should, of course, stay below the fish packets. Bring the liquid to a boil over a medium-high flame. Arrange the fish packets on top of the chopsticks or trivet. Cover. Turn the heat down to medium low and steam gently for 15 minutes or until the fish is just done.

MRS DARUWALA'S
FISH IN A DARK SAUCE
Patia

Very slightly sweet and sour, this Parsi dish is another favourite with our family. We serve it with rice – Plain Rice or Rice with Tomatoes and Spinach. In India, firm-fleshed pomfrets are used. Unfortunately, they are very difficult to find in the West. You could use chunks of either halibut or haddock, or steaks of bass, pompano or red snapper. I used steaks with bone but boneless fish pieces would work as well. You can also make this dish with prawns (shrimps).

Serves 4
5 tbs/75 ml/6 tablespoons vegetable oil
10 oz/275 g, 2 good-sized onions, peeled, cut in half lengthwise and then cut into fine half rings
2 tsp/10 ml very finely grated, peeled fresh ginger
2 tsp/10 ml finely crushed garlic
2 tsp/10 ml very finely chopped fresh green chillies
2 tsp/10 ml ground roasted coriander and cumin seed mixture (page 199)
½ tsp/2.5 ml red chilli pepper (cayenne pepper)
12 oz/350 g, 3 small tomatoes
1 tsp/5 ml sugar

2 tsp/10 ml distilled white malt vinegar or cider vinegar
1¼ tsp/6 ml salt
1½ lb/700 g fish steaks, cut about 1 in/ 2.5 cm thick (see note above)

Heat the oil in a frying pan over a medium-high flame. When hot, put in the sliced onions. Stir and fry them until they are a rich reddish-brown colour. Turn the heat down to medium and put in the ginger and garlic. Stir for ½ minute. Now put in the coriander and cumin seed mixture and the red chilli pepper (cayenne pepper). Stir once or twice. Put in the tomatoes, sugar, vinegar, salt and ½ pint/300 ml/1¼ cups of water. Bring to a boil. Cover, lower the heat and simmer gently for 30 minutes. Remove the cover and put in the fish pieces. Spoon the sauce over the fish and bring to a simmer. Cover and simmer gently for about 15 minutes or until the fish is just done.

THE FARIYAS HOTEL'S
CHICKEN WITH APRICOTS AND POTATO STRAWS
Sali Jardaloo Murgi

Amongst the Parsis, two things seem to be very popular – sweet and sour foods and potato straws. This particular festive dish, eaten, so far as I know, only by the Parsis of India, happily combines the two.

You may, if you like, use boned, cubed lamb instead of chicken. You will need to cook it for a little over an hour and it should feed at least 6 people. If you want a simple Western style meal you could serve it with a salad or, if you like, with rice and Mushrooms with Fennel and Ginger.

Serves 4–6
3 lb/1.4 kg chicken, or chicken pieces, skinned
4 whole dried hot red chillies
2-in/5-cm cinnamon stick, somewhat broken up
1½ tsp/7 ml whole cumin seeds
7 cardamom pods
10 whole cloves
2 tsp/10 ml finely grated peeled, fresh ginger
1 tsp/5 ml finely crushed garlic
4 oz/100 g/15–16 stoned (pitted) dried apricots
6 tbs/90 ml/½ cup vegetable oil
½ lb/225 g, 2 good-sized onions, peeled, cut in half lengthwise and then cut crosswise into very fine half rings
2 tbs/30 ml tomato purée (paste) mixed with 8 fl oz/250 ml/1 cup water
1¼ tsp/6 ml salt
2 tbs/30 ml distilled white malt vinegar
1½ tbs/22 ml sugar

For the potato straws (sali):
1 tbs/15 ml salt
7 oz/200 g, 1 large potato, peeled
vegetable oil for deep frying

If using a whole chicken, cut it into small serving pieces. Divide the legs into 2 and the whole breasts into 4 pieces.

Put the red chillies, cinnamon, cumin seeds, cardamom pods and cloves into the container of a coffee grinder or other spice grinder. Grind as fine as possible.

Put the chicken in a big bowl. Put 1 tsp/5 ml of the ginger, ½ tsp/2.5 ml of the garlic and half the dry spice mixture on the chicken. Mix well with your hands, rubbing the seasonings into the chicken pieces. Set aside for 1 hour.

Put the apricots in a small pan with ¾ pint/450 ml/2 cups of water. Bring to a boil. Turn the heat down and simmer, uncovered, until the apricots are tender but not mushy. (The time will vary depending upon the quality of the dried fruit and on whether they are whole or halved.) When the apricots are tender, turn off the heat and let them sit in their own juice.

When the chicken has completed its marinating time, heat the 6 tbs/90 ml/ ½ cup of oil in a wide, heavy pan over a medium-high flame. When hot, put in the onions. Stir and fry until they turn a rich, reddish-brown colour. Turn the heat down to medium and add the remaining 1 tsp/5 ml of ginger and ½ tsp/2.5 ml of garlic. Stir once or twice. Now put in the remaining dry spice mixture from the coffee grinder. Stir once or twice and put in all the chicken. Stir and brown the chicken lightly for 5 minutes. Now put in the tomato purée (paste) liquid and the salt. Bring to a boil. Cover, reduce the heat to low and simmer gently for 20 minutes. Add the vinegar and sugar. Stir to mix. Cover again and simmer for another 10 minutes. Turn off the heat. Spoon off as much fat from the surface as possible.

Put the apricots into the pan with the chicken. (If the apricots were sitting in only a little bit of liquid, say 2–3 tbs/30–45 ml put that in as well. If there is more liquid than that, discard it.) Gently slip the apricots in between the chicken pieces and let them soak in the sauce for at least 30 minutes.

Make the potato straws: fill a large bowl with about 3 pints/1.75 litres/8 cups of water. Add the salt and mix.

Grate the potato on the coarsest grating blade. Put the grated potato into the bowl of water. Stir the potatoes about with your hand. Now remove one handful of potatoes at a time, squeezing out as much liquid as you can. Spread the potatoes out on a tea towel (dish towel). Pat with absorbent kitchen paper (paper towel) to dry off as much moisture as possible.

Pour vegetable oil into a wok, *karhai* or frying pan to a depth of 2 in/5 cm. Heat over a lowish heat. Let the oil heat slowly. When it is hot – this may take 10 minutes – put in one smallish handful of the uncooked straws. They will begin to bubble. When the bubbling stops, stir them until they are crisp and a pale golden colour. Remove with a slotted spoon and leave to drain on a plate lined with absorbent kitchen paper (paper towel). Make all the potato straws this way.

When you are ready to eat, heat the chicken gently and put it in a serving dish. Garnish the top with the Potato Straws.

AYMAN MUCCHALA'S
BEEF CREAM KEBABS
Malai Tikka

These beef kebabs, eaten by the Muslim Bohris of Gujarat, are unusual, delicately spiced, and quite wonderful. Beef is cubed and marinated in, amongst other things, thick cream. It is then dipped in egg and crumbs,

skewered and deep fried. I have not bothered to skewer the pieces as I prefer them to brown evenly on all sides.

You may serve these kebabs with an Indian meal or else as part of a simple Western meal with perhaps a salad and potatoes.

Serves 4
1½ lb/700 g, 1-in/2.5-cm thick sirloin steak
2 tsp/10 ml very finely grated, peeled fresh ginger
1 tsp/5 ml very finely crushed garlic
1–2 tsp/5–10 ml very finely chopped (minced) fresh hot green chilli
4 tbs/60 ml/⅓ cup double cream (heavy cream)
¾ tsp/4 ml salt
vegetable oil for deep frying
1 large egg
3 oz/75 g/1 cup dried breadcrumbs

Cut away and discard heavy edgings of fat from the meat, if there are any. Cut the steak into 1-in/2.5-cm cubes and put in a bowl. Add the ginger, garlic, green chilli, cream and salt. Mix well. Cover and refrigerate for at least 3 hours or overnight.

Just before you are ready to eat, pour enough oil into a wok, *karhai* or deep frying pan to come to a depth of 2 in/5 cm. Set to heat over a medium-low flame.

Meanwhile, put the egg into a shallow dish and beat lightly. Put the breadcrumbs in a second, similar dish. Dip the meat cubes, one at a time, first in the egg and then in the crumbs, rolling them around until they are quite encrusted.

When the oil is heated, put in as many meat cubes as the vessel will hold in a single layer. Stir and fry until they are nicely browned on the outside and done to your taste inside. It takes about 4 minutes of frying on a medium-low heat for the meat cubes to be the way I like them – just lightly pink inside. (Most Indians have them well-done.)

JYOTI DESAI'S
STEAMED SAVOURY CAKES
Dhoklas

Spongy to the touch and covered with mustard and sesame seeds, *dhokla* squares are a savoury and may be served with tea or as part of a meal. Chutneys – such as Yoghurt Chutney and Sesame Seed Chutney – may be used as a dip.

Dhoklas are very simple to make but they do need about 30 hours for soaking and fermentation.

Serves 6–8
6¼ oz/180 g/1 cup skinned *chana dal*
3 oz/75 g/½ cup long-grain rice
1¼ oz/35 g/¼ cup skinned *urad dal*
1 tsp/5 ml salt
1¼ tsp/6 ml peeled and very finely grated fresh ginger
1 tsp/5 ml very finely minced fresh green chillies
¼ tsp whole cumin seeds
2 fl oz/50 ml/¼ cup vegetable oil
¼ tsp bicarbonate of soda (baking soda)
3 tbs/45 ml vegetable oil
1 tbs/15 ml whole black mustard seeds
2 tbs/30 ml whole sesame seeds
2–3 whole, dried hot red chillies
4 tbs/60 ml chopped fresh green

coriander (Chinese parsley)
2–3 tbs/30–45 ml grated fresh coconut (page 197), optional

Pick over the *chana dal*, rice and *urad dal* and wash together in several changes of water. Drain. Cover with water by 3 in/7.5 cm and leave to soak for 8 hours. Drain.

Put the *dal* and rice mixture into the container of a food processor or blender. Blend, pushing down with a rubber spatula whenever necessary. When you have a coarse paste, add 8 fl oz/250 ml/1 cup of water in a steady, but gentle stream. Continue to blend, again pushing down with a rubber spatula when necessary for a good 6–8 minutes or until you have an airy batter. Empty the batter into a bowl. Cover loosely with an overturned plate and put in a *warm* place (80°F/28°C temperature is ideal) for 20–22 hours or until the batter is *filled* with tiny bubbles. (In very hot climates, this will happen much faster.)

Put the salt, ginger, green chillies and cumin seeds into the bowl with the batter but do *not* stir them in yet.

Get everything ready for steaming. Ideally, you should have two cake tins. They could be 8-in/20-cm rounds, with a height of 1–1½ in/2.5–4 cm or they could be 8-in/20-cm squares of the same height. At a pinch, one cake tin will do. The cake tin should fit easily into some contraption for steaming. I use a Chinese bamboo steamer that has its own lid. I sit this over a large wok with water in it. The water stays just below the steamer. You could also use a very large pan with a lid or a deep frying pan with a lid. Just set a trivet in the bottom of it and pour in just enough water so it stays below the top of the trivet.

Bring the water for steaming to a rolling boil. Have extra boiling water ready in case you need to replenish it.

In a small pan combine the 2 fl oz/50 ml/¼ cup of vegetable oil with 2 fl oz/50 ml/¼ cup of water and bring to a boil. Take it off the flame. Immediately stir in the bicarbonate of soda (baking soda), and pour this mixture into the batter. Stir to mix. Divide the batter into 2 equal portions and pour 1 portion into a cake tin. Set the baking tin in your steamer. Cover and steam for about 20 minutes or until a toothpick inserted in the middle comes out clean. Turn off the flame. Carefully, remove the cake tin from the steamer using two sets of tongs or oven mittens. Let the *dhokla* cool for 10–15 minutes (Meanwhile, start steaming the second portion.) Now cut it into 1-in/2.5-cm cubes and remove from the cake tin.

When both batches of *dhoklas* have been cooked and cut, heat the 3 tbs/45 ml of oil in a large frying pan over a medium flame. When very hot, put in the whole black mustard seeds and the sesame seeds. When the seeds start to pop, put in the whole red chillies. Stir them around once or twice and then spoon out the oil and spices over the *dhokla* squares as evenly as you can. Cover with plastic film so the *dhoklas* do not dry out. Garnish with fresh coriander and coconut just before you eat. Serve warm or at room temperature.

FAIJI FATTEH'S
SMOKED AUBERGINE/ EGGPLANT WITH YOGHURT
Bharat

There are many ways to smoke foods. The Muslim Bohris of Gujarat often cook a dish, then set an onion skin 'cup' in the middle of it. Into this 'cup' they put some *ghee* (clarified butter) and then a hot, live piece of charcoal. They cover the dish immediately, allowing the ensuing smoke to perfume the cooked food. Instead of the coal, you could use a broken piece of ceramic tile or a small spoon, well-heated over a flame.

This dish may be served with all Indian meals. It also makes a good dip for raw vegetables and cocktail crisps and crackers.

If you plan to use the charcoal, arrange to have it glowing and handy sometime before you eat.

Serves 4–6
2 spring onions (scallions)
about 14 oz/400 g, 1 medium-sized aubergine (eggplant)
8 fl oz/250 ml/1 cup plain yoghurt
3 tbs/45 ml finely chopped fresh green coriander (Chinese parsley)
½ tsp/2.5 ml ground, roasted cumin (page 199)
½ tsp/2.5 ml salt
freshly ground black pepper
1 tbs/15 ml very hot *ghee* (clarified butter – page 201)

Cut the spring onions (scallions) crosswise into paper-thin rounds all the way up their green sections. Leave to soak in cold water for 30 minutes. Drain and pat dry.

Roast the aubergine (eggplant) over a low naked flame, turning it whenever necessary, until the skin is completely charred and the vegetable is soft. You could, if you prefer, do the same thing under your grill (broiler).

Peel the aubergine (eggplant) under running water, making sure you remove all the charred bits. Cut off the stem end and mash the vegetable. Put in a serving dish. Add the spring onions (scallions).

Beat the yoghurt lightly with a fork or a whisk until it is smooth and creamy. Add it to the dish with the aubergine (eggplant). Also put in the green coriander (Chinese parsley), roasted cumin, salt and black pepper. Mix well.

Now put a very small bowl or a cup-shaped pice of onion skin in the centre of the aubergine-yoghurt mixture. Pour the hot *ghee* into it. Put a small glowing piece of charcoal into the *ghee* and cover the serving dish immediately. Open it after 5 minutes.

This *bharat* may be served at room temperature or cold.

MAHARASHTRA

The seaside city of Bombay may be the capital of the state of Maharashtra, but Poona, much further inland, is its soul. It is here, in a house shaded by mulberry and jackfruit trees, that a Brahmin bride is just about to start her married life. The house, festooned with mango leaves and marigolds, is new, designed by the groom's brother, but the first ritual for the bride seems as old as the distant Deccan hills that form a brown and sombre backdrop.

As she crosses the threshold of her new home, the bride lifts her pretty henna'd foot and gently kicks a wooden measure piled high with grains of rice. The grains spill over, scattering themselves inside the living-room door. It is as it should be. The bride is, at this moment at any rate, Laxshmi incarnate, the Goddess of Wealth, bringing Plenty, as signified by the rice, into the home of her in-laws.

Starting around Maharashtra, one can almost begin to draw a line – albeit a hazy one – that divides the basically wheat-eating north (Kashmir is an exception) from the rice-eating south. Maharashtrians eat both wheat and rice, but rice is given a special place of prominence. It is used in every form imaginable, from steamed rice flour dumplings (*modaks*) served at the feast day of the elephant-headed god, Ganesh, to delicate rice flour biscuits (cookies) called *anarsa* that are served at Divali, the Festival of Lights.

I succumbed to *anarsa* the very first time I tasted it. A hostess in Poona had decided that it was late enough in the afternoon to serve tea. She quickly fried up some *sagodana vada*, fritters made by combining boiled potatoes, crushed peanuts and soaked sago.

Then she went into her store room to pull out an old English biscuit tin with George VI smiling from its lid. As she poured my tea, she said, 'You open the box. What is inside is very special.' And indeed it was.

It is hard to describe *anarsa*, even harder to make it. Somewhat like a lacy, airy, light – but slightly chewy – biscuit, its preparation takes time. Lots of it. First rice must be soaked for several days, each day in fresh water. Then the fermented grains are dried and pounded into a fine flour. This flour is mixed with jaggery (raw sugar) and a little hot oil and left in a closed tin for five days. When the tin is opened, the mixture is ready to be formed into a soft dough. The dough is patted into thin rounds on a leaf lined with poppy seeds and then slid into moderately hot oil to be deep fried. The results, served at religious festivals – and, if one is lucky, at tea-time – are quite heavenly.

Anarsa typifies the best of Maharashtrian food. This cuisine from India's heartland aims more to delight and satisfy than to dazzle. It depends, for its final taste, not so much on rare ingredients as on the gentle but expert blending of sweet, salty, hot and sour flavours.

Consider the wedding banquet that our bride with henna'd feet is attending.

She sits, like all other diners, on a red *paat* (a low, individual platform) set on the floor. Her body is draped in a nine-yard, Paithani saree of thick royal blue silk, edged with maroon and gold. A black dot of kohl has been placed on her cheek – to keep away the evil spirits, naturally.

The floor in front of every diner had been decorated with *rangoli*, curlicues made with red, green and white powders. Incense burns. Large metal plates are set down in the centre of each *rangoli* pattern. Most of the food is already on the plates, neatly laid out in a very special, unchanging order, just inside the rim. It is all vegetarian. Each food has its designated place on the plate, like the numbers on a clock. The left side is for seasonings, relishes and savouries, the right for vegetables, split peas and sweets.

At the twelve o'clock position is the most basic seasoning of all, salt – a tiny hillock of it. Following it, on the left, are a wedge of lime, a fresh coconut chutney flavoured with cumin seeds, then two fresh relishes, or *koshimbirs*, one made with cucumber bits

and crushed peanuts, the other with boiled and mashed pumpkin, perked up with ground mustard and yoghurt. A glistening
preserve follows next, a sweet-and-sour mango *achar*, studded
with plump raisins. Then come the savouries – a *papadum*, on
which sit a few white sago crisps, and a few *bhajjias*, or vegetable
fritters.

To the right of the salt, in a small *vati* or bowl, is *aru chi bhaji*, a
melange of colacassia leaves, *chana dal*, cashews and peanuts
cooked in tart tamarind water, followed by two vegetable dishes,
one dry one, *batata bhaji* – potatoes cooked with cumin seeds,
curry leaves, lime juice, a touch of sugar and coconut – the other
a somewhat wet one, an unusual combination of tiny, striped
aubergines (eggplants) and lima beans flavoured with Maharashtra's famous *kala masala*, or black spice mixture . (This
varies from home to home but often contains roasted and
ground spices such as cinnamon, cardamom, cumin, sesame
seeds and pieces of blackened coconut.)

Next come sweets which include squiggly, syrup-filled *jalebis*
and a special *kheer* or pudding made with semolina dough carefully rolled and cut to resemble rice. Somewhat in from the rim
will be placed, a bit later, the *masala bhat*, a spicy fried rice
flavoured with vegetables such as cabbage, and perhaps a bread
with a sweet *dal* stuffing, *puran poli*.

The first course is placed just slightly above the six o'clock
position. It is a simple, almost bland starter, consisting of rice
moulded in a round bowl, covered partially by an 'icing' of
varan, a simple *toovar dal*, very lightly seasoned with salt, turmeric and asafetida. Some hot ghee will be poured over the *dal*,
and that will be it. The meal can begin. This exceedingly plain
first course seems to say, 'Taste every grain you eat. Savour it.
Enjoy it. And be thankful for it.'

While the foods of certain Brahmin communities around
Poona may be classically restrained and vegetarian, one has only
to look at the extravagance and richness of the diet of the
Mahrattas headquartered in Kolhapur or the spicy ebullience of
that of the coastal fisherfolk to realize that, even within the state
of Maharashtra, there are several different cuisines.

The Mahrattas, belonging to a caste of working-class agricul-
turists, were once Hindu India's best warriors. From tiny inland
forts perched on craggy Deccan hills, they rushed out like angry

moles, fighting the Portuguese, Arabs, Moghuls and English with equal ferocity. Inspired by their seventeenth-century leader, Shivaji, they once had an empire that stretched all the way from the coast of Gujarat and Maharashtra to Uttar Pradesh. They have, traditionally, eaten and enjoyed whatever has come their way. On hunts they marinate quail in yoghurt, cloves and black pepper, wrap them in wet clay, and then throw them into smouldering fires to bake. Or else they cook up a hare, shred it, and then fry up the shreds with a healthy dose of red chillies. Mahrattas eat their food hot and unsweetened. In fact the villagers around Kolhapur are known to drink up – and enjoy – the red, hot fat that floats up to the surface of their blistering and utterly delicious meat stews.

Travelling west from Kolhapur, one reaches Ratnagiri on the Konkan coast. This area has the distinction of producing what is to my mind the best mango in the entire world. It is called the Apus, or Alphonso. Pleasingly plump on the outside with a clear yellow skin touched with red, the flesh of the Alphonso is juicy, satin-smooth, firm enough to offer a slight hint of resistance but soft enough to yield with beguiling eagerness, 'sweet-sweet' as we Indians might say but with just a possibility of sourness. I often think that summers in India would be unbearable without the God-given compensation of mangoes – Alphonsoes in particular. Maharashtrians not only eat their mangoes as a fresh fruit but convert their summer's bounty into fresh juice – which they eat with freshly fried *pooris* (breads), or into the most exquisite sweetmeats, such as the scrumptious morsels known as *amba barfi*.

It is along the same Konkan coast, a little farther north, that one can find the ancient tribe of Koli fisherfolk. In a nice division of labour, the Koli men go out to fish, the Koli women sell the fish – and cook it as well for their families. It is the Maharashtrian custom for married women to wear green glass bangles on both their arms. Koli women wear theirs only on their left arms. At the time of their marriage, their right arms are immersed in the sea. It is these right arms that are supposed to save their husbands from the dangers of the deep.

Savitri is a Koli fisherwoman. She lives in an idyllic setting. The warm sun filters gently through a permanent canopy of mango, tamarind, and palm trees. Green parrots flit about. The sea breathes just a stone's throw away, its edges scalloped by sandy beaches.

She and her husband share a single room which has been arranged to fulfil three clear functions. One area is for praying – a picture of Vithoba (an incarnation of Vishnu) hangs on the wall with a fresh hibiscus balanced on it; another is for sleeping and dressing, and the third at the back is for cooking. There is a hole in the ceiling just above the dung and clay stove to let out the wood smoke.

Wearing a blue cotton saree tightly pulled between her legs, thus accentuating the curves of her buttocks and thighs, Savitri moves with sinuous grace as she prepares a spicy fisherman's banquet, a seafood extravaganza the likes of which no casual tourist to India is ever likely to see.

Tiny dried fish, bought that morning in a wrapping of newspaper, are washed, then sautéed in a very shallow, wok-like vessel with asafetida, onion and lots of green chillies and garlic. The prized pomfret, a firm-fleshed, flat fish, is cut crosswise into steaks on a lethal, curved blade, dipped in a thrice-ground paste of fresh coconut, green coriander, green chillies, cinnamon, cloves and turmeric, and then slapped on to a hot griddle until it is crisp on the outside, soft and tender inside. Prawns are next. They are salted and rubbed with a coconut paste. Some oil is heated, and mustard and cumin seeds thrown in. When they pop, onions and garlic go in as well. There is some quick stirring, some pulling out and pushing in of burning logs to adjust the flame. In go the prawns – some of the freshest and firmest I have seen. There is more stirring and the dish is done. Now it is the turn of the squid. I have specially requested them, having a particular weakness for the slithery creatures. They are to be flavoured with *chircoot*, a spice very similar to Szechuan peppercorns and used on the Konkan coast for the preparation of fish dishes. The delicacy of the day is *newta* or mudfish. They have been procured after careful selection and much bargaining. They are expensive. They are also alive. Savitri would not consider buying them dead. They look like black tadpoles. They are swiftly dispatched and their inedible portions thrown to the family rooster, who seems delighted, in his own nervous sort of way. The mudfish are cooked with a ground red spice mixture that contains inordinate amounts of red chillies as well as black pepper, coriander and cinnamon.

We sit under the trees to enjoy our superb meal. With the seafood, we are served black-eyed beans, partially milled rice with flecks of red bran still clinging to it, some of the most scrumptious rice flour breads I have ever eaten and crisp, white, rice flour wafers that glisten in the sun like sea-shells.

Bombay, the state capital and western India's principal seaport, is just over a hundred miles away from where Savitri lives, but it might as well be another world. Its inhabitants, about nine million of them, are a vibrant blend of Gujarati Hindu merchants, Parsi industrials, Maharashtrian intellectuals, Baghdadi Jews in the advertising business, Muslim movie stars, Goan lawyers, the original Koli fishermen, to say nothing of the other Indians from the south, east and north who came here to make good.

Bombay was once a group of seven verdant, if somewhat sleepy, islands inhabited mainly by Koli fisherfolk and not taken too seriously by Hindu and Muslim empire-builders. The Shah of Gujarat handed them over to the Portuguese, who in 1661 passed them on to England as part of the dowry when Catherine of Braganza married Charles II. Encouraged by the religious tolerance promised by the English Governor, cotton weavers, merchants and ship-builders began pouring in from the neighbouring mainland. As the population boomed, the seven islands were gradually connected with causeways and landfills. In 1865, when the Prince of Wales (later Edward VII) visited India, he was welcomed enthusiastically in Bombay, with one banner saying, somewhat deliriously, 'Tell Mama (Queen Victoria) we are happy.' Bombayites had every reason to be happy. During the years 1861–5, when Americans were bloodying each other in the Civil War, the cotton trade between America and England all but dried up. Lancaster turned to Bombay for cotton, and Bombay supplied it. Fortunes were made. Today, many of Bombay's millionaires owe their palatial homes and productive industries to the misfortunes of the Americans and the perspicacity of their ancestors.

Even though Bombay's cotton boom ended after the American Civil War, enough prosperity was generated to put Bombay on a sound financial footing. Bombay set up its own textile mills, docks were expanded, and massive public buildings in exotic Gothic styles came heaving out of the earth.

One such building was Crawford Market, built in 1871 as a collection of handsome, spacious halls to be used for the sale of fresh produce. The flagstones for its floors came from Caithness. The bas-reliefs on its entrance gate and its fountain were designed by Rudyard Kipling's father. Today, even though the building itself is in desperate need of restoration, the institution remains as vibrant as ever, in many ways the pulsating heart of the city.

The best produce from the nation is sold here: easy-to-peel oranges from Nagpur; 'glass' cherries from Kashmir; plump, sweet-and-sour litchis from Dehradun; sugary baby melons from Lucknow; and Alphonsoes from Ratnagiri – when the Middle East does not buy them up with its coveted hard currency.

Crawford Market is always filled with shoppers, though early mornings bring in the discerning. A Bohri lady in a long skirt is buying sliver-thin shoots of garlic which will be used to make *lessan,* a much loved dish for cold days. A Baghdadi Jewish lady is selecting pieces of liver for her Friday dish of *kubba hamad.* The liver will be ground to a paste with soaked rice and used as a wrapping for minced (ground) beef. The resulting dumplings will be poached in a delicious soupy stew containing lots of sliced beetroots. The same lady stops off at the poultry section as well. The children will come in hungry from school, and she had better fry them some minced chicken fritters – *arooq* – making sure they are nice and spicy. The children seem addicted to spicy food. A stout Goan gentleman is buying rather a lot of eggs. He is going to mix them with coconut milk and jaggery and patiently, over several hours, bake one pancake over the next, to produce that amazing Goan cake known as *bibinka.* A tall, elegant Parsi lady in slim white slacks brushes past the stout Goan gentleman. She also wants eggs for her *Bharuchi akuri.* She checks her list. Yes, she already has the pure *ghee* from the Parsi Dairy . . . into that will go the ginger, garlic and green chillies – she has those – then the beaten eggs and matchstick potatoes . . . yes she has everything . . . but she is carrying too much. The shopkeeper is eager to oblige: 'Shall I get a basket boy?' he asks. A young man appears as if on command. All the paper bags are put into his basket which he then lifts on to his head. The Parsi lady leads the way, and the basket boy follows, all the way to the distant parked car.

If Parsi, Jewish and Gujarati shippers and industrialists were once the sought-after élite of Bombay, they have now been completely replaced by film stars. Bombay is India's Hollywood, churning out hundreds of extravaganzas every year. Cinema fever grips everyone – taxi drivers, coconut vendors and fisher-women. Stars walking into the monolithic Sheraton Oberoi to have a Châteaubriand steak or into the Taj Mahal Hotel's Harbour Bar to have a 'Johnnie Walker, Black Label, please,' are mobbed before they can get in by adoring fans in the streets.

But there is one equalizer in Bombay to which everyone succumbs – Parsi millionaires, movie stars and taxi drivers alike – and that is *bhel-poori*. *Bhel-poori* is a snack. The place to have it is Chowpatty Beach, the time sundown, when most of Bombay likes to promenade by the sea to 'eat the air'.

A hissing hurricane lamp lights up the *bhel-poori* vendor's cart. All the ingredients for the snack are neatly laid out in a orderly fashion so his fingers can move with dizzying speed. Some puffed rice is put into a bowl. Then, some wheat-flour crisps are crumbled over it. Generous sprinklings of chopped onion and chopped boiled potato follow. The vendor cups the bowl in both hands and tosses its contents. Two chutneys are now spooned in: a tart, hot green one made with fresh green coriander and green chillies, and a thick sweet-and-sour one made with tamarind and dates. Some *sev*, fine, squiggly vermicelli made out of chickpea flour, are thrown in as well, followed by more of the two chutneys. The bowl is given a final toss and emptied into the saucers of waiting customers. Hot, sweet-and-sour, and crunchy, the *bhel-poori* is now ready to be gobbled up.

RECIPES FROM MAHARASHTRA

HOT YOGHURT SOUP
Dahi Shorba

The Taj Mahal Hotel in Bombay is perhaps India's finest hotel. It is certainly one that I have stayed in since the days of my childhood and watched both interiors and menus change over the years.

This yoghurt soup is a relatively new addition – and a very pleasant one, I might add. It draws its inspiration from similar dishes found in the dining rooms of many Gujarati and Maharashtrian homes.

Serves 4

¾ pint/450 ml/2 cups plain yoghurt
3 tbs/45 ml chickpea flour (gram flour/ *besan*)
2 tsp/10 ml sugar
¾–1 tsp/4–5 ml salt
2 oz/50 g, 3–4 nice, firm radishes, trimmed
2 tsp/10 ml vegetable oil
⅛ tsp ground asafetida
1 tsp/5 ml whole black mustard seeds
1 tsp/5 ml whole cumin seeds
1 tsp/5 ml whole coriander seeds
6–8 curry leaves, fresh or dried
4 whole, dried hot red chillies
4 cloves garlic, peeled and chopped
4 peeled slices of ginger, finely chopped (about 1½ tsp/7 ml)

Put the yoghurt into a bowl. Beat lightly with a fork or a whisk until smooth.

Put the chickpea flour in a bowl. Slowly add ¾ pint/450 ml/2 cups of water, mixing well as you do so. (Put through a strainer if lumps form.) Now add the yoghurt to the chickpea flour mixture with the sugar, salt, and whole radishes. Mix and pour into a pan. Bring to a boil over moderate heat. Turn heat down and simmer, uncovered, for 10 minutes. Remove the radishes and set aside.

Organize all your spices for the next step, which goes very fast. Heat the oil in a small frying pan over a medium flame. When hot, put in, first the asafetida, then, a second later, the mustard seeds, cumin seeds and the coriander seeds. When the mustard seeds begin to pop, put in the curry leaves and whole red chillies. As soon as the red chillies start to darken, put in the chopped garlic and ginger. Stir until the garlic pieces brown a bit. Now put the entire contents of the frying pan into the soup. Continue to simmer the soup with the spices for another 5 minutes.

Strain the soup. Cut the radishes into small, ⅛-in/0.25-cm dice and add to the soup just before serving.

MRS BAKLE'S
TOMATO WITH COCONUT MILK
Tomato Saar

Saars are not exactly soups. They *are* soupy, however, and are eaten – in Maharashtra – with Indian breads or rice dishes, accompanied by meats and vegetables. Generally, they are served in small, individual bowls. You could put a spoon in the bowl, if you so choose.

Serves 4
1½ lb/700 g, 6 smallish tomatoes
1 tbs/15 ml rice flour
8 fl oz/250 ml/1 cup coconut milk (page 198)
1 tbs/15 ml vegetable oil
¼ tsp whole cumin seeds
1 fresh hot, green chilli, very finely chopped
¼ tsp red chilli powder (cayenne pepper)
about ½ tsp/2.5 ml salt
⅛ tsp sugar
freshly ground black pepper
1 tbs/15 ml finely chopped fresh, green coriander (Chinese parsley)

Drop the tomatoes into boiling water for 15 seconds. Remove and peel. Chop up the tomatoes and put them into a small pan. Bring to a simmer. Cover and simmer for about 15 minutes or until the tomatoes are soft. Put the tomatoes into the container of a food processor or blender. Blend until smooth.

Put the rice flour in a bowl. Slowly add 8 fl oz/250 ml/1 cup of coconut milk, mixing as you go, to avoid lumps. Put this liquid into a food processor or blender and blend with the tomatoes.

Heat the oil in a medium-sized pan over a medium flame. When hot, put in first the cumin seeds and, about 30 seconds later, the green chillies. Stir once. Now put in the tomato mixture, the red chilli powder (cayenne pepper), salt, sugar and black pepper. Stir and bring to a simmer. Cook, uncovered, on a low flame for 5 minutes, stirring every now and then. When serving, sprinkle with fresh, green coriander (Chinese parsley).

MRS RAJADHYAKSHA'S
CAULIFLOWER, PEAS AND POTATOES
Fulvar, Ola Watana Ana Batatya Chi Bhaji

This is a mild, soul-satisfying everyday dish, served in nearly all Maharashtrian homes. As it cooks very quickly – in about 15 minutes – most working people find it no trouble at all to put together. Even though I have made the sugar optional, the Maharashtrians almost always use it.

You could serve it with all Indian meals – I find that it is not at all out of place with simple Western meals of grilled (broiled) or roasted meats.

Serves 4–6
12 oz/350 g/2 cups, when cut, cauliflower (about half a medium-sized head)
8½ oz/230 g, 3 smallish potatoes, preferably new or red
4 tbs/60 ml/⅓ cup vegetable oil
⅛ tsp ground asafetida
1 tbs/15 ml whole black mustard seeds
8–10 curry leaves, fresh or dried
4½ oz/125 g/1 cup shelled peas, fresh

84

or frozen (if frozen, thaw enough to separate)
2 fresh, hot, green chillies, very finely chopped
¼ tsp ground turmeric
¾ tsp/4 ml salt
½ tsp/2.5 ml sugar
2 tbs/30 ml grated fresh coconut
2 tbs/30 ml chopped fresh green coriander (Chinese parsley)

Cut the cauliflower into small flowerets – no larger or wider than 1½ in/4 cm.

If the potatoes are new or the American, small red variety, do not bother to peel them. Cut them into ¾-in/2-cm dice or a bit smaller.

Warm the oil in a good-sized frying pan over a medium-high flame. When hot, put in first the asafetida, then, a second later, the mustard seeds. When the mustard seeds begin to pop – this takes just a few seconds, put in the curry leaves. Stir once. Now put in the potatoes, cauliflower, peas, green chillies, turmeric, salt and sugar. Stir for 2 minutes. Add about 2 fl oz/50 ml/¼ cup of water and stir. As soon as the water begins to bubble, cover and turn the heat to low. Cook for 10–15 minutes or until the potatoes are just done. Sprinkle the coconut and coriander (Chinese parsley) over the top and stir.

ANJALI NARAHARI KHARE'S
GREEN BEANS COOKED WITH SPLIT PEAS
Farasvi Bhaji

This delicious bean dish from the Chittapavan Brahmins uses an unusual cooking technique. It can only be des-cribed as a reversed double-boiler method – the food is in the bottom pot and water on top – with the result that the food cooks in the minimal water that drips down as condensation. This is simple to do and is exceedingly nutritious as all the properties of the vegetables are conserved. I find myself cooking all my vegetables this way now. If you have a double-boiler, do use it. Otherwise, find a second pot that can sit on the first one, nesting inside it slightly, or a lid that can hold water on top of it.

You will notice that *dal* (or split peas) has been added to provide protein. This bean dish may be served with almost any Indian meal.

Serves 4
2 tsp/10 ml skinned *urad dal* or *moong dal* or yellow split peas (page 200)
10 oz/275 g green beans
3 tbs/45 ml vegetable oil
⅛ tsp ground asafetida (optional)
½ tsp/2.5 ml whole black mustard seeds
¼ tsp whole cumin seeds
8–10 curry leaves, fresh or dried (page 199)
1 whole hot green chilli, very finely chopped
about ½ tsp/2.5 ml salt
about ½ tsp/2.5 ml sugar
⅛ tsp ground turmeric
¼ tsp ground cumin seeds
1 tsp/5 ml ground coriander seeds
2 oz/50 g/½ cup freshly ground coconut
2 tbs/30 ml finely chopped fresh green coriander (Chinese parsley)

Pick over the *dal* or yellow split peas and wash. Drain and put in a small bowl. Add enough water so it covers the *dal* or split peas by about 1 in/ 2.5 cm. Let the *dal* soak for 30 minutes and the split peas for 1 hour. Drain.

Trim the ends of the beans and cut crosswise into ¼-in/0.5-cm rounds. Put some water to boil.

Heat the oil in a heavy pan over a medium heat. When hot, put in first the asafetida, then, a second later, the mustard seeds and whole cumin seeds. When the mustard seeds begin to pop (this just takes a few seconds) put in the curry leaves. Stir once and put in the drained *dal* or split peas. Stir a few times until the *dal* is very lightly browned. Now put in the green beans, the green chillies, salt, sugar, turmeric, ground cumin and ground coriander. Stir for 1 minute. Turn the heat to low. Put a second pan on top of the first pan and half fill it with boiling water. (If you are using a lid to hold water, just pour as much as it will hold and replenish it now and then.)

Cook for about 10 minutes or until the beans are just done. Remove the pan with the water. Add coconut and fresh green coriander (Chinese parsley). Stir to mix.

DURGA KHOTE'S
POTATOES WITH TOMATOES
Batate Ambat

Cooked by the Sarasvat Brahmins of Maharashtra, this potato dish is flavoured with tomatoes and fresh coconut. Serve it hot with Indian meals or cold as a deliciously spicy potato salad.

Serves 6
1 lb 2 oz/500 g new potatoes, or any other firm, waxy potatoes
10 oz/275 g, 3 medium-sized tomatoes
4 tbs/60 ml vegetable oil
⅛ tsp ground asafetida (optional)
1 tsp/5 ml whole black mustard seeds
½ tsp/2.5 ml ground turmeric
⅛–½ tsp red chilli powder (cayenne pepper)
2 tsp/10 ml tamarind paste (page 202) or lemon juice
1 tsp/5 ml salt
2 oz/50 g/½ cup fresh grated coconut (page 197)

Cut the potatoes lengthwise (with skin, if using new potatoes) into 1-in/2.5-cm thick fingers. Chop the tomatoes very finely.

Heat the oil in a frying pan or wide pan over a medium-high flame. When hot, put in first the ground asafetida and, a second later, the mustard seeds. As soon as the mustard seeds begin to pop take the pan off the fire and quickly put in the turmeric, red chilli powder (cayenne pepper) and the tomatoes. Cover and put the pan back on the heat for 1 minute. Uncover. Put in about 8 fl oz/250 ml/1 cup of water, the potatoes, the tamarind paste and salt. Bring to a boil. Cover, lower the heat and simmer gently for 30 minutes or until the potatoes are tender. Add the coconut and continue cooking for 2–3 minutes. Increase the heat a bit during this period if the sauce seems too thin and watery. You should end up with a very thick sauce that clings to the potatoes somewhat.

Sealdah vegetable market, Calcutta.

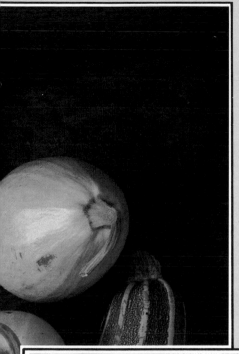

Fish in a Bengali Sauce, Prawns with
Mustard Seeds.

Okra with Mustard Seeds, Plain Rice,
Delicious Fried Morsels, Roasted
Moong Dal with Spinach.

Fish on sale in Calcutta.

Chicken in a Green Sauce, Hyderabadi Pilaf of Rice and Split Peas.

Flaky Pan Bread, Sesame Chutney and Yoghurt Chutney, Quick Kebabs.

A market trader, surrounded by the
ingredients for a thousand vegetarian
recipes, with gourds and pumpkins
suspended overhead.

Kulcha, a popular Hyderabadi bread,
is laid to rise on mats and then marked
with its distinctive pattern.

Sacks of dried beans and split peas.

MRS KAMAL GOLE'S
PRAWNS/SHRIMPS COOKED IN THE MAHARASHTRIAN MANNER
Kolumbi Tse Kalvan

Here is a quick dish which you may make with prawns (shrimps) or any firm-fleshed fish that can be cut into thick steaks or chunks. Serve with rice and vegetables such as Stuffed Okra, Carrots with Dill and Puréed Vegetables.

Serves 4

1 lb/450 g medium-sized uncooked prawns (shrimps) unpeeled (but no heads) or 12–13 oz/350–375 g, peeled, uncooked prawns (shrimps)
1 clove garlic, finely crushed
1 tsp/5 ml finely grated, peeled fresh ginger
3 tbs/45 ml tamarind paste (page 203)
⅛ tsp ground turmeric
¾ tsp/4 ml salt
¼ tsp hot, red chilli powder (cayenne pepper).
2 tbs/30 ml vegetable oil
3 cloves garlic, peeled, mashed lightly, but left whole
4 fl oz/125 ml/½ cup unsweetened coconut milk, tinned or fresh (page 198)
1 tbs/15 ml finely chopped fresh coriander (Chinese parsley)
2 fresh hot green chillies, very finely chopped

If the prawns (shrimps) are unpeeled, peel them. Devein them (page 203). Put them in a bowl. Add the crushed garlic, ginger, tamarind paste, turmeric, salt and chilli powder (cayenne pepper). Mix well and set aside for 10 minutes (not longer, as raw ginger tends to affect the texture of the prawns/shrimps).

Heat the oil in a frying pan over a medium-high flame. When hot, put in the whole, mashed cloves of garlic. Stir until they brown lightly. Now put in the prawns (shrimps). Stir for 1 minute so the prawns (shrimps) can also brown lightly. Turn the heat to medium-low. Put in the coconut milk, fresh coriander (Chinese parsley) and green chillies. As soon as the sauce begins to simmer, turn off the heat and serve.

MRS MOZELLE SOFAER'S
MINCED/GROUND CHICKEN FRITTERS
Arooq

This dish comes from a family of Iraqi Jews who settled in India over 100 years ago. The *arooq*, an Iraqi dish, has, what with the green chillies and turmeric in it, been Bombayized. It is quite delicious and is the sort of thing that one just cannot stop eating. Amongst Bombay's Iraqi Jews, it is sometimes served with rice and a *dal*. When children come home starving after a day in school, it is stuffed inside a pitta-like bread, along with a little chopped lettuce and tomato and served as a snack. I like it best when it just comes out of the wok, either plain or with a mint or fresh coriander chutney acting as a dip. My husband loves it with a generous squeeze of lemon juice.

As the fritters are deep-fried, I find a wok or Indian *karhai* the best utensil to use for the cooking. If you do not have a wok, a frying pan will do. *Arooq* can also be made with minced (ground) fish or very finely minced (ground) lamb.

Serves 4
2 spring onions (scallions)
1 lb/450 g raw minced (ground) chicken (I use raw minced/ground boneless chicken breast)
⅛ tsp ground turmeric
¼ tsp red chilli powder (cayenne pepper)
½ tsp/2.5 ml very finely chopped (minced) fresh, hot green chilli
½ tsp/2.5 ml salt
freshly ground black pepper
2 tbs/30 ml plain white flour
2 eggs, beaten
vegetable oil, for deep frying

Cut off 1 in/2.5 cm of the white, onion-like part of the spring onion (scallion) as well as the top, very green section. You do not need them. Cut the middle sections in half, lengthwise, and then cut these strips crosswise as finely as possible.

Put the minced (ground) chicken in a bowl. Add the turmeric, chilli powder (cayenne pepper), green chilli, salt, black pepper, spring onions (scallions) and flour. Mix well. Add the eggs and mix again. Cover and refrigerate for at least 1 hour. (You can even make the mixture a day ahead of time.)

Just before you are ready to eat, pour enough oil into a wok or *karhai* to come to a depth of 2 in/5 cm. Heat the oil over a lowish flame. Give it time to heat.

Use two soupspoons to make the fritters. Lift up a ball of the chicken mixture, about 1 in/2.5 cm in diameter, on the front end of one of the spoons. Help release it into the hot oil with the second spoon. Make as many balls as will fit easily in one layer. Stir and fry them until they are golden brown on the outside and cooked inside. This should take about 5 minutes. Adjust your heat, if necessary. Take the fritters out with a slotted spoon and drain on absorbent kitchen paper (paper towels). Make all the fritters this way. Serve them hot.

MRS KUMAR RASTE'S
LAMB COOKED IN THE KOLHAPURI STYLE
Kolhapuri Mutton

Within Maharashtra, as in much of India, districts, even towns, have their own distinct cuisines. Kolhapur is associated with the foods of the Mahrattas, who were once the bravest of Indian warriors, fighting both Moghul emperors and imperial British forces with great success.

This dish, with its superb, dark sauce, is quite fiery if eaten in Kolhapur. The recipe calls for 10–12 whole red chillies. I find 4 chillies fiery enough. You can use more or less as you desire.

You may serve this meat with rice and any Indian bread. A relish, such as Cucumbers with Fresh Coconut or Tomato and Onion with Yoghurt, could be served on the side.

Serves 4–6
2 lb/900 g boned lamb from the shoulder, cut into 1½-in/4-cm cubes

For the marinade:
4 tbs/60 ml plain yoghurt
2 tsp/10 ml very finely grated peeled
  fresh ginger
1 tsp/5 ml very finely crushed garlic
¼ tsp turmeric

For the sauce:
½ tsp/2.5 ml vegetable oil
2–4 dried, hot, red chillies
1½-in/4-cm cinnamon stick
10 whole cloves
10 whole cardamom pods
2 tbs/30 ml whole coriander seeds
10 oz/350 g, 3 medium-sized onions,
  peeled
6 tbs/10 ml vegetable oil
2 tsp/10 ml very finely crushed garlic
1 tsp/5 ml very finely grated peeled
  fresh ginger
½ lb/225 g, 3 small tomatoes, very
  finely chopped
about 1¼ tsp/6 ml salt

Put the meat in a bowl. Add all the marinating seasonings and mix well. Cover and refrigerate for 3 hours or overnight if you prefer.

Lightly grease a small cast-iron frying pan with the ½ tsp/2.5 ml of vegetable oil and heat it over a medium-low flame. When it is hot, put in the dried hot red chillies and the cinnamon stick. Stir these around until the red chillies darken. Remove the spices and put them in a plate. Put the whole cloves, cardamom pods and coriander seeds into the same frying pan. Stir and roast the seeds until they darken a few shades. You will be able to smell the roasted coriander seeds. Put these spices into the same

plate as the chillies and cinnamon.

Put all the roasted spices from the plate into the container of a clean coffee grinder or other spice grinder. Grind as finely as possible.

Cut all the onions in half, lengthwise. Now slice half of these sections crosswise into very fine half rings. Chop up the other half as finely as you can.

When the meat has finished marinating, heat the 6 tbs/90 ml/½ cup of oil in a wide, heavy pan over a medium-high flame. When hot, put in just the sliced onions. Stir and fry them until they are reddish-brown in colour. Now put in the very finely chopped onions and stir them for 1 minute. Turn the heat down to medium-low. Put in the 2 tsp/10 ml of garlic and 1 tsp/5 ml of ginger. Stir for a few seconds. Put in the ground spices from the coffee grinder and stir once. Now add 4 fl oz/125 ml/½ cup of water. Continue to stir and cook on a medium-low flame, stirring as you do so, for 3–4 minutes. You will begin to see the oil as it separates from the spice mixture.

Now put in the marinated meat. Turn up the heat to medium-high. Stir and fry the meat with the spice paste for 10 minutes. Add the tomatoes and salt. Continue to stir and cook for another 5 minutes. Now add about 8 fl oz/250 ml/1 cup of water and bring to a simmer. Cover, turn heat to low and simmer for about 1 hour or until the meat is tender.

Just before serving, you can spoon the fat off the top if you so desire.

SHEILA JACOB'S
RICE WITH TOMATOES AND SPINACH
Tomato Palak Bhat

Here is one of those wonderful rice dishes that I can eat all by itself, accompanied, at times, by just plain yoghurt and a pickle. You will find that a thin crust might form at the bottom of your pan after you finish cooking. Do not throw it away. It tastes quite wonderful and should be eaten!

This particular recipe comes from the Bene Israel community – a Jewish group that settled in Maharashtra centuries ago.

This rice dish is very mild and can be served with almost any meal.

The roasted, ground coriander and cumin seed mixture used here is quite simple to make – it requires only whole coriander and whole cumin seeds. The recipe for it is on page 199.

Frozen spinach leaves work very well here. Use fresh spinach if you prefer.

Serves 6
Basmati or any long-grain rice, measured to the ¾ pint/450 ml/2 cup mark in a glass measuring jug
1 × 10-oz/275-g packet of frozen leaf spinach
9 oz/250 g, 2 small tomatoes
3 tbs/45 ml vegetable oil
2½ oz/65 g, 1 small onion peeled, cut in half and then cut crosswise into very thin slices
¼ tsp ground turmeric
1 tsp/5 ml roasted, ground coriander and cumin seed mixture (page 199)
1 tsp/5 ml salt

Wash the rice in several changes of water and drain. Add enough water to cover by 1 in/2.5 cm. Set aside for 30 minutes.

Cook the spinach according to package directions in just 4 fl oz/125 ml/½ cup of water. It should be tender and have no liquid left. (Fresh spinach may be cooked the same way.) Chop up the spinach very, very finely. Chop the tomatoes finely.

Heat the oil in a heavy pan over a medium-high flame. When hot, put in the onion. Stir and fry until the onion is nicely browned. Add the rice and turn the heat to medium. Stir and sauté the rice for 2 minutes. Now put in the spinach, tomatoes, turmeric, the roasted coriander and cumin seed mixture and salt. Stir gently to mix and keep stirring for 1 minute. Now add ¾ pint/450 ml/2 cups of water and bring to a boil. Cover very tightly, turn heat to very low and cook for 25 minutes. Remove cover and stir the rice gently, leaving the crust on the very bottom alone. Cover and cook on a very low heat for another 10 minutes.

MRS GOLE'S
CUCUMBERS WITH FRESH COCONUT
Koshimbir I

Koshimbirs are simple everyday relishes that are served with most meals. There are many variations. Since I like them all, I have chosen two to put in this book. This relish calls for roasted peanuts. You may use any that you find. Even fried peanuts will do. If they happen to be salted, taste the *koshimbir* just before you add the salt, then put in however much you need.

Serves 4
2 oz/50 g, 4 tablespoons roasted, shelled peanuts
10 oz/275 g/1½ cups, chopped, 2 small or 1 large cucumber
2 tbs/30 ml grated fresh coconut (page 197)
2 small green chillies, very finely chopped
2 tbs/30 ml lemon juice
½ tsp/2.5 ml sugar
½ tsp/2.5 ml salt
1 tbs/15 ml vegetable oil
⅛ tsp ground asafetida
¼ tsp whole black mustard seeds
⅛ tsp red chilli powder (cayenne pepper)

Put the peanuts in a mortar and crush them lightly. You can, if you prefer, chop them coarsely with a knife.

Peel the cucumbers and cut them into ¼-in/0.5-cm dice.

In a bowl, combine the peanuts, cucumber, coconut, green chillies, lemon juice, sugar and salt. Mix.

Heat the oil in a small frying pan over a medium flame. When hot, put in first the asafetida, then, a second later, the mustard seeds. As soon as the mustard seeds begin to pop, put in the red chilli powder (cayenne pepper). Lift up the frying pan and tilt it

around to stir the spices. Now pour the contents of the pan over the relish. Stir to mix. Serve at room temperature.

THE RAVIRAJ HOTEL'S
TOMATO AND ONION WITH YOGHURT
Koshimbir II

This relish, like the last, may be served with most Indian meals.

Serves 4
4 oz/100 g, 1 medium-sized tomato, cut into ¼-in/0.5-cm dice
2 oz/50 g, 1 small onion, chopped fine
2 tbs/30 ml yoghurt
¼ tsp salt
½ tsp/10 ml vegetable oil
pinch ground asafetida (optional)
¼ tsp whole, black mustard seeds
⅛ tsp red chilli powder (cayenne pepper)

Put the tomato, onion, yoghurt and salt into a bowl and mix.

Heat the oil in a small frying pan over a medium flame. When hot, put in first the asafetida, then, a second later, the mustard seeds. As soon as the mustard seeds begin to pop, put in the red chilli powder (cayenne pepper). Lift up the frying pan, tilting it around gently once to stir its contents and then pour the contents over the relish. Stir to mix. Serve at room temperature.

KASHMIR

Every year, on a certain full moon night in the late autumn, the landlocked people in India's northern-most state of Jammu and Kashmir can catch a glimpse of the sea.

While the sun sets over the village of Pampur, they picnic on minced (ground) meat kebabs wrapped in thin *lavasa* bread or on lamb stewed with dried ginger and fennel seeds which they eat with scoops of rice and pickled kohlrabi. They sip *noonchai*, salted mountain tea, from handleless cups, puff on their hookahs and wait. Soon a pale moon fills the clear, crisp night with its ethereal sheen. And then, suddenly, there it is – a vast, magical, silver-blue sea, its rippling surface breaking every now and then into swirls of advancing waves.

Kashmiris are a poetic lot, and their illusory sea is composed of acre upon acre of mauve crocuses, flowers that will provide them, and indeed all of India, with an ancient crop, saffron. Each threadlike stigma will be worth almost its weight in gold. The local people will use the saffron, sparingly of course, to flavour rice and meat dishes. They will float it in their tea-filled samovars if an honoured guest should drop in. They will also sprinkle it over the bowl of yoghurt that is sent out ritually with the dowry of every Hindu bride.

Summering Moghul emperors compared Kashmir to Elysium and came here, with their entire court in tow, in leviathan processions that included elephants, cavalry, artillery, wives, concubines, leopards for hunting antelope, to say nothing of the mules and porters used to carry everything from fine porcelains to gilt beds. The beauty of Kashmir is awesome. Snow-covered peaks surround, protect and conceal a lush valley that a Britisher of the Raj described as an emerald set in pearls. It is believed that the Vale of Kashmir, higher in latitude than Tibet, was once a vast lake plagued by a water demon. In order to rid her favourite playground of this pest, the goddess Parvati, wife of Shiva, cracked an opening in the mountainous wall – in an area now known as Baramula – letting out all the water and the demon with it. What was left was a green, fertile plateau, sitting coolly and comfortably at about six thousand feet above sea level, filled with gurgling streams, crystal-clear lakes, and a meandering river around which the capital, Srinagar, a town rather like Venice, would soon spring up. This naturally pretty town would be given an overlay of elegance by Moghul emperors who would edge boulevards and poplars and lakes with spreading *chinars* (oriental planes). They would build formally landscaped royal gardens where generations of common people could picnic in the years to come.

For their cuisine, the Hindu – and later on the Muslim – inhabitants of the land drew on whatever they could find, raise or grow, acknowledging, at times quite cursorily, the culinary whims of their changing overlords – Afghans, Moghuls, Sikhs and Britons. The upland forests of Kishtwar were carpeted with fat, juicy, spongy morels. Other mushrooms grew everywhere and could be harvested at no cost. (They still are. Whole wedding parties have been known to die off because someone picked the wrong fungi!) There was rhubarb that could be cooked with honey, and plenty of wild asparagus. There were enough grassy meadows to raise goats and sheep. But the Kashmiris rarely slaughtered their household animals. They chose to depend for their meat upon the Gujars, nomadic Muslim herdsmen who travelled north with the receding snowline in the spring and south again in the autumn. Household animals, raised for their milk and wool, lived on the ground floor of simple, three-storey peasant homes where, during the cruel winters, they could help out the freezing families with their ample body heat.

Growing food was and is more of a problem. Many precious terraces are reserved for the staple, rice. Kashmiris love their rice, which the cold dew, penetrating through the husk to the grain, makes hard and sweet. Wheat, too, is grown, to make Kashmir's superb breads such as the flaky, bun-shaped *kulcha* and the sesame-encrusted *tsachvaru*, both very popular accompaniments for tea.

Because so much land is covered by mountains and lakes, the Kashmiris have take to harvesting the water. The same blue lakes – the Dal, Nagin, Manasbal and Wular – on which tourists glide in upholstered *shikaras* (gondolas), admiring the lotus flowers around them, are also filled with the rhizomes of the lotus, often called lotus roots. These resemble linked sausages and taste, quite surprisingly, of artichoke hearts. Called *nedr*, they are cooked with fish, with *wastahaak* (tender spring greens) and with lamb; they are made into 'meatballs', cooked with yoghurt as a *yakhni*, dipped into a rice flour batter and made into fritters (*nedr moinj*); best of all they are fried in mustard oil to make yummy, crunchy chips (*nedr churm*). The lake waters also produce edible lotus seeds, water chestnuts, and many fish that fin their way around them.

Still, this is not enough. So the Kashmiris have learnt to slap together, layer by layer, islands of water reeds on which they pile lake weeds and mud, about four to five inches high. These man-made islands can be towed and they can be moored with the help of long poles anchored on the bottom of the lake. They can also float serenely down the lakes, allowing the world to marvel at moving crops of mint, cucumbers, watermelons, sugar melons, tomatoes and radishes.

The Kashmiri day begins at the crack of dawn while a delicate mist still hovers over the lakes. Inside beautifully carved, multi-storeyed wooden homes, floor mattresses are rolled up and put away. Charcoal is lit in *kangris*, lined baskets which act as portable hot water bottles and which the Kashmiris carry around with them as casually as walking sticks. (When the weather is really severe, the *kangris* are tucked *under* the long woollen robes – *pherens* – so that their last bit of heat may be conserved. At times a potato or even a duck egg, if that is what is available, is thrown in to bake!)

Life in a traditional Kashmiri home is carried out on the floor. There are no tables, no chairs. To take the chill off these floor and to keep them as warm and cosy as upholstered furniture, they are first lined with reeds, then with simple cotton durees, then with burlap and finally with thick, black felt. Shoes are left out in the hall.

The first order of business in most homes is the setting up of the samovar. Some live charcoal from the *kangri* is thrown down its chimney. Water is poured into its belly and after much blowing, huffing and puffing on the coals, it finally begins to heat. Once it is boiling, loose green tea (called 'Bombay tea' for some reason, even though it is more like teas drunk in China and Tibet) is sprinkled in and a little sugar, if the family wants it. Those who can afford it crush some cardamom and almonds in a mortar and put them in as well. This is *kahva*. It will be drunk for breakfast and then sipped through the course of the day until the last person beds down again in a huddle of quilts and shawls.

For breakfast, handleless metal cups make their appearance neatly stacked in a special iron cage, a *pyalanoor* or 'cupholder', which also has loops for spoons. *Kahva* is poured into the cups. They get so ferociously hot that they can only be held with the help of small towels or handkerchiefs. Breads sitting in a basket are now nibbled with the tea. They might be dunked in it first or else broken into chunks and dropped into the cup, only to be retrieved later with a spoon when all the tea has been consumed.

I cannot say enough in praise of Kashmiri breads. They are hardly known outside the state but certainly deserve to be. Related more to the breads of Afghanistan, Central Asia and the Middle East than to the *chapatis*, *pooris* and *parathas* of the rest of the subcontinent, they are generally baked by professional bakers in clay or brick ovens and bought fresh every day. They range from shortbread-like buns, to discs of flaky pastry, to spongy, chewy creations that are crosses between bagels and doughnuts. Most breads, like buns, are sized for single individuals, though more than one may be eaten. They can be sweet or salty, though never overly so. (One baker in Pampur charmingly advertises his as 'sweetish' and 'saltish'.) Some breads are encrusted with poppy seeds, others with sesame seeds. Some breads last just a day, others, wrapped in towels and placed in baskets, can last for a week. There is nothing quite as satisfying as a chewy *girda*, still warm from the bakery, smothered with a mound of clotted cream, or for that matter, a crumbly *kulcha* from Bandipora, the soft *bakirkhani* from Sopore with a hole in its centre, or the delicate *krep* and the biscuit-like *sheermal* from Pampur.

At about 9.30a.m., before everyone leaves for work, lunch is served. Dinner will not be eaten until a good ten or eleven hours later, with only tea and bread again around 4p.m. What is served at the two main meals, what is is called and how it is cooked depend to a large extent on whether the family is Hindu or Muslim. Two dishes are almost always present, rice and either kolhrabi or a green of the cabbage family that is similar to spring greens in Britain and collard greens in the United States. These vegetables and many other seasonal greens that go under names like *moinja haak, vappal haak, wastahaak, hernj haak* and *aaram haak*, are considered staples and are invariably cooked in mustard oil and water with the addition of red and green chillies. For extra flavouring, Hindus throw in asafetida, a strong-smelling resin whose odour the late James Beard, America's venerated authority on food, once compared to that of fresh truffles. Muslims add garlic and sometimes cloves and cinnamon as well. In Kashmir, it is the asafetida and garlic that seem to separate the Hindus from the Muslims.

Many of the Hindus in Kashmir are Brahmins, the high priestly class, where the men go by the title of 'pandit' (hence Pandit Jawaharlal Nehru). While the Brahmins of the rest of India abhor meat, Kashmiri pandits have worked out quite a different culinary tradition for themselves. They eat meat with great gusto – lamb cooked with yoghurt (*yakhni*), lamb cooked in milk (*aab gosht*), lamb cooked with asafetida, dried ginger, fennel and lots of ground red chillies (*rogan josh*) – but frown upon garlic and onions. Garlic and onions, they say, encourage base passions.

On the whole, Kashmiri Muslims eat many of the same meat dishes, but just spice them somewhat differently, using lots of garlic, dried red cockscomb flowers (*maval*) for food colouring, and onion. But the onion is different from anything I have ever seen. It is not the shallot of South India, nor the pink-skinned round onion of the northern plains. Instead, it is *praan*, the onion of Kashmir, a strange cross between a spring onion (or scallion) and a shallot.

Hindus tend to eat many more vegetables than the Muslims, and at times in unusual and exquisite combinations such as aubergines (eggplants) cooked with greens, aubergines cooked with apples, and cabbage cooked with tomatoes. But all these vegetables have to be cut in a certain predetermined style, a style that has to be taught to women while they are still quite young.

Every morning, all the females in a Hindu household gather around baskets of vegetables, some picked minutes before from the family kitchen garden (most families seem to have such a patch, however small) or bought from the wholesale 'floating market' in the middle of the Dal Lake where about two hundred small boats, all laden with freshly harvested produce, converge at daybreak.

Under the watchful eyes of mothers, grandmothers and mothers-in-law, who look quite unbudgeable in long, flowing robes, white head scarves and tasseled, shoulder-length earrings, young girls learn to wield sharp knives with alarming dexterity and precision. Lotus roots, they are taught, must be cut into ¼-inch (0.5-cm) rounds if they are to be cooked with spinach, into ¼-inch (0.5-cm) thick diagonals if they are to be cooked with the red-leafed *wastahaak*, into 1¼-inch (3-cm) long chunks if they are to be made into a yoghurt-enriched *yakhni*; the same chunks need to be halved, lengthwise, if the lotus root is to be cooked with fish, and so on. Great frowns appear on ancient faces at signs of carelessness.

These same matriarchs are not only masters of the kitchen knife but also repositories of a family secret, the recipe for *ver*. *Ver* is a spice mixture. Ask any Kashmiri woman for the recipe and she turns evasively coy: 'Well, you see, I don't actually make it myself,' she says cagily. 'My mother-in-law sends, just a little at a time.' *Ver* comes in the form of a thin, hard cake with a hole in its centre. It can contain garlic and *praan* for Muslims, asafetida and fenugreek for Hindus as well as lots of freshly ground red chillies, cumin, coriander ('*we* never use coriander in *our* house,' one woman told me quite emphatically), dried ginger, cloves, cardamom, and turmeric. All the spices are ground, then made into a patty with the help of some mustard oil. A hole is made in the patty and it is left to dry on wooden planks in the shade. ('Oh no! *Ver* must *never* be dried in the sun or it will turn quite black.') Here it is turned over expertly many times until it is quite hard, after which it is strung and kept for the rest of the year. Small amounts are broken off as needed, crumbled and then sprinkled over many foods to give them a recognizably Kashmiri flavour.

While summer and autumn produce an abundance of vegetables, there is constant awareness of the inevitability of winter. Every vegetable that can be cut and dried, is. Unpeeled turnips are sliced into thick rounds with holes in their centres and strung up. The long, green leaves of *vappal haak* are plaited and tomatoes are slit open. By autumn, all wood-shingled roofs are ablaze with drying chillies, superb red specimens, known throughout India for their delicately tart flavour and for the deep colour they impart. Every wooden beam inside the houses and all the eaves outside them are festooned with garlands of swaying vegetables. In the distance, professional fishermen dry their daily catches with the same urgency. Their dried fish, *hogaad*, will have to last until the spring.

The first snowfall is celebrated by the Muslims with a dish of *harissa*, a kind of porridge made of meat and grains that is eaten with the delicious *girda* bread. Hindus might huddle around their *bokharis* (chimneyed, indoor stoves) to enjoy hearty bowls of *razma gogji*, red kidney beans simmered gently with turnips.

By April, it is spring again. Willows turn green, cherry blossoms bloom and irises begin to sprout gaily from earthen rooftops. The entire valley is enamelled with narcissi, gladioli, tulips and daffodils. No wonder the British felt at home here. They could hunt – there are plenty of wild ducks and migrating Siberian geese – and they could fish for the sweet-fleshed *mah aseer* or for trout which a nineteenth-century Scotsman had introduced into the streams. Nothing is as succulent as a freshly caught fish. I treasure the memory of a recent meal of trout, just caught from a stream in Pehlgam, sliced crosswise and fried. It was served simply and elegantly on a plate, all by itself, with just two small mounds of spices beside it, one of coarse salt and the other of Kashmir's red, red chilli powder. Nothing else was needed. Crisp on the outside, sweet and juicy inside, it remains totally unforgettable.

The British might have had the flora and fauna to make them feel comfortable but there was one problem. They had no place to stay, as a maharaja in the late nineteenth century had issued an edict that forbade foreigners from owning land. So the British took to living in houseboats moored on the Jhelum River and the numerous lakes. The tradition of rental houseboats for tourists continues – indeed, flourishes – today, even though there are now several hotels including the splendid Oberoi

Palace Hotel which was once the home of the Maharaja of Kashmir.

The better houseboats, made out of pale pine contrasting to fine effect with the darker walnut, are like complete houses, with bedrooms (two, three, four – whatever one desires and can pay for), bathrooms, dining rooms, living rooms, porches and roof terraces. They have decided advantages. Children can fish from the windows – we found ours glued to their rods even before we had our morning cup of tea – and the boat can be moved, at extra cost, of course, if a change of view is desired.

Attached to the back of the houseboat, overflowing invariably with many kohl-eyed, rosy-cheeked, (and often red-haired) children, is the kitchen boat. It is from here that a strange cuisine, half English and half spicy Kashmiri, emerges at least four times a day. Foreigners are generally fed soup, roast lamb or grilled trout, followed in the spring with rhubarb stew. If you insist on an all-Kashmiri dinner, you will probably still start with soup, some pale, weak, tasteless lamb broth, thickened to no purpose with flour. Houseboat chefs seem convinced that all foreigners would simply cease to exist without regular doses of soup.

Having got that out of the way, you might find yourselves enchanted by the next course: *timatar goli*, meatballs cooked with tomatoes and yoghurt; *dhaniwal korma*, lamb cooked with fresh green coriander; *marzwangan korma*, lamb cooked with the strained red puree of Kashmiri chillies; and perhaps a chutney of some kind. Kashmiris make exquisite fresh chutneys using either walnuts, or sour cherries, or yellow pumpkin or white radishes. There will, of course, be lots of rice and, if you request it, some kind of greens, *heddar* (mushrooms cooked with tomatoes, dry ginger and fennel), *shikar* (slightly vinegared duck cooked with garlic and red chillies) and *gard muj* (fish cooked with white radish). If Kashmiri custom is followed, the fish might well be at room temperature. Kashmiris do not believe in reheating fish dishes as they say it disintegrates them. Your meal will probably end with a thud as some heavy English steamed pudding is grandly passed around.

My favourite time on these houseboats is early evening when tea is served. You may ask for *kahva*, Kashmiri tea served with a selection of Kashmiri breads, or you could have English black tea with superb scones, complete with butter and jam. As you sit on your front porch, sipping your tea, tradesmen will drift by in their boats, trying to sell you silk carpets made by little boys who sing the pattern as they weave, and the finest *pashmina* (cashmere) shawls made from the soft hair of Tibetan goats. The Kashmiri shawl industry was fostered by the Moghul emperors. Baby-soft wool threads, dyed with indigo, madder, safflower and a hundred other natural tints, were woven or embroidered with striking paisley designs. One such shawl could take three or more workers a whole year to make. Moghul emperors wore them over their shoulders and presented them as gifts to those they wished to acknowledge. The British in India had insisted that the Maharaja of Kashmir pay his annual tribute to them with one horse, twelve shawl goats (both male and female so that an industry could be started in England) and three pashmina shawls. Such shawls have always carried with them the status of a fine mink or a sable. They still do.

As you sit on your porch, you may finger such a shawl and watch the kingfishers flit over the lotus flowers. In the distance, the sun will begin to descend behind some purple peak, leaving the sky to glow in shades of gold, pink, and burning red.

By early summer, the cherries will be ripe. Whole busloads of school children will be let into orchards to pick their fill. Blankets will be spread under mulberry trees and their branches shaken to release their sweet fruit. What humans cannot eat will be munched by cattle, ponies and dogs. Marrow (squash) flowers will appear on vines, only to be dipped in a chickpea flour or rice flour batter and devoured as fritters. Tiny aubergines will be plucked from kitchen gardens and hastily cooked with liver.

Autumn will bring the hard cooking pears, *naak*, that are peeled, cut in half, and stewed with tomatoes, green chillies and green coriander. There will also be quinces that are cooked with aubergines in a fennel-flavoured sauce, almonds that may be stuffed into meatballs and crisp *amri* apples, red on one side, green on the other, that will be crunched, sending their juices flying.

It is a good season for banquets too. The Kashmiri Muslim banquet, *waazwaan*, named for the *waaza*, or professional cooks, who prepare it, begins with the appearance of an unlikely procession. A team of about twenty or thirty chefs and assistants enter, all carrying gargantuan cauldrons and herding before them goat and sheep of varying ages. All the meat that the *waaza* intend to cook is on the hoof. Their recipes are secret, locked away in their heads.

The animals are slaughtered ceremonially according to Muslim custom and then butchered expertly on the spot. There are seventy-two parts to an animal, the *waaza* say, and most of them will be cooked. Organ meats, such as kidneys, liver and hearts, will be served to the host family for lunch. The rest will be saved for the five hundred or more guests who are to arrive later.

Tents are set up, one as the kitchen and another as the dining pavilion. Long logs on which a dozen or so pots can be placed in a row are preferred, though planks from demolished buildings, some with nails still sticking out of them, seem to work as well. Earnest young men in skull caps cut the meat into cubes, mince it and pound it repeatedly into a smooth paste. All of this is done with mallets and cleavers over several hours. Not a single machine is used. Hawks buzz overhead, swooping down occasionally to pick stray bits of discarded tendon that will never get to see a rubbish bin.

As cauldrons are stirred, long, white sheets, *dastarkhans*, are spread on the carpeted floor of the dining pavilion. Guests come in quietly and take their places, the men segregated from the women. Jugs of water and basins are brought in so hands may be washed.

It is time for the food. This comes in covered *tramis*, plates that are large enough to seat four people around them. The cover (*sarposh*) is removed, the name of god invoked with the cry of 'bismillah' and the eating begins. In the centre of the *trami* is a huge mound of rice on top of which are placed 'dry', unsauced meats – roasted chicken halves, skewered, mincemeat *seekh kababs*, the much prized muscle from a shank and the Kashmiri speciality, *tabakmaaz*. To make the last, rib chops are braised in an aromatic broth and then shallow-fried until they are nice and crisp. Yoghurt is served in large, clay bowls and sweet pumpkin chutney in saucers.

Once the 'dry' course is eaten, the 'wetter' dishes begin to arrive. Etiquette demands that, even though the food in a *trami* is communal, you must, neatly, using just your fingertips, burrow your own private tunnel into the rice without letting the mound collapse or breaking through into your neighbour's territory. (Young girls are taught: 'Build your *own* house. Do not break into your neighbour's house!') Your particular serving will always be placed at the entrance of your own tunnel, be it *rista*, spongy meatballs; *rogan josh*, meat cubes cooked with yoghurt, red chillies and saffron; *palag korma*, tiny meatballs in a spinach sauce; *ruangan tsaman*, fresh cheese chunks cooked with tomatoes; or *goshtaba*, large, silky meatballs that Pandit Nehru once described as 'the *pashmina* (cashmere) of meats'.

On Shivratri, Shiva's birthday, Kashmiri Hindus have a banquet too and then gamble with cowries. Just before retiring, they leave servings of cooked fish and rice outside their front doors. By morning, nothing is left but some tell-tale fish bones. It is quite clear to local residents that Shiva and Parvati keep at least one condominium here on some choice hilltop and that their love for Kashmiri food has not diminished over the years.

RECIPES FROM KASHMIR

•

MUSHROOMS WITH FENNEL AND GINGER
Heddar

This very simple mushroom dish may be served with almost any Indian meal. It may also be served cold, as a salad.

Serves 4
12 oz/350 g mushrooms
4 tbs/60 ml vegetable oil
6 oz/175 g, 2 smallish tomatoes, chopped
¼ tsp ground fennel seeds (fennel seeds may be crushed in a mortar or ground in a clean coffee grinder)
¼ tsp ground ginger (*sont*)
¼ tsp ground turmeric
¼ tsp red chilli powder (cayenne pepper)
½ tsp salt

Wipe the mushrooms with a wet cloth and cut into ¼-in/0.5-cm thick slices.

Heat the oil in a frying pan over a medium-high flame. When hot, put in the mushrooms. Stir and fry the mushrooms for about 2 minutes. Add all the other ingredients. Stir and cook until the tomatoes are soft.

AUBERGINES/EGGPLANTS WITH APPLE
Tsoont Vaangan

I have never come across this delightful combination anywhere else.

Aubergines (eggplants) come in all sorts of shapes and sizes. Use the more delicate slim, long ones if you can find them otherwise the more common big fat ones will do.

Use hard, tart apples such as Granny Smiths for this dish. In Kashmir, quinces are often used instead of apples. Both taste equally wonderful. You can serve up this dish with both Indian and Western meals. I like it with Lamb or Chicken with Fresh Green Coriander and rice as well as with a roasted leg of lamb and boiled new potatoes!

Serves 4
1¼ lb/550 g aubergines (eggplants)
about 7½ oz/210 g, 1–2 good-sized, hard, tart apples such as a Granny Smith
¼ tsp ground fennel seeds (the seeds may be crushed in a mortar or ground in a clean coffee grinder)
½–¾ tsp salt
¼ tsp ground turmeric
¼ tsp red chilli powder (cayenne pepper)
6 tbs/90 ml/½ cup mustard or vegetable oil
⅛ tsp ground asafetida

Cut the aubergines (eggplants) cross-wise into ¾-in/1½-cm thick slices. If the aubergines (eggplants) are slim, the slices should be cut at a slight diagonal. If the aubergines (eggplants) are the big, fat kind, halve or quarter the rounds so that no straight side is more than 2 in/5 cm long.

Cut the apple into 6 wedges without peeling it. Core the pieces.

Put the fennel, salt, turmeric and chilli powder (cayenne pepper) into a small bowl. Add 1 tbs/15 ml of water and mix to a smooth paste.

Heat the oil in a large frying pan over a medium flame. If you are using mustard oil, let it get very hot and smoke for a few seconds to release its pungency. Put in the asafetida and, a second later, the apple wedges. Brown the apple wedges lightly on all sides. Remove them with a slotted spoon and set aside in a plate. Put the aubergine (eggplant) slices into the same oil, as many as the pan will hold in a single layer, and brown on both sides. As the slices get browned, remove them with a slotted spoon and set aside with the apple. Do all the aubergines (egg-plants) this way.

Put the aubergines (eggplants) and apples back into the frying pan. Put in the spicy paste from the bowl and mix gently. Turn the heat to low and cook for about 10 minutes, turning the aubergine (eggplant) and apple pieces over gently so that they do not break.

To serve, lift the apples and auber-gines (eggplants) out of the oil with a slotted spoon and place in a serving dish.

YASMIN AHMED'S

KOHLRABI GREENS

Moinja Haak

Kohlrabi, also called knol-kohl, is eaten in its entirety in Kashmir – the leaves as well as the turnip-like ball to which they are attached. This dish calls for just the greens. (The ball may be peeled, sliced, and put into a salad or else sprinkled lightly with salt and pepper – red chilli powder (cayenne pepper) too, if you like – and served with drinks.) If the kohlrabi is picked when the leaves are still tender, the leaves should be used whole, with just their coarse stems broken off. I rarely find such kohlrabi in Western markets. I find that I have to cut up the maturer leaves that are more readily available. This particular dish may also be made with spring greens in Britain and with collard greens in the United States.

Kashmiris use bicarbonate of soda when cooking leafy vegetables in order to keep them green. You may do so if you are particular about the colour of the dish or else leave it out.

This versatile dish may be served with any Kashmiri meat and Plain Rice or with any North Indian meal. I find that it also tastes particularly good with grilled (broiled) pork chops!

If this dish is to have an authentic Kashmiri taste, it should be cooked with mustard oil. You could, however, substitute olive oil for a different but equally interesting flavour. Do not let the olive oil heat to smoking point.

At a typical Kashmiri meal it would be served with Plain Rice and Lamb with Kashmiri Red Chillies.

Serves 4
1¼ lb/550 g kohlrabi leaves
5 tbs/75 ml mustard oil or olive oil (see
  note above)
½ tsp/2.5 ml bicarbonate of soda
  (baking soda) (optional)
½ tsp/2.5 ml salt
2 hot, dried red chillies, deseeded
4–6 cloves garlic, peeled and very
  coarsely chopped

Wash the kohlrabi leaves and cut away
the very coarse stems. If the leaves are
large, hold several of them together
and cut them crosswise at 2-in/5-cm
intervals.

Heat the oil in a very large pan over
a medium-high flame. Let it get smokingly hot. Let it smoke for a few
seconds. (This burns away its pungency and makes it sweet.) Now put in
4 pints/2.25 litres/10 cups of water, the
kohlrabi leaves, the bicarbonate of
soda, salt, red chillies and garlic. Bring
to a boil. Cook, uncovered, over a
medium-high flame for about 1 hour,
stirring now and then, until there is
just a little liquid left in the pan, about
4 fl oz/125 ml/½ cup, and the leaves are
tender.

KASHMIRI SPINACH

I do not have a Kashmiri name for this
dish as I have substituted ordinary
spinach for the very different varieties
found in Kashmir. This dish is normally hot and spicy. It is often eaten
with plain rice and a mild meat dish. I
have frequently served it with a very

Delhi-style dish – Moghlai Chicken
braised with Almonds and Raisins.
The two complement each other
rather well. Instead of Kashmiri *ver*, I
have used *garam masala*. The bicarbonate of soda helps keep the spinach
green, but may be omitted.

Serves 4–6
5 tbs/75 ml mustard or vegetable oil
⅛ tsp ground asafetida
2½ lb/1.1 kg fresh spinach, washed
  and chopped
½ tsp/2.5 ml ground turmeric
½ tsp/2.5 ml red chilli powder
  (cayenne pepper) – use more or less
  as desired
about 1¼ tsp/6 ml salt
½ tsp/2.5 ml bicarbonate of soda
  (baking soda) (optional)
¼ tsp *garam masala* (page 200)

Heat the oil in a very large pan over a
high flame. If you are using mustard
oil, let it get so hot that it smokes. Let it
smoke for a few seconds to burn away
its pungency. Now put in the asafetida
and then all the spinach. Stir the
spinach around. Add the turmeric,
chilli powder (cayenne pepper), salt
and bicarbonate of soda. Continue to
cook and stir until the spinach has wilted. Add ¾ pint/475 ml/2 cups of
water. Cook, uncovered, over a
medium-high flame, for about 25
minutes or until just a little liquid is
left. Stir a few times during this
period. Turn the heat to low and mash
the spinach with the back of a spoon.
Continue to cook, uncovered, for
another 10 minutes. Sprinkle *garam
masala* over the top and mix.

JAWAHARA MOHAMMAD'S
LAMB OR CHICKEN WITH FRESH GREEN CORIANDER
Dhaniwal Korma

This exquisite dish is not the slightest bit hot – it is not meant to be. Meat here is cooked gently in a yoghurt sauce flecked and flavoured with lots of fresh green coriander.

You need rather a lot of coriander. It is hard to tell you exactly how much to buy as it is sometimes sold with roots (which makes it weigh more) and sometimes without. After cutting off the roots and coarse lower stems, the coriander I bought weighed about 7 oz/200 g.

Dhaniwal Korma is generally served with Plain Rice. You may serve other Kashmiri vegetables with it or vegetables from almost any other part of India.

This *korma* can also be made with chicken. Cook 3 lb/1.4 kg of jointed chicken just the same way as the lamb but reduce the initial boiling time to about 20 minutes or even a bit less if the chicken pieces are very small and tender.

Serves 6

3 lb/1.4 kg lamb meat taken from the shoulder with bone cut into 1½-in/4-cm cubes or 2½ lb/1.1 kg lamb meat from the shoulder without bone, cut into 1½-in/4-cm cubes
½ tsp/2.5 ml ground turmeric
1¼ tsp/7 ml salt
2 large, black cardamom pods (optional)
5 tbs/75 ml vegetable oil
7 oz/200 g, 2 medium-size onions, peeled, cut in half lengthwise and then cut crosswise into fine half rings
3 whole cloves
5 whole black peppercorns
3 cardamom pods
1½-in/4-cm cinnamon stick
2 pints/1.1 litres/4 cups plain yoghurt, preferably made from whole milk, lightly beaten with a fork or whisk
5 cloves garlic, peeled and crushed
freshly ground black pepper
enough fresh green coriander (Chinese parsley) to fill a measuring jug to the ¾ pint/450 ml/2 cup mark after it has had its coarse stems removed, been washed and finely chopped

Put the meat into a pan along with the turmeric, salt, large black cardamom pods and 1¼ pints/750 ml/3 cups of water. Bring to a boil. Cover, turn the heat to low and simmer for about 50–60 minutes or until the meat is almost tender.

Heat the oil in a heavy, wide-based pan over a medium-high flame. Put in the onions. Stir and fry them, lowering the heat a bit as they darken, until they are a reddish brown colour and crisp. Remove the onions with a slotted spoon and spread them out in a plate lined with absorbent kitchen paper (paper towels). Leave behind as much oil as possible.

Put the cloves, peppercorns, cardamom pods and cinnamon into the same oil. Stir once and put in all the yoghurt and the garlic. Turn the heat back up to medium-high. Keep stirring the mixture until it has reduced to a very thick, white sauce. Oil should begin to show through along its edges.

When the meat is almost tender,

strain it. Save the stock (broth). Add the meat pieces to the yoghurt sauce. Stir and cook the meat over a medium heat for 3–4 minutes. The white sauce should now cling to the pieces of meat. It might even turn golden in spots. Now put in all the stock (broth). Continue to stir and cook until the stock (broth) is reduced and comes about a third of the way up the meat. Crumble the onions and sprinkle them over the meat. Mix in some freshly ground black pepper. Put in all the chopped green coriander (Chinese parsley) just before you serve and stir it in.

Note: the large whole spices in the dish are not meant to be eaten. Also, you will notice a lot of fat floating around the sauce. It should be spooned off just before you serve.

LAMB WITH KASHMIRI RED CHILLIES
Marzwangan Korma

The traditional recipe for this dish involves deseeding, soaking and puréeing 20 of Kashmir's famous long red chillies. Since those mildly hot chillies are unavailable outside Kashmir, I have substituted a paste made from paprika and red chilli powder (cayenne pepper). Good quality Hungarian paprika gives the same red coloured to foods that Kashmiri chillies do.

This *korma* should be served with Plain Rice and any green vegetable out of this book. At Kashmiri banquets, both this dish and *Dhaniwal Korma* are served, one red and hot, the other pale and mild.

Serves 6

1 oz/25 g, a walnut-sized ball of tamarind, (page 203)
3 lb/1.4 kg lamb meat cut from the shoulder with bone or 2½ lb/1.1 kg meat from the shoulder without bone, cut into 1½-in/4-cm cubes
½ tsp/2.5 ml ground turmeric
1¼ tsp/6 ml salt
2 tbs/30 ml bright red paprika
½ tsp/2.5 ml red chilli powder (cayenne pepper)
½ tsp/2.5 ml ground fennel seeds (the seeds may be finely crushed in a mortar or ground in a clean coffee grinder)
½ tsp/2.5 ml ground ginger (*sont*)
5 tbs/75 ml/½ cup vegetable oil
3 whole cardamom pods
1½-in/4-cm cinnamon stick

Break the tamarind lump up into smaller pieces and put in a small bowl. Add 4 fl oz/125 ml/½ cup of boiling water and leave to soak for 1 hour. Rub the tamarind pieces with your fingers to release their pulp. Set a strainer over a clean bowl and empty the contents of the bowl containing the tamarind into it. Push out as much pulp as possible.

Put the meat in a pan along with the turmeric, salt, and 1¼ pints/750 ml/3 cups of water. Bring to a boil. Cover, lower the heat and simmer for 50–60 minutes or until the meat is almost tender. Strain the meat and save the stock (broth).

Put the paprika, chilli powder (cayenne pepper), fennel seeds, and ground ginger into a small bowl. Add 4 tbs/60 ml of water and work to a smooth paste.

Heat the oil in a wide, heavy-based

pan over a medium flame. When hot, put in the cardamom and cinnamon, the paprika paste and the tamarind paste. Stir and fry until the paste is so well reduced that you can see oil around its edges. Now put in the pieces of meat. Stir and fry them for 3–4 minutes. Now put in all the stock (broth). Stir well and turn the heat up to medium-high. Continue to stir until the stock (broth) is greatly reduced. It should come just about a quarter of the way up the meat.

Before serving, spoon off some of the fat.

FAREEDA KAUL'S
RED KIDNEY BEANS COOKED WITH TURNIPS
Razma Gogji

This is a perfect dish for cold days. It may be served with Plain Rice and any Kashmiri greens in this chapter if one wants an all vegetarian meal, or it may be served with almost any lamb or chicken dish in this book. I sometimes eat it all by itself with some crusty wholemeal bread and a green salad!

Serves 6
5½oz/160g/1 cup red kidney beans, picked over and well washed, soaked overnight, drained
14oz/400g, 4 medium-sized turnips
¼tsp ground ginger (*sont*)
¼tsp ground turmeric
1 tsp/5 ml salt
⅛–½tsp red chilli powder (cayenne pepper)
4 tbs/60 ml vegetable oil

1 medium-sized onion, peeled, cut in half lengthwise and then cut crosswise into fine half rings
2–3 cloves garlic, peeled and finely chopped

Put the red kidney beans in a large pan. Add 2 pints/1.1 litres/5 cups of water and bring to a boil. Boil vigorously for 10 minutes. Turn the heat down and simmer, partially covered, for 1–1½ hours or until cooked through.

Meanwhile, peel the turnips and cut into 4 wedges each.

Put the ground ginger, turmeric, salt and chilli powder (cayenne pepper) into a small bowl. Add 1 tbs/15 ml of water and mix to a smooth paste.

Heat the oil in a frying pan over a medium heat. When hot, put in the turnip pieces and brown them on all sides. Remove the turnip pieces with a slotted spoon and set aside. Now put the onion into the same oil. Stir and fry until the onion is a medium brown colour. Turn the heat down slightly and put in the garlic. Stir for a few seconds. Now put in the spice paste from the small bowl. Stir once and turn the heat off.

When the beans have cooked for 45 minutes, add the turnips as well as the onion mixture in the frying pan to the pan of beans. Stir. Ladle a little of the bean liquid into the frying pan, swish it around and pour it back into the bean pan. Bring the beans to a vigorous simmer. Turn heat down to low, cover partially and simmer gently for another 45 minutes or until cooked through.

WALNUT CHUTNEY
Akhrote Chutney

This delightful chutney is found in all Kashmiri homes. I have kept mine relatively mild but you could make yours as hot as you like.

This chutney may be served with almost all Indian meals. If thinned out with 6 tbs/90 ml of yoghurt instead of 4 tbs/60 ml, it can be used as a dip for raw vegetables.

Serves 4
2 oz/50 g/⅔ cup shelled walnuts
¼ tsp salt
½ tsp/2.5 ml red chilli powder
 (cayenne pepper)
4 tbs/60 ml plain yoghurt

Put the walnuts, salt and chilli powder (cayenne pepper) in a mortar and pound until smooth. (Alternatively, you could use a clean coffee grinder, but you may need to stop and start the machine several times.) Put the mixture in a bowl. Add the yoghurt and mix.

BENGAL

'I am frying some *elish*,' says a lady over the telephone in mellifluous, round-toned Bengali. 'Why don't you come over?'

Elish – or hilsa – is a fish. For Bengalis, it is also an event. Rather like the American shad, with which the hilsa shares its taste, texture and heritage, this elusive, silvery fish spends several winter months in the deep, turbulent waters of the open sea. Then, around late February, it leaves the Bay of Bengal and, in large shoals, begins finning its way up the Ganges and other rivers and rivulets of the Ganges delta to spawn – and to take its chances with Bengali fishermen.

Bengalis are, on the whole, an infectiously passionate lot and few things unite them more than their common passion for food – especially for fish. No meal is considered complete without it. Symbols of fertility, fish are touched by husbands and then sent to their brides before the wedding ceremony. Fish heads are put into pots of split peas to add richness and flavour; tiny shrimp are stir-fried with vegetables; fish are steamed, fried, smoked, made into balls and patties, even stuffed into creamy green coconuts and baked.

In a strange idiosyncrasy, most Bengalis will not touch salt-water fish, complaining that they lack sweetness. Luckily for them, there is abundant fresh water in the spreading fingers of the vast Ganges estuary. The verdant earth, too, is pitted with lakes and ponds. Every ditch, every major puddle seems to swarm with some variety of fish – perch, mullet, crab, carp, prawn, crayfish and lobster. All are loved. But it is the expensive, seasonal hilsa that is prized above all.

At a recent soccer match between Bangladesh (East Bengal) and India's West Bengal, fans – in shows of good-natured jingoism – waved hilsas from their own waters as banners, the Bangladeshis claiming that their fish from the Padma River were the sweetest, and the West Bengalis shouting them down with equal – and louder – claims of their own. Bengalis, anxious to satisfy deep cravings of their relatives abroad, have been known to rub fresh hilsa pieces in salt and turmeric – the latter being an antiseptic – drown them in mustard oil and then pack them in polythene bags and carry them all the way to New York. This, it may be a relief to know, is only tried in the winter season and the only accidents reported have been loss of suitcases, *not* spoilage of fish!

Bengalis not only love fish, they are exceedingly particular about it when they shop. Early mornings, heads of households can be seen in Calcutta's nineteenth-century New Market, sporting plastic or jute shopping bags. They not only examine the eyes of the fish for clearness and the inside of the gills for redness, they know that *leta* fish is good for invalids and must be bought live, as should be *koi* or climbing perch, as well as the carp-like *rui* and female crabs, all rich with roe. They know that only fools discard prawn heads, as that is where most of the flavour resides, and that local hilsa should be snapped up whenever the availability of fish happily coincides with the availability of the extra cash needed to buy it.

Hilsa may be cooked in many ways. The Hotel Oberoi Grand in Calcutta, an oasis tucked into a crowded thoroughfare, serves a superb Anglo-Indian version, all beautifully smoked and boned, while every Bengali home prepares that most elegant of hilsa dishes, *elish bhapa*. In a breathtakingly simple procedure, cut pieces of hilsa are mixed with a mayonnaise-like paste of ground mustard seeds (yellow if mildness is desired, black if a certain bitter pungency is favoured), mustard oil, red chillies, green chillies, turmeric and salt. The combination is either wrapped up in an airtight package of banana leaves and cooked along with rice or, if banana leaves are not handy, the mixture is put in a covered metal bowl and the bowl left in a larger pot with just enough water to steam the fish. The fish stays moist and tender while allowing the simple spices to permeate it to its very core.

Seasonings that could be classified as 'Bengali' would have to include two used in the steamed hilsa dish, mustard oil and mustard seeds. Both have Jekyll and Hyde characteristics. If whole mustard seeds are thrown into hot oil and allowed to pop, they turn nuttily sweet; if they are ground to a paste as many Bengali recipes require, they develop a delicious, nose-tingling pungency. Mustard oil is sharp when used raw; it turns docile and sweet if it is heated. Many Bengali dishes require mustard seeds to do triple duty – as an oil, as a popped, nutty seed, and as a fiery seed paste as well.

Calcutta, Bengal's capital city of about ten million people, has, of all Indian cities, lived the longest under continuous and very direct foreign rule, and has therefore a mixed culinary history. In the 1600s there was no Calcutta, only three green villages along the Hooghly River. Bengal had silk, sugar, cotton and indigo (tea and jute were to come later). The Portuguese were already trading there when the British arrived. The Moghuls were still ruling the country from Delhi but they could be asked for favours – in the form of land or trade permissions – in exchange for, say, the services of a good doctor. The British first acquired the three villages and then took over the land between and around them by moving out the landed gentry (such as the Tagore family) who owned these verdant tracts. The East India Company, set up for trade, began sending out young, eager 'writers' or clerks to man its offices in Calcutta on little pay but with the understanding that they could indulge in private trade. Fortunes were made, and sometimes lost as well. Calcutta, growing daily with palatial buildings patterned after country mansions and London churches, became the capital of British India and remained so until 1911.

Many of the young English East Indiamen lived in a style they could hardly have managed back home. An ordinary household could have as many as thirty servants. There was one to cool the water, one in charge of the wine, others for the garden and the children. There was a tailor, a laundryman, a head steward, waiters and stableboys, a servant of pull fans, and even one to light and take care of the hookah or hubble bubble pipe – which had become quite the rage.

By the nineteenth century, amusements included amateur theatricals, riding in the morning, promenading by the water in the evening, fancy-dress balls and all manner of banquets. Almost every major English family had a relative in Calcutta – and the history of the city is filled with names like Dickens, Turner, Thackeray, Macaulay and Cornwallis.

Because of the heat, mornings started before dawn, often with a ride for the men. According to the diary of a nineteenth-century East Indiaman, breakfast could be 'a preparation consisting of a little butter, two or three green chillies, a pyramid of boiled rice, a ditto egg, and a pound of dried fish, with salt and cayenne at discretion, all mashed up on a hot water plate and baled down the throat with a spoon.' This Anglo-Indian dish, sounding suspiciously like what the British were to call kedgeree, was served with tea, coffee and lots of Indian fruit.

Ice began coming into Calcutta in the 1830s – strangely enough, all the way from America, as the ballast in ships. 'Up to then it had been collected in small quantities and hoarded like gold dust.' The day that it came, 'everybody invited everybody to dinner, to taste claret and beer cooled by the American importation.' Banquets, already glittering affairs, glittered even more with lumps of ice shining from butter dishes and water goblets. Such banquets served soups, beefsteaks (Americans, it is said, marvelled at the beefsteaks, saying that they were better than those in their homeland), 'quails or ortolans piled up in hetacombs', an overgrown turkey, a ham, a sirloin of beef, a saddle of mutton, legs of mutton boiled and roasted, geese, ducks, tongues, pigeon pies, curry and rice, mutton chops and mutton cutlets. Wine was served in 'petticoated' bottles (wet 'clothing' to keep them cool), port, claret and Burgundy in crimson with white flounces, sherry and madeira in white. Dinner was followed by the gurgle-gurgle of the hookahs which were placed behind each chair. Many people died in Calcutta during this period of what was called 'the vapours'. This may well have been a euphemism for over-indulgence.

If many Indians were reduced to living on the periphery of English society, not all suffered financial deprivation. Some families traded, along with the British, and held on to their rice fields and coconut groves. Highly educated and versed in both English and Bengali literature as well as in commerce and technology, the upper-class Bengali was already a product of both cultures. Some of the palace-like homes of the Bengali gentry were marble and stone fantasies, built to resemble Scottish castles and Corinthian temples, where 'lords of the manor' slept in canopied beds, complete with a crest on the headboard, tassels, cherubs, and – because it was Calcutta – fitted with a fan as well. When the British finally left in 1947, these Bengalis moved into exclusive all-English clubs and British jobs with ease, carrying on their own 'Englishness' with golf, cricket, horse-racing and beer on Sunday mornings at 'the Club'.

But, just as the Bengali – however westernized – never gave up his language, neither did he give up his Bengali food and his passion for fish, rice – and sweets. In fact, Bengalis have – with justification – such high regard for their food that one gentleman at a dinner turned to me and said with quiet conviction, 'There are only four great cuisines in the world – French, Chinese, Italian and Bengali!'

Today, a Bengali's day in the country might well begin, gastronomically speaking, with a big bowl containing *moori* (puffed rice), thick creamy milk and healthy dollops of freshly mashed fruit such as sweet, ripe mangoes or musky jackfruit. In the city, a clerk rushing to the office in a white *kurta* and *dhoti* (voluminous lower garment) might hurriedly partake of a steaming cup of tea and *moori* in its savoury form, just tossed with mustard oil and chopped green chillies. Being Bengali and terribly sweet-toothed, he might nibble a lump of date palm jaggery on the side to balance the savouriness of the one with the sweetness of the other. Then, he is likely to pick up his brolly and rush to catch a clanging tram or a careening red double-decker bus already bursting at the seams with a profusion of humanity.

Date jaggery is quite a delicacy and it made by tapping the date palm. An elegant hostess in Calcutta laid out – as one of the final dinner courses – a 'jaggery board', just as one might a cheese board, with six different varieties of jaggery. Only one of them was made from the juice of sugar-canes. The others were made from date palms, varying from dark brown and ochre lumps sitting on the board to golden and brown treacle-like syrups in bowls. They were to be eaten with *loochi*, a deep-fried bread made out of white flour, and were delicious beyond description.

Any Bengali will confess to you that he has a great weakness for sweets. Because millions of sweetmeats are consumed hourly in Bengal, I thought it best to visit a gentleman whose cable address is 'Rossogolla' and whose family runs the old and very successful firm of K. C. Das that specializes in Bengali sweets.

Mr Rabindra Nath Das lives in North Calcutta, on a street lined with ancient town houses. The doors and windows are shuttered to keep out the sun's glare. There is an inner court-yard with three tiers of balconies looking down upon it. A large joint family calls this home. The living-room contains a piano and some stunning and rare paintings by the Bengali painter Jamini Roy. A ceiling fan whirrs overhead. Servants can be seen, trays in hand, disappearing around corners with nourishment. It is time for the mid-morning snack, or *jalkhabar*. I protest that I have already breakfasted, but the rejoinder comes, 'Oh, you can always find room for *rossogolla*, *sondesh* and *singhara*.' I fall into the spirit of Bengal – and do.

A *singhara* is a Bengali *samosa*, consisting of vegetables such as cauliflower or potatoes, all nicely spiced, wrapped in a triangular pastry, and deep fried. *Rossogollas*, or *rasgullas*, often described to foreigners by Indian waiters as 'cheese balls in syrup' (my children called them squeaky balls because they do squeak), are served at almost every festive gathering in the country. They were invented by his great-grandfather in 1868, Mr Das says, though others claim that what his great-grandfather, Nabin Chandra Das, did was to mass-produce and market an already existing sweet.

In the family factory, *rossogollas* are still 'mass-produced' by hand. To make them, milk is first curdled and the curds separated from the whey. Enormous *karhais*, even discarded bathtubs are used to contain the results. Moisture is squeezed out of the curds through muslin. The resulting 'cheese dough' (*chhana*) is the raw material for hundred of Bengali sweets.

Several expert hands now form the dough into balls, some-times rolling three at a time between their palms. The balls are then dropped into boiling syrup where they are allowed to puff up and become India's premier sweet – *rossogollas*.

Perhaps the most classical, and perhaps the oldest as well, of all the *chhana* sweets is *sondesh*. *Chhana* is simply mixed with thick sugar syrup and cooked over a very low flame until the moisture evaporates. It is then pressed into pretty wooden moulds, emerging with imprints of flowers and trailing vines. *Sondesh* is a delicacy served throughout the year but is specially good in spring when, instead of sugar syrup, it is prepared with the season's new jaggery. This *mutan gurer sondesh* has a lovely, caramel colour and flavour and is quite a rare delight.

Once the morning's *jalkhabar* is done, housewives can rest, read, shop, sing Tagore songs or begin preparations for lunch.

A lunchtime favourite is *sukto.* It starts the meal and consists of a mélange of diced and fried vegetables, some bitter (like bitter gourd), some pungent (like white radish), some starchy (like potato), some stiff (like *sheem*, a hard-skinned flat bean), and others soft, such as delicious stems and leaves which only Bengalis seem to eat. To this are added *bori* (sun-dried morsels fashioned out of ground split peas). The resulting mélange is then cooked with some milk and water and flavoured with ground ginger, ground mustard seeds, cumin and turmeric. As a final fillip, some roasted and ground *panchphoran* is sometimes added. *Panchphoran* is a spice mixture used only in Bengal and consists of whole cumin seeds, whole fennel seeds, whole *kalonji*, whole fenugreek seeds and whole *radhuni*, which resembles parsley seeds.

At this same lunch would follow some rice and *dal* accompanied by a fried titbit or *bhaja. Bhajas* can be made out of most vegetables and fish, but one of my favourites remains *alur khosha bhaja*, made with the potato skins that most people just throw away. (An English bishop, arriving in Calcutta in 1823, remarked that potatoes, once unpopular, '[are] now ... much liked, and are spoken of as the best thing the country has received from its European masters.') There might be some *rui machher jhol*, carp pieces cooked in a simple sauce of cumin, coriander, turmeric, red chillies and water. This would be followed by sweet-and-sour chutney (perhaps my favourite), *aam jhol*, a thin, watery, sweet-and-sour 'soup' made out of green mangoes flavoured very lightly with mustard oil and mustard seeds. Since Bengalis must have a sweet, there might be *mishti doi*, a thick, sweetened yoghurt set in earthen cups, and perhaps some pretty diamond-shaped pieces of *sondesh* to finish off.

Early evenings might see families strolling near the enormous white pile known as the Victoria Memorial, or along the cooling banks of the Hooghly to enjoy snacks like *jhal moori*, a spicy combination of *moori* (puffed rice), potatoes and cucumber.

These families may, on the other hand, enjoy the river more with a *puchka* in their mouths. This mouthful – and it *is* that – is a scrumptious delight. First you fry up a small, *very* crisp, ball-shaped *poori*, crisp enough to hold its shape. Then you poke a hole in the top and stuff in some spicy potatoes. Then – and here is the best part – you fill it to the top with tart, cumin- and red chilli-flavoured tamarind water, and, before it can drip, carry it, whole, to your mouth and stuff it in. There is no pleasure like that of eating *puchkas*, one after another, though I suppose it is not quite the thing for politer circles.

As dusk falls over this Indo-British town, with its ghosts of English damsels who came searching for rich husbands, and East Indiamen who seldom lived long enough to enjoy their fortunes or their new wives, the labourers of this maritime city might gather in local taverns to sip liquors made out of distilled jaggery while they tear up and devour the tasty flesh of spicy crabs (*kakra chaat*). Around this same time, the more westernized rich – those who own advertising agencies and tea plantations – might relax with their whiskies and their recordings of Mozart, slowly moving on to a grand dinner served on large *kansa* (an alloy of tin, copper and zinc) plates.

The leisurely meal, punctuated by accounts of a son at Oxford or a daughter at Harvard, would start traditionally with rice, *dal* and *bhaja*. The rice might be an elegant pilaf, the *dal*, flavoured with a fish head (*machher matha diye mooger dal*), and the *bhaja*, delicate pumpkin flowers dipped in a chickpea flour batter and deep-fried.

Next would come the fish – perhaps large estuary prawns simmered in coconut milk (*chingri malai*) – and vegetables such as the pungent *sorse dharush* (okra cooked with a paste of mustard seeds) and *kopir dantar dalna chingri maccher diye* (cauliflower stems cooked with tiny shrimp).

Meat would follow – perhaps *mangsho jhol*, nicely marinated lamb cooked in mustard oil with potatoes and onions. The chutney course would be next – this could be made with tomatoes, nicely studded with bits of preserved sweet mango – accompanied by soft *loochis* (breads). Then would come the sweet yoghurt, *bhapa doi* (steamed yoghurt) perhaps, smelling elegantly – and expensively – of saffron. Finally, would come the sweets – the glory of Bengal: *rasmalais* (a *chhana* sweet) floating

A family enjoys a picnic of okra, *sambar* and *idlis*.

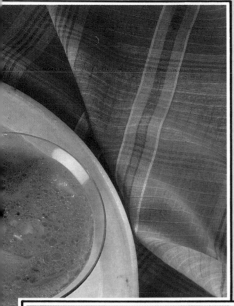

Chettinad Fried chicken, Cauliflower with Dried Chillies and Mustard Seeds, Mysore Split Peas with Whole Shallots.

Rice Pancakes, Cucumber Salad with Moong Dal, Mango Salad.

Fishermen taking to the sea at sunrise
from the beach at Madras.

Yoghurt Rice, 'Pickled' Mackerel.

Chicken Stew, Hoppers.

Green Beans with Coconut.

in cardamom-flavoured cream, *kala jamuns* (dark round balls made out of fried *chhana*), and Lady Kennys (fried *chhana* balls stuffed with raisins) – the last named after a foreign woman, Lady Canning, the wife of a Governor-General, who once, a long time ago, admitted that she had a partiality for those dark Bengali morsels. The gentlemen in their fresh bush shirts and the ladies in their crackling cotton sarees would now be able to indulge themselves to their hearts' content.

RECIPES FROM BENGAL

FROM THE HOUSEHOLD OF TAPASK ROY
DELICIOUS FRIED MORSELS
Bhaja

A first course at many formal Bengali meals consists of rice, *dal* and *bhaja*. A *bhaja* is fried tidbit. It could be fish – or better still, tender fish roe, or it could be a vegetable or an assortment of vegetables. Slices of aubergine (egg-plant) or potatoes could be rubbed with a little salt and turmeric and then deep fried. Sometimes the vegetables are dipped into batter before they are deep fried. Batters can vary slightly from house to house and from vege-table to vegetable. My favourite batter, the one in this recipe, uses both rice flour and chickpea flour. You could make a slightly different batter by using all chickpea flour and adding about 1 tsp/5ml of nigella seeds (*kalonji*).

A great many vegetables can be deep fried. My favourites are pump-kin (sweet potato or yam makes a good substitute), onion, cauliflower, pump-kin or courgette (zucchini) flowers, eggplant (aubergine), potato and potato skins. The last, known as *alur khosha bhaja* is simply superb. Bengalis love to eat it on rainy days with *kichri*, a pilaf of rice and split peas.

Bhajas should be made at the last minute and eaten hot.

Serves 4–6
For the batter:
2oz/50g/½ cup chickpea flour (gram flour/ *besan*)
2½oz/65g/½ cup rice flour
¼tsp bicarbonate of soda
½tsp/2.5ml ground turmeric
½tsp/2.5ml red chilli powder (cayenne pepper)
¾tsp/4ml salt
1½tbs/22ml white or blue poppy seeds
vegetable oil, for deep frying

Vegetables:
Singly or in a combination of your choice:
potato skins: scrub 2 medium-sized potatoes well and pat dry. Peel the skins in strips that are about ¼in/0.5cm thick, 1in/2.5cm wide and 2–3in/5–7.5cm long. The remaining potato may be cut, crosswise, into ¼-in/0.5-cm thick slices
yam, sweet potato or pumpkin: peel and cut the pumpkin into about 12 strips, each ¼in/0.5cm thick, 1in/2.5cm wide and 2–3in/5–7.5cm long. A medium-sized sweet potato or yam should be peeled and cut into ¼-in/0.5-cm thick rounds
aubergine (eggplant): cut a third of a medium-sized vegetable into ⅓-in/0.7-cm rounds. Cut each round into three long strips

about 12 flowers from courgette (zucchini), pumpkin or marrow (squash) vines
12 spinach leaves: wash and pat dry the leaves

Put the chickpea flour, rice flour, bicarbonate of soda, turmeric, chilli powder (cayenne pepper) and salt in a bowl. Slowly add about 8 fl oz/250 ml/1 cup of water to make a thin batter.

Add the poppy seeds to the batter just before you are ready to use it and mix in.

Pour enough oil into a wok, *karhai* or frying pan to come to a depth of 2 in/ 5 cm. Heat the oil on a lowish flame to about 350°F/180°C/gas mark 4.

Cut the vegetables as suggested above. Dip as many vegetable pieces into the batter as you think will fit a slightly overlapping single layer in your wok, *karhai* or frying pan. Make sure they are evenly coated with batter and then slide them into the hot oil. Fry, stirring now and then, for about 7 minutes or until the vegetables are golden on both sides and cooked through. Remove with a slotted spoon and drain well on absorbent kitchen paper (paper towels), changing the paper at least once or twice. Do all vegetables this way. Flowers and spinach leaves should be fried separately as they tend to cook a bit faster.

FROM THE HOUSEHOLD OF TAPAS K ROY
OKRA WITH MUSTARD SEEDS
Sorse Dharush

Ground mustard seeds are used to make the sauce for this dish. They can be slightly bitter – in fact, that is their charm. If you cannot find black mustard seeds, use 2 tbs/30 ml of the common yellow kind.

You may serve this with almost any Indian meal.

Serves 4
1 lb/450 g whole, fresh okra
1 tbs/15 ml whole black mustard seeds
1 tsp/5 ml whole yellow mustard seeds
½ tsp/2.5 ml ground turmeric
½–¾ tsp/2.5 ml red chilli powder (cayenne pepper)
1 tsp/5 ml salt
3 tbs/45 ml vegetable oil
⅛ tsp nigella seed (*kalonji*)
2 fresh, hot green chillies

Wash the okra and pat it dry. Cut off the very tips of the pods. Peel the cone-shaped top.

Put the black and the yellow mustard seeds into the container of a clean coffee grinder or other spice grinder. Grind. Put the ground mustard seeds into a small bowl. Add the turmeric, chilli powder (cayenne pepper), salt and ¼ pint/125 ml/½ cup + 2 tablespoons of water. Stir to mix.

Heat the oil in a large frying pan over a medium flame. When hot, put in the nigella seeds. Ten seconds later, put in the okra and stir. Stir and fry the okra on a medium-low heat for 10 minutes or until it is lightly browned. Add the spice mixture and the green chillies. Bring to a simmer. Cover, lower the heat and simmer gently for 5–8 minutes or until the okra is tender.

JAYA DUTT'S
POTATOES WITH POPPY SEEDS
Aloo Posto

Poppy seeds, like sesame seeds, add a wonderful nutty taste to foods. Bengalis grind them and use them in quantity with vegetables like potatoes and cauliflower to provide a thick, clinging sauce. The result is unusual and quite superb.

This potato dish may be served with most Indian meals. It could also be served with roast lamb, lamb chops or with grilled (broiled) or roasted chicken.

Note: cauliflower may be cooked in exactly the same way. Break it into flowerets first.

Serves 4
1½ lb/700 g, 6 firm, smallish potatoes
6 tbs/90 ml vegetable oil
3 whole red chillies
2 oz/50 g/½ cup white poppy seeds
  ground as finely as possible in a
  clean coffee grinder or other spice
  grinder
½ tsp/2.5 ml ground turmeric
¼–½ tsp red chilli powder (cayenne
  pepper)
1 tsp/5 ml salt
3 fresh hot green chillies

Peel the potatoes and cut them in ¾-in/2-cm dice.

Heat the oil in a non-stick frying pan over a medium heat. When hot, put in the potatoes. Stir and fry the potatoes so they are very lightly browned – just golden – and only half cooked. Remove with a slotted spoon.

Put the red chillies into the same oil. As soon as they start to darken, put in the ground poppy seeds and 2 tbs/30 ml of water. Stir and sauté this paste until it turns a medium-brown colour. Now put in the potatoes, about 6 fl oz/175 ml/¾ cup of water, the turmeric, red chilli powder (cayenne pepper), salt and green chillies. Stir to mix and bring to a simmer. Cover and simmer for 5–10 minutes or until the potatoes are done and most of the water is absorbed.

Note: the whole chillies should only be eaten by those who know what they are doing.

MAYA'S
ROASTED MOONG DAL WITH SPINACH
Bhaja Moong Dal

This earthy dish has a delightful flavour which comes from roasting the grains of *dal* before cooking them in water. In Bengal, it is generally served with rice and a fried vegetable – such as Delicious Fried Morsels – as a first or second course. You may serve it as part of any Indian meal.

Serves 4–6
6½ oz/190 g/1 cup skinned *moong dal*
  (page 200)
½ tsp/2.5 ml ground turmeric
1 bay leaf
¾ lb/350 g spinach, washed and cut
  into 1-in/2.5-cm wide shreds
1 tsp/about 5 ml salt
½ tsp/2.5 ml red chilli powder
  (cayenne pepper)
1 tbs/15 ml *ghee* or vegetable oil
½ tsp/2.5 ml *panchphoran* (page 202) or
  cumin seeds

2 fresh, hot red or green chillies, cut
into 1-in/2.5-cm pieces

Pick over the *dal*. Put it on a clean tea
towel (dish towel). Rub it gently to
remove as much surface dust as possible. Heat a cast-iron frying pan over
a medium-low flame. Allow it to get
hot and then put the *dal* in it. Stir and
roast until many of the grains turn
golden-red. (The colour will not be
uniform, but that is all right.) Put the
roasted *dal* in a bowl and wash it in
several changes of water. Drain.

Put the *dal* in a heavy-based pan.
Add the turmeric, bay leaf and
1½ pints/900ml/4 cups of water. Stir
and bring to a simmer. Turn the heat
to low, cover, leaving the lid slightly
ajar, and cook gently for about 1 hour
until the grains are quite tender.

Add the spinach, salt, red chilli powder (cayenne pepper) and ¼ pint/
125 ml/⅔ cup of water. Stir and bring
to a simmer. Cover and simmer gently
for 30 minutes, stirring once or twice
during this cooking period.

Heat the *ghee* in a small pan or
frying pan. When hot, put in the
panchphoran. A few seconds later,
when the seeds start to pop and sizzle,
put in the red or green chillies. Stir
once and then pour the contents of the
small pan or frying pan over the
cooked *dal*. Cover immediately.

Note: the whole chillies should only
be eaten by those who know what they
are doing.

MAYA'S
FISH IN A BENGALI SAUCE
Maachher Jhol

This is Bengal's 'everyday' fish dish – a
staple, along with dishes like the *Bhaja
Moong Dal*, (see preceding recipe) without which no meal seems complete. It is
eaten with Plain Rice. You may serve
any other vegetables and *dal* of your
choice with it as well.

Rui, a carp-like fish is often cooked in
this 'sauced' style. I used carp, with
bone, cut crosswise into 1½-in/4-cm
thick 'steaks' and it worked very well.
Heads can be cooked by those who can
handle them. They need to be cut up
first. If you cannot find carp, use any
firm, white-fleshed fish such as haddock, red snapper, halibut, cod or even
swordfish. (In the case of swordfish, I
always remove the skin and cube the
flesh.) Just make sure the fish pieces are
at least 1 in/2.5 cm thick. If you can't get
'steaks' you may use cut up fillets.

Serves 4
1¾ lb/800 g carp steaks, red snapper
    steaks, or any other firm white-
    fleshed fish (see note above) cut
    about 4 cm/1½ in thick – large fillets
    should be cut into pieces no longer
    than 2 in/5 cm
½ tsp/2.5 ml ground turmeric
½ tsp/2.5 ml salt
¼ pint/150 ml/⅔ cup mustard oil or
    vegetable oil
1 tbs/15 ml ground coriander seeds
1 tsp/5 ml ground cumin seeds
1½ tsp/7.5 ml finely grated, peeled
    fresh ginger
1 tsp/5 ml ground turmeric
½ tsp/2.5 ml red chilli powder
    (cayenne pepper)

½ tsp/2.5 ml salt
¼ tsp nigella seeds (*kalonji*)
4 whole, dried, hot red chillies
2 bay leaves
4 oz/100 g, 1 large onion, peeled and
   fairly finely chopped
3 whole hot green chillies

Rub the fish well with the ½ tsp/5 ml of turmeric and ½ tsp/2.5 ml of salt and set aside for 10–15 minutes.

Heat the oil in a non-stick frying pan over a medium flame. If you are using mustard oil, let it get smokingly hot. Now put in the fish pieces and brown lightly on all sides without cooking them through. Gently lift the fish out of the oil and put it on a plate. Turn off the heat.

Combine the ground coriander seeds, the cumin, ginger, 1 tsp/5 ml turmeric, chilli powder (cayenne pepper) and ½ tsp/2.5 ml of salt in a small bowl. Add 3 tbs/45 ml of water and mix.

Remove all but 5 tbs/75 ml/½ cup of oil from the frying pan. Heat the frying pan over a medium flame. When hot, put in the nigella seeds. A few seconds later, put in the red chillies. As soon as they darken a bit, put in the bay leaves. When the bay leaves start to darken, put in the onion. Stir and fry the onion, lowering the heat, if necessary until it is translucent and lightly browned. Add the spice paste. Stir and fry it for about 1 minute. Now put in the fish in a single layer as well as 8 fl oz/250 ml/1 cup of water. Lay the green chillies over the fish. Simmer over a medium heat for 2 minutes, spooning the sauce over the fish pieces as you do so. Now cover, turn the heat to low and cook the fish for 10–15 minutes or until it is just done.

Note: the whole chillies should be eaten only by those who know what they are doing.

FROM RUBY PALCHOUDHURI'S
HOUSEHOLD
SPICY CRABS
Kankra Jhal

It is not the very large king crabs that are used for this dish, but the smaller kind whose length, from eyes to the 'tail', is about 3 in/7.5 cm. They must be bought live.

Here is how the Bengalis deal with them: hold a crab firmly by the tail end with its large claws facing front and away from you. Pull off the claws. Pull off the legs. Lift up the flap on the underside. Now continue to open up the crab as if it were a rouge box or powder compact. Clean and discard the area near the eyes. On the fleshier side, it will have, apart from the meat, some spongy fern-like matter. Discard this matter. Now wash the claws, legs and the rest of the crab, scrubbing the shell thoroughly. The empty half of the body may be thrown away or put into the dish for extra flavour.

That is how the Bengalis do it. *I* do not have quite the nerve to tear up a live crab. This is what I do: I fill a large bowl three-quarters full of hot water. Then I lift the crabs, one at a time, with a set of tongs and drop them into the hot water. This anaesthetizes them. I keep adding fresh hot water to the bowl until the crabs are calm. Now, one at a time, I hold them firmly from the tail end and scrub them with a brush under hot, running water. As I clean them, I put them in a fresh bowl and then cover the bowl. I cook my crabs whole and crack them open at the table to get at the meat.

In the working class 'pubs' of Calcutta, crabs are often served with country liquor. You may serve them with rice or all by themselves. They can only be eaten with bare hands!

Unfortunately, these live crabs are not always available in Britain. But do make the dish if you can find or catch them.

Serves 3–6
about 1¾lb/800g, 6 live crabs (see note above)
2 tsp/10 ml finely grated, peeled fresh ginger
1 tsp/5 ml finely crushed garlic
½ tsp/2.5 ml ground turmeric
½ tsp/2.5 ml red chilli powder (cayenne pepper)
4 tbs/60 ml/⅓ cup mustard or vegetable oil
3 oz/75 g, 1 medium-sized onion, peeled and finely chopped
½ tsp/2.5 ml salt
2–3 fresh hot green chillies

Clean the crabs as suggested above and set aside.

Put the ginger, garlic, turmeric, red chilli powder (cayenne pepper) and 2 tbs/30 ml of water in a small bowl. Mix.

Heat the oil in a large wok, *karhai* or pan over a medium flame. If you are using mustard oil, allow it to get smokingly hot. Put in the onion. Stir and fry for 2–3 minutes or until the oil separates from the spice paste and it gets

lightly browned. Now put in the crabs and salt. Stir and fry for 2–3 minutes or until the crabs have turned red. Add the green chillies and 4 fl oz/25 ml/ ½ cup of water. Bring to a boil. Cover and simmer for 10 minutes or until the crabs are cooked.

Note: the whole chillies should be eaten only by those who know what they are doing.

MRS RAMA CHAKRAVARTY'S
PRAWNS/SHRIMPS WITH MUSTARD SEEDS
Chingri Maachher Jhal

For me, no dish could be more typical of Bengal than this one. It is simple to cook – and yet quite distinctive in the nose-tingling pungency it acquires from the ground mustard seeds in its sauce. In Calcutta, it is cooked only with inland, estuary prawns (shrimps) that are known for their sweetness. Heads are always cooked and are preferred by many diners for their richness and flavour. As prawns (shrimps) with heads are hard to find in the West, I have, reluctantly, left them out. If you cannot find black mustard seeds, use 2 tbs/30 ml of yellow mustard seeds.

Serve the dish with Plain Rice. Any *dal* and a vegetable may also be served.

Serves 4
1 tbs/15 ml whole black mustard seeds
1 tbs/15 ml whole yellow mustard seeds
½ tsp/2.5 ml ground turmeric
½ tsp/2.5 ml red chilli powder (cayenne pepper)
½ tsp/2.5 ml salt

1 lb/450 g uncooked prawns (shrimps)
with shell but no head (about 13 oz/
375 g shelled)
4 tbs/60 ml mustard oil or vegetable oil
⅓ tsp/3 ml nigella seeds (*kalonji*)
4 whole, dried, hot red chillies
3 fresh hot green chillies

Put the black mustard seeds and the
yellow mustard seeds into the container of a clean coffee grinder or food
processor. Grind. Empty the ground
spices into a small bowl. Add the turmeric, red chilli powder (cayenne pepper), salt and 6 tbs/90 ml/½ cup of
water. Mix.

Peel the prawns (shrimps), but leave
their tails on.

Heat the oil in a frying pan over a
medium flame. Let it get smokingly
hot for a second, if using mustard oil.
Now put in the nigella seeds (*kalonji*)
and a second later, the red chillies. Stir
once and put in the prawns (shrimps).
Stir for 1 minute. The prawns
(shrimps) will just start to turn pink.
Now put in the mixed spice paste and
the green chillies. Stir on a medium
heat for 1–2 minutes or until the
prawns are just done and the sauce is a
bit thicker.

Note: the whole chillies should be
eaten only by those who know what
they are doing.

MRS KAMALA BOSE'S
LAMB COOKED WITH ONIONS
AND POTATOES
Mangsho Jhol

This simple lamb dish may be served
with rice or Indian breads.

Serves 6
1¾ lb/800 g boned lamb meat from the
shoulder, cut into 1½-in/4-cm cubes
1 tsp/5 ml ground turmeric
1 tsp/5 ml ground cumin seeds
1 tsp/5 ml ground coriander seeds
¼–1 tsp/ red chilli powder (cayenne
pepper)
1 tbs/15 ml finely ground, peeled fresh
ginger
1 tsp/5 ml finely crushed garlic
4 fl oz/125 ml/½ cup mustard or
vegetable oil
1 tbs/15 ml sugar
1 lb/450 g, 4 large onions, peeled, cut in
half lengthwise and then cut crosswise
into fine rings
1 lb/450 g, 4 medium-sized potatoes
peeled and quartered
1¾ tsp/9 ml salt
¾ tsp/4 ml Bengali *garam masala* (page
200)

Put the lamb in a bowl. Add the turmeric, cumin, coriander, red chilli powder (cayenne pepper), ginger and garlic.
Mix well, cover and set aside for 2–3
hours.

Heat the oil in a wide, heavy-based
pan over a medium-high flame. Let it get
smokingly hot. Now scatter in the sugar.
Immediately, put in the onions. Stir and
fry the onions until they get a rich brownish colour. Add the meat. Stir and fry
the meat for about 10 minutes or until it
browns lightly. Now put in the potatoes.
Stir and fry them for about 5 minutes.
Now put in the salt and ½ pint/300 ml/
1¼ cups of water and bring to a boil.
Cover, lower the heat and simmer gently
for about 1 hour and 10 minutes or until
the meat is tender. Stir gently once or
twice during this cooking period. Add
the *garam masala* and stir.

MRS RAMA CHAKRAVARTY'S
TOMATO CHUTNEY
Timator Chutney

In Bengal, sweet or sweet and sour chutneys are served after all the main courses and just before dessert as palate cleansers. They are generally accompanied by crisp *papadums*. You may, of course, serve the chutney with almost any Indian meal.

Here is a very easily made, and delicious chutney whose flavour takes me back to Calcutta's dining rooms in one swift leap. In Bengal, small cubes of dried mango are added towards the end of the cooking period. These are hard to find in the West. I find that dried apricots make a perfectly good substitute.

Serves 6

1-in/2.5-cm cube of ginger, peeled
2 tbs/30 ml vegetable oil
½ tsp/2.5 ml *panchphoran* (page 202)
2 whole, hot, dried red chillies
6 good-sized cloves of garlic, mashed
    to a pulp
1 lb/450 g tomatoes, chopped

1 tsp/5 ml salt
2½ oz/72 g/½ cup sugar
4–5 dried apricots, cut into ½-in/1-cm
    cubes
2 whole, fresh hot green chillies

Cut the ginger, crosswise, into very fine slices. Stacking several slices together at a time, cut them into very fine slivers.

Heat the oil in a heavy-based pan over a medium flame. When hot, put in the *panchphoran*. Let the spices sizzle and pop for a few seconds. Now put in the red chillies. Stir once and put in the ginger and garlic. Stir for about 5 seconds. Now put in the tomatoes, salt and sugar. Simmer on a medium to medium-low flame or until the chutney begins to thicken. This may take about 15–20 minutes. Now add the apricot cubes and the green chillies. Simmer and cook on a lowish heat for another 10–15 minutes or until the chutney is thick and has a glazed look. Serve at room temperature.

Note: the chillies should only be eaten by those who know what they are doing.

HYDERABAD

The mansion needs paint. Its ochre wash, done perhaps twenty or thirty years ago, is now stained with the drippings of as many monsoons. Gardeners have long since abandoned the grounds – only a few determined weeds stick out of the hard, caked earth. A curtain – a sheet of printed cloth, really, that covers an arched entrance – parts, sending dozens of pigeons flying in all directions, and a tall gentleman appears. He is a nawab, a nobleman of ancient heritage, who, after many welcoming salaams, leads us into a vast chamber decked out with dusty chandeliers and whirring ceiling fans. We sit and talk with members of his large family as exquisite, home-made fruit drinks – *sharbats* – some flavoured with sweetly aromatic *khas* roots (vetivert), others with the purple, sweet-and-sour juice of tiny *falsa* berries (grewia Asiatica), are served in Venetian glasses. *Tootak*, morsels of delicate semolina pastry filled with spicy minced (ground) meat, are passed around on a silver tray to provoke and then satisfy the palate. The nawab's family is fast running out of money and can hardly sustain the style of life it was once used to. But unfailing courtesy and an almost overwhelming sense of hospitality are in its blood and will be with it until the last breath is drawn. That is the Hyderabadi way.

Times have changed in Hyderabad. An old order has passed, with some families coming out of the changes better than others. But if there is one common link that connects gracious old families in straightened circumstances with those who have managed to translate old wealth into new, it is the cuisine of the region, of which every Hyderabadi is justifiably proud and which no Hyderabadi, rich or poor, can do without.

And what a cuisine it is! Nurtured by what was once a wealthy Muslim court in the heart of Hindu South India, the cuisine combines the very best of Muslim foods – kebabs, pilafs, *kormas* and yoghurt dishes – with the hauntingly aromatic, tart, pungent, and creamy flavourings of the South – mustard seeds, cassia buds (*kabab cheeni*), cinnamon, curry leaves, hot chillies, peanuts, tamarind and coconut milk. A sauce of roasted and ground sesame seeds which, in the Middle East, might appear under the guise of mild-flavoured *tahini*, is mixed here with fiery green chillies and tart tamarind paste to become the mouth-wateringly good *til ki chutney*. Dried beans and lamb, which are often stewed together in Persian cookery, are perked up here with tamarind, cumin seeds, red chillies and curry leaves to become the delectable *dalcha* of Hyderabad.

Hyderabad city was, until 1948, the capital of Hyderabad state, the largest semi-autonomous royal kingdom within India, two and a half times the size of Ireland. Its Muslim ruler, the last Nizam, was a direct descendant of a Moghul governor who had declared his independence in the early eighteenth century just as central Moghul authority in Delhi was beginning to weaken. Reputed to be the richest man in the entire world, the Nizam had his own currency and his own private railway system. Shortly after India became independent, the Nizam was prodded into merging his state with the new democratic country that surrounded it on all sides. Later, the state was to lose some of its western dominions to Maharashtra and Karnataka, while gaining others to the east and south, and become the brand new state of Andhra Pradesh with Hyderabad city as its capital.

Hyderabad state is now no more, but such was the grandeur of its court that almost no Hyderabadi over fifty years of age can speak for long without referring to the 'old days'. The Nizams, of course, lived in their own stratosphere, borne aloft by caparisoned elephants, coaches (one Nizam turned up at the British Resident's house in a dashing yellow coach and four, the yellow clothing of the postilions and grooms carefully dyed to match the shade of the coach), and, as the twentieth century rolled in, fleets of the most expensive cars. They wore jewels the size of pigeon's eggs, and when they entertained, the city was lit up, fountains played and dining tables set for hundreds glittered with gold plate.

The nobles, mainly Muslims of Turkish, Arab, Persian, Turkoman and Afghan descent, did not do so badly for themselves either. They had vast land holdings, armies of retainers, and enjoyed both royal patronage and the fruits of the trickle-down economy. Some hardly needed to work at all. One nobleman was known to have asked a British Resident why he bothered to paint pictures with his own hand when he could so easily get someone else to paint the pictures for him.

In this atmosphere of wealth and leisure, noble families looked for distractions and amusements and often turned to food to provide both. If liquor was being distilled in a private *sharaab-khana*, or winery (only a few Hindu nobles were granted royal permission to do this as Muslims were, technically, not supposed to drink), then rare flavours such as concentrates of venison or quail were added for the delight of guests to come. If pickles were laid out on *chowkies* (low, square dining tables seating four or eight on the floor at formal occasions), then diners might find, apart from the more common lime and mango, exquisitely pickled partridges and, believe it or not, delicate bits of pickled chicks as well.

While there was a certain exotic quality to some royal foods, it was also known that a true Hyderabadi would go anywhere in the city for a well-prepared dish, however humble its origins. Not so long ago a certain widowed begum was known to travel around during the evening hours in her curtained car, stopping outside local taverns – *saindhi-khanas* – in the heart of the busy, sixteenth-century, Char Minar (Four Minarets) area but never stepping out of her car. She would, periodically, send her chauffeur in to buy an earthen vessel's worth of *saindhi* (palm toddy), another of *chakna*, a superb, spicy stew made out of abdominal offal, and some deliciously fluffy oven breads called *sheermals*. It was rumoured that inside the car she ate with silver cutlery. I know many Hyderabadis who delight in the same combination of foods today, going the same route as the old begum, though not with her style and elegance!

One no longer sees ostentatious signs of wealth in Hyderabad. What wealth there is has found fewer, more discreet forms. Just outside the old city is a hilly, rocky area, once known only for the massive, Stonehenge-like rocks that are strewn across it, and for the gaily clothed Banjara tribesmen who decided to settle amidst

Nature's magnificent pre-historic wreckage. Far-sighted Hyderabadis bought land here when the prices were low. Among the rocks, they planted frangipani and jasmine, bougainvillaea and hibiscus, palms, papayas, tamarinds and mangoes. They also built new houses, some brilliantly incorporating giant rocks as inside walls and as the sides of pools. Today, the Banjara Hills are the city's most sought after – and pricey – extension. There, sleek kitchens, manned by a minimum of staff, produce excellent Hyderabadi fare to satisfy the cravings of some very sophisticated residents.

Early mornings can begin with *nahari*, a slow-simmering (*very* slow-simmering – it cooks all night on embers) stew of lamb trotters and tongue, seasoned with cassia buds, cardamom, and an unusual, highly aromatic bouquet garni – *potli ka masala* – that can include sandalwood powder, earthy *khas* roots (vetivert), and even whole, dried roses! The rising steam perfumes the cool morning air, beckoning late sleepers – rather like the smells of coffee and bacon – to hurry to the breakfast table where the *nahari* is poured into soup bowls and devoured with the help of obliging, dunkable *sheermals*.

Those who wish to start their day more vigorously, who prefer to jog, ride, or play tennis before they eat, may sustain themselves through their physical exertions by thoughts of another, larger breakfast, immortalized by the Urdu couplet:

> *Khichri* has but three bosom buddies
> Minced meat, *ghee, papadums*, and pickles.

I do not know who originally thought up this Hyderabadi combination, but it is quite superb. *Khichri*, a fluffy mixture of rice and red split lentils, is first lubricated with a dollop of *ghee* and then eaten with a simple *kheema*, minced meat stewed with onions, garlic, ginger and red chillies. Rice flour *papadums* provide crunch and texture while a creamy, minty, sesame chutney and a tart mango pickle add pep and pungency. To round out the breakfast, there is always *khagina*, gingery scrambled eggs, as well as *parathas* (flaky griddle breads) and cups of sweet tea to wash everything down.

Such satisfying breakfasts usually beg to be followed by a nap, and most people succumb, especially on weekends. After that, there is time enough to go antique hunting. What the old rich must sell every day to survive, the new rich quickly buy up. Available in the market-place, and at private sales, are excellent, turn-of-the-century photographs, eighteenth-century *hookahs* (hubble bubble pipes) made of the finest *bidri* work (gun metal inlaid with silver), and betel boxes of gleaming silver. Those with smaller budgets head towards Lal Bazaar in the old city to stock up on brightly tasselled ribbons and bangles. There are bangles everywhere in every colour imaginable. Children buy them, laides enshrouded from head to toe in black *burkas* stick out pale arms for fittings and even men come in to pick up special shades requested by their sweethearts. An arm without bangles, they say here, is as ugly as a stick of bamboo.

It is soon time for lunch, and, if one is lucky – as we were – one has friends in the vicinity. We take one of the busy crossroads leading away from Char Minar and enter a walled compound through an arched gateway. Inside is a palatial town house, a jigsaw puzzle of gardens, courtyards, stairs and inner chambers, all inhabited by an aristocratic old family. A *dastarkhan* (long dining cloth) is spread out on the Persian carpet and we take our places on either side of it. The midday feast includes some of Hyderabad's most glorious dishes: *lukmi*, ravioli-like squares of pastry dough filled in the centre with spiced minced meat and deep-fried; *chippe ka gosht*, chunks of meat marinated in a paste of onion, green chillies, coconut, garlic, *garam masala* and yoghurt and then cooked very slowly in a new clay pot so the meat smells a bit like parched earth after a rainfall (this odour, loved by all Indians, is even made into an attar); *ambaday ki bhaji*, a dish of sour, sorrel-like greens; *baghare baigan*, small, whole aubergines (eggplants), slit, browned, and then cooked gently in a nutty sauce containing sesame seeds and peanuts; *tomato kut*, an aromatic purée of fresh tomatoes perked up with tamarind, curry leaves and bits of browned garlic; *murgh methi*, free-range chicken cooked with freshly sprouted fenugreek greens; *kacchi biryani*, a difficult pilaf to prepare as raw, marinated meat and rice must cook together so the first gets tender and the second does not turn to mush; and one of my all-time favourites, *kacche dahi ke koftay*. For this last, minced meat, nicely spiced with green coriander, mint, browned garlic and *garam masala* is ground to a very fine, paté-like paste, formed into delicate balls and fried. Just before eating, these balls are slipped into beaten yoghurt and the entire dish seasoned with a quick *baghar* of garlic, mustard seeds, curry leaves and red chillies. It is incredible!

As we all protest that not another morsel can pass our lips, the sweets arrive. Who can resist the *baadaam ki jaali*, light, round marzipan 'sandwiches' where the top layer, with its filigreed cut-outs, reveals real silver *varak* (fine tissue) and coloured sprinkles? The *unday ki piyosi*, saffron-flavoured diamonds made with eggs, *ghee*, ground almonds and reduced milk, looks equally good so we nibble on that as well. And as for the *dubble ka meetha*, a glorious bread pudding liberally sprinkled with pistachios and raisins, well, I have always had a weakness for it and my host insists that I try it. So I do. My host adds, almost apologetically, that he cannot offer us the wonderful *balai* (cream) that, in the old days, was often sent over from the Nizam's palace, to put over the pudding. He need not worry. We all like it just the way it is.

Another rest is called for. And then some exercise. We take ourselves off to the Banjara Hotel for a swim, and, let's admit it, a taste of the deliciously soft kebabs they make by the lake side. After that it is time to dress up for a banquet thrown by a nawab who is known to set one of the best tables in town. The women slip into their Moghul jewellery – nothing ostentatious, mind you, just little 'pieces' – and the men don *sherwanis* (fitted, knee-length jackets).

After florid courtesies at the door, our host ushers us into a large drawing-room lined on all side with stuffed chairs. The two sexes, as if drawn by programmed magnets, seat themselves at opposite ends of the room. My hostess, a charming, betel-chewing lady, talks wistfully of the 'old days' when good cooks were in ample supply, then praises Allah for blessing her with many talented daughters-in-law who have taken up the slack. Our first course is served in the drawing-room: it is *marag*, a clear Arab meat broth with bits of meat floating in it, served in Chinese bowls. It is light, soothing, and beautifully prepared – a very pleasant start to the meal that is to follow.

As we take our last spoonfuls of soup, a curtain at one end of the drawing-room parts to reveal, on a dais, an enormous dining table, covered with platters of food from end to end. Our host leads us to a servant who is waiting with an *aaftaaba*, a beautifully carved brass jug filled with warm water. One by one, we stretch our hands over a *sylaabchi*, a matching basin, to have our hands washed. The basin has a recessed cover with tiny holes in it. The dirty water drains through these holes so as not to offend the next guest.

Members of the family hardly leave our sides, urging us to eat this and have more of that. We start with *haleem*, a smooth, velvety (and *very* hard to make) paste of wheat kernels and meat. It is as good as caviar. In fact, it is eaten here very much like caviar, with bits of hard-boiled eggs and generous squeezes of lime.

Next we sample the *shikhampuri kababs*, patties made out of finely pounded meat, stuffed with a pleasant mixture of paneer (very fresh cheese), mint, green coriander, and green chillies. They are uncommonly good, as are the cigar-shaped *seekh kababs*. Our host suggests that we have the *qabooli* and the *kheema methi*. The first is a layered casserole made of partially cooked rice, yellow split peas cooked with ginger, garlic and yoghurt, a purée of green herbs, and browned onions. It is gently baked in a large pot. The second is minced lamb perfumed with masses of tiny green fenugreek leaves. The two, when eaten together, are simply wonderful. We have a bit of the *mirch ka salan*, a fiery dish of large green chillies in a sesame seed and coconut sauce, and then dip into the *sarkari dalcha*, a stew of mixed split peas and meat. We note that the *shahi dahi baras* are divine. In a large bowl of lightly sweetened, very creamy yoghurt bob lots of airy *moong dal* dumplings. Sultanas and almonds are scattered about. The dumplings are so good that we are forced to go back for seconds. Then I, for one, decide to call it quits, even though I see whole stuffed chickens, breads, more pilafs and vegetables on the table – to say nothing of the sweets looming in the distance on yet another table. I wish for a large pocket to carry away some of the food so I can eat it the next day!

We return to the drawing-room where the hostess offers us beautifully folded betel leaves, each impaled on a silver hook attached to a single merry-go-round of many silver chains. We removed the betel leaves from the hooks and put the aromatic digestives in our mouths. As we get set to leave, our host approaches us with tiny phials of attar and dabs a little on the backs of our hands.

We get into our cars and drive off. The perfume lingers with us all night, reminding us not only of the superb meal that we have been lucky enough to eat but of the courtesy and hospitality of our Hyderabadi hosts.

RECIPES FROM HYDERABAD

BILKIZ ALLADIN'S
GREEN PEPPERS IN A SESAME SEED SAUCE
Mirch Ka Salan

This rather rich, pickle-like dish from Hyderabad is actually made with long hot peppers, rather like those known as 'Italian hot peppers'. As these peppers are not always available, and also because they may be too hot for some palates, I have used the large green (bell) peppers. They have a good flavour and you can adjust the 'heat' by adding as much chilli powder or hot green chillies as you like.

There are many recipes for the dish – I have three myself. I have picked the simplest one.

You can serve the peppers with almost any Indian meal.

Serves 4–6
2 tbs/30 ml dessicated, unsweetened coconut
3¼ oz/82 g/¾ cup sesame seeds
1–1¼ lb/450–550 g, 6 medium-sized green peppers
6 fl oz/175 ml/¾ cup vegetable oil
1 tsp/5 ml whole black mustard seeds
½ tsp/2.5 ml nigella seeds (*kalonji*)
7 oz/200 g, 2 medium-sized onions, peeled and finely chopped
1 tbs/15 ml ground cumin seeds
4–5 fresh, hot green chillies, cut into very fine rounds
1¼ tsp/6 ml salt

¼–½ tsp/1–2.5 ml red chilli powder (cayenne pepper)
3 tbs/45 ml lemon juice

Put the coconut and sesame seeds into the container of a clean coffee grinder or other spice grinder. Grind, in several batches if necessary, as finely as possible.

Core the green peppers, removing the stem end and the seeds. Cut, lengthwise, into slices that are ¾-in/2-cm at their widest.

Heat the oil in a large, non-stick frying pan over a medium flame. When hot, put in the sliced green peppers. Stir and fry them for a few minutes or just until they are lightly browned and slightly wilted. Remove the pepper slices with a slotted spoon and set aside.

Put the mustard seeds into the hot oil. As soon as they begin to pop, put in the nigella seeds. A few seconds later, put in the onions. Stir the onions around for a bit. They should not brown. Now put in the coconut-sesame mixture, the cumin seeds, green chillies, salt and chilli powder (cayenne pepper). Stir and sauté for a few minutes or until the spice mixture turns a shade darker. Now put in 8 fl oz/250 ml/1 cup of water and stir. Bring to a simmer. Turn the heat to low and simmer for 2–3 minutes, stirring in the green peppers and serve.

In Hyderabad, this dish is served

with all its oil. I prefer to remove the oil just before serving.

HARD-BOILED EGGS IN A TOMATO SAUCE
Tomato Kut

As the juiciness of tomatoes varies so much, it is hard to give an exact recipe here. You may have to make your own adjustments. A *tomato kut* is a delicately spiced tomato purée which may be eaten, as is, or may have hard-boiled eggs partially imbedded in it, making it a very useful dish for breakfasts, brunches and lunches. It goes particularly well with Rice with Tomatoes and Spinach.

Serves 4

2 lb/900 g ripe tomatoes, chopped finely
2 tbs/30 ml whole coriander seeds
2 tbs/30 ml tamarind paste (page 203)
2 tsp/10 ml very finely grated, peeled fresh ginger
1 clove garlic, mashed to a pulp
½ tsp/2.5 ml red chilli powder (cayenne pepper)
20 fresh or dried, curry leaves
2 tbs/30 ml chopped, fresh green coriander (Chinese parsley)
1 tsp/5 ml ground, roasted cumin seeds (page 199)
2 tsp/10 ml chickpea flour (gram flour/ *besan*)
1 tbs/15 ml vegetable oil
⅛ tsp whole mustard seeds
⅛ tsp whole cumin seeds
2–3 whole fenugreek seeds
⅛ tsp nigella seeds (*kalonji*)

1 whole dried, hot red pepper
1 large clove garlic, cut in quarters, lengthwise
4 hard-boiled eggs, peeled

Put the tomatoes, coriander seeds, tamarind paste, ginger, garlic, chilli powder (cayenne pepper), 10 of the curry leaves and the fresh coriander into a heavy-based pan. Place on a low flame. Cover. The tomatoes will begin to release their juices. Start to simmer and keep simmering gently until the tomatoes are very soft. Now sieve them into a bowl. Discard the contents of the sieve. Add the ground, roasted cumin seeds to the purée and mix. Rinse out the cooking pan and put the purée back in it.

Examine your purée. If it is very thin, it might require more than the 2 tsp/10 ml of chickpea flour. My purée is generally just a little thinner than the average tomato soup and I have about ¾ pints/450 ml/2 cups.

Put the chickpea flour in a small cast-iron frying pan over a medium-low flame. Stir it about until it turns slightly brown. Empty it into a small bowl and mix with 1 tbs/15 ml of water. Add this mixture to the tomato purée. Bring the purée to a simmer over a medium-low flame, stirring. Turn the flame down and let it cook gently for 2–3 minutes.

Heat the oil in a small frying pan. When hot, put in the mustard seeds, whole cumin seeds, fenugreek seeds, nigella seeds, red pepper and remaining 10 curry leaves. As soon as the red pepper begins to darken, put in the garlic. When the garlic browns a little, pour the contents of the frying pan into the pan with the purée.

Put the purée into a serving dish. Cut the hard-boiled eggs in half, crosswise, and arrange them, cut side up, in the serving dish so that they are at least half buried in the purée.

Note: the whole, hot red chilli should be approached with caution.

SAKINA MEHTA'S
CHICKEN IN A GREEEN SAUCE
Murgh Methi

This dish is nothing short of inspired. The only problem with it is that it requires fenugreek greens – or *methi*. Not just ordinary fenugreek leaves, the kind used in the rest of India, but delicate shoots that are just sending out their first budding leaves. It is this fuss and delicacy that is so typical of the Hyderabadis and their food. I have substituted the equally popular dill for the fenugreek greens. The dish remains wonderful and should, perhaps, be called *Murgh Sooa*. You may serve it with rice or Flaky Pan Bread and any vegetable of your choice. Salads or crunchy relishes should be served on the side.

Serves 4–6
3 lb/1.4 kg chicken, cut into serving pieces and skinned or 3 lb/1.4 kg chicken pieces, cut into serving pieces and skinned
4×2.5-cm/1-in cubes fresh ginger, peeled and coarsely chopped
8–10 cloves garlic, peeled
1 tsp/5 ml ground turmeric
6 tbs/90 ml/½ cup vegetable oil
12 oz/350 g, 3 large onions, peeled, cut in half lengthwise and then crosswise into fine half rings
½ pint/300 ml/1¼ cups plain yoghurt
1¼–1½ tsp/6–7.5 ml salt
enough well-packed, chopped, fresh coriander to fill a glass measuring jug to the 8 fl oz/250 ml/1 cup level
6 fresh, hot green chillies, coarsely chopped
enough well-packed, chopped, fresh dill to fill a glass measuring jug to the 8 fl oz/250 ml/1 cup level

Examine the chicken pieces and remove all extra bits of fat. When cutting the chicken into serving pieces, cut the breast into quarters and the legs into half.

Put the ginger, garlic and 4 fl oz/ 125 ml/½ cup of water into the container of a food processor or blender. Blend until you have a paste. Add the turmeric and blend to mix.

Heat the oil in a very wide-based pan over a medium-high flame. When hot, put in the onions. Stir and fry them until they brown lightly in a few spots. Now put in the chicken pieces. Stir them around until they also turn golden, with a few brown spots. Put in the ginger-garlic mixture. Stir and cook on a medium-high heat for another 10 minutes or until the ginger-garlic mixture has browned lightly. Now put in the yoghurt and salt. Stir. Scrape up anything that may have stuck to the bottom of the pan. Bring to a simmer. Cover, lower the heat and simmer for about 15 minutes or until the chicken is almost done.

While the chicken is simmering, put the fresh coriander, green chillies and 4 fl oz/125 ml/½ cup of water into the container of a food processor or blender. Blend until smooth.

When the chicken is almost done, remove the lid and turn the heat up to medium. Boil away some of the liquid to thicken the sauce. Now pour in the mixture from the food processor or blender. Stir to mix and then put in all the chopped dill. Simmer for 5 minutes.

Spoon off as much fat as possible before serving.

QUICK KEBABS
Tala Gosht

This dish is just as easy as it is delicious and cooks in about 15 minutes. There is, however, a marinating period of 2 hours. Hyderabadis often eat it with Flaky Pan Bread or rice, and a tamarind-flavoured *dal*. You could also offer them as cocktail snacks – just stick toothpicks into them and serve them as soon as they come out of the pan!

Serves 6
2 lb/900 g boneless lamb meat from the shoulder cut into 1¼–1½-in/3–4-cm cubes
4 tsp/20 ml very finely grated, peeled fresh ginger
2 tsp/10 ml very finely crushed garlic
4 fresh hot green chillies, very finely chopped
½ tsp/2.5 ml red chilli powder (cayenne pepper)
1½ tsp/7.5 ml salt
freshly ground black pepper
2 tbs/30 ml vegetable oil
½ tsp/2.5 ml *garam masala*
mint sprigs and wedges of lime or lemon

Cut each cube of meat into narrower ¼-in/0.5-cm thick pieces. Pound the pieces with a meat mallet or potato masher so that they flatten out slightly.

Combine the ginger, garlic, green chillies, red chilli powder (cayenne pepper) and salt. Rub this mixture into the meat. Grind lots of black pepper over the meat. Rub that in as well. Set the meat aside for 2 hours.

Heat the oil in a large non-stick frying pan over a medium-low flame. Put in all the meat and slowly, bring it to a simmer. Cover and continue to cook on a medium-low heat for about 15 minutes or until the meat is tender. The meat will cook in its own juices. Remove the cover and turn up the heat a bit. Add the *garam masala*. Boil away all the liquid and gently fry the meat so it turns slightly brown. Serve with mint sprigs and lime wedges.

FROM THE HOUSEHOLD OF NAWAB SHAH ALAM KHAN
LAMB WITH ONIONS AND MINT
Do Piaza

A stew-like dish, this tastes of the sweetness of onions that have simmered for a long time and the freshness of lemon, mint and fresh coriander. It goes well with Hyderabadi Pilaf of Rice and Split Peas and Carrots with Dill.

Serves 6
2 lb/900 g boned meat from lamb shoulder, cut into 1-in/2.5-cm cubes
1 lb/450 g, 5 medium-sized onions, peeled, cut in half, lengthwise, and then cut crosswise into fine half rings

140

2 tsp/10 ml salt

1 tsp/5 ml red chilli powder (cayenne pepper)

2 tsp/10 ml finely grated, peeled fresh ginger

1 tsp/5 ml finely crushed garlic

1 tsp/5 ml ground turmeric

3 tbs/45 ml vegetable oil

enough well-packed fresh green coriander (Chinese parsley) to fill a glass measuring jug to the 4 fl oz/ 125 ml/½ cup mark

enough well-packed mint to fill a glass measuring jug to the 4 fl oz/125 ml/½ cup mark

6 fresh hot green chillies, coarsely chopped

3 tbs/45 ml lemon juice

Combine the meat, onions, salt, chilli powder (cayenne pepper), ginger, garlic, turmeric, vegetable oil and ¾ pint/ 400 ml/2 cups of water in a wide-based pan. Bring to a simmer. Cover, lower the heat and simmer gently for about 1 hour. Remove the lid, turn up the heat and boil down the sauce until it is very thick.

While the meat is cooking, put the green coriander, mint, green chillies, lemon juice and 2 tbs/30 ml of water in the container of a food processor or blender. Blend until as smooth as possible.

When the meat sauce has reduced, pour the contents of the food processor or blender into the pan with the meat. Bring to a simmer. Stir and simmer gently for 3–4 minutes.

FROM THE HOUSEHOLD OF MAHARAJ KARAN

RED SPLIT LENTILS COOKED WITH LAMB
Dalcha

Not much lamb is used in this Hyderabadi dish – just ½ lb/225 g – making it perfect for those who are trying to cut down on their meat intake. You may serve it with rice, some green vegetables and a yoghurt dish.

Serves 6

8 oz/225 g/1½ cups skinned red split lentils (*masoor dal* – page 200)

½ tsp/2.5 ml ground turmeric

4 tbs/60 ml vegetable oil

1½-in/4-cm cinnamon stick

6 whole cardamom pods

3 oz/75 g, 1 medium-sized onion, peeled, cut in half lengthwise and then cut crosswise into fine half rings

½ lb/225 g boneless meat from lamb shoulder, cut into 1-in/2.5-cm cubes

1 tsp/5 ml peeled and finely grated fresh ginger

1 tsp/5 ml finely crushed garlic

¼ tsp/ red chilli powder (cayenne pepper)

¼–⅓ tsp/ salt

3 tbs/45 ml tamarind pulp or about 2 tbs/30 ml lemon juice

about 1½ tsp/7.5 ml salt

½ tsp/2.5 ml red chilli powder (cayenne pepper)

2 tbs/30 ml *ghee* or vegetable oil

½ tsp/2.5 ml whole cumin seeds

1–2 dried whole hot red chillies

8–10 fresh or dried curry leaves

2 cloves of garlic, peeled and cut in half lengthwise

Pick over the lentils and then wash them in several changes of water. Drain. Put them in a heavy-based pan. Add 1½ pints/900ml/3¾ cups of water and the turmeric. Bring to a simmer. Cover, leaving the lid slightly ajar and simmer gently for about 1¼ hours or until the lentils are quite tender.

While the lentils are cooking, prepare the meat. Heat the 4tbs/60ml of oil in a wide based pan over a medium-high flame. When hot, put in the cinnamon and cardamom. Stir for a few seconds or until the cardamom begins to darken a bit. Put in the onions and stir fry until slightly browned. Now put in the meat. Stir the meat around until it browns a little. Now put in the ginger, garlic, ¼tsp red chilli powder (cayenne pepper) and the ¼–⅓tsp of salt. Stir for 1 minute to allow the spices to brown. Now put in about 6floz/175ml/¾ cup of water and bring to a simmer. Cover tightly and simmer very gently for 1–1¼ hours or until the meat is tender. If the water boils away, just add a tiny bit more.

When the lentils are tender, mash them lightly with the back of a spoon. Add the tamarind, the 1½tsp/7.5ml of salt, and the ½tsp/2.5ml of red chilli powder (cayenne pepper). Stir to mix and taste for the balance of seasonings. Adjust, if necessary.

When the meat is tender, pour the cooked, seasoned lentils over it. Stir to mix. Bring to a simmer and simmer gently, uncovered, for 1 minute.

Heat the *ghee* in a small frying pan over a medium flame. When hot, put in the whole cumin seeds. A few seconds later, put in the whole red chilli and the curry leaves. Stir. As soon as

the chilli darkens a bit, put in the garlic cloves. Stir until the garlic turns a medium-brown in colour. Pour the contents of the frying pan over the lentil-meat combination. (You may do this last step after you have put the *dalcha* into a serving dish. The seasonings scattered over the top serve as a garnish.)

Note: the large whole spices in this dish are not meant to be eaten.

FROM THE HOUSEHOLD OF NAWAB SHAH ALAM KHAN
HYDERABADI PILAF OF RICE AND SPLIT PEAS
Hyderabadi Qabooli

Although a dish of rice and beans, this is very elegant one – indeed, the first time I had it in Hyderabad, it was at a very lavish and grand banquet.

You could serve it with any meat dish and some nice, simple vegetable, such as Carrots with Dill. Relishes and salads, and yoghurt dishes also, go particularly well with this pilaf.

Serves 6
2½oz/65g/½ cup skinned *chana dal* or yellow split peas (page 200)
Basmati or any other long-grain rice, measured to the ¾ pint/450ml/2 cup mark in a glass measuring jug
½tsp/2.5ml ground turmeric
4tbs/60ml vegetable oil
4½oz/115g, 1 large onion, peeled, cut in half lengthwise and then cut crosswise into very fine half rings
2tsp/10ml finely grated, peeled fresh ginger
1tsp/5ml finely crushed garlic

5 tbs/75 ml/½ cup plain yoghurt
salt
⅛–¼ tsp/ red chilli powder (cayenne
   pepper)
2 tbs/30 ml *ghee* or 1 oz/25 g/2
   tablespoons unsalted butter, cut into
   small pieces
2 tbs/30 ml lemon juice
2 tbs/30 ml milk
1 tbs/15 ml finely chopped fresh, green
   coriander (Chinese parsley)
1 tbs/15 ml finely chopped fresh mint
2–4 fresh green chillies, very finely-
   chopped
2 tsp/2.5 ml *garam masala* (page 200)

Pick over the *chana dal* and wash it in
several changes of water. Leave to soak
in enough water to cover it by 3 in/
7.5 cm from 1½ hours.

Pick over the rice and wash it in
several changes of water. Leave to soak
in enough water to cover it by 2 in/5 cm
for 30 minutes. Drain.

Put the *dal* and its soaking liquid
into a pan. Add ¼ tsp of the turmeric
and bring to a boil. Cover, leaving the
lid slightly ajar, turn the heat down
and simmer for about 30 minutes or
until it is almost tender but the grains
are still whole. Drain.

Heat the oil in a non-stick frying pan
over a medium-high flame. When hot,
put in the onions. Stir and fry them
until they are a rich, reddish-brown
colour and crisp. Remove with a slotted spoon and spread out on a plate
lined with absorbent kitchen paper
(paper towels). Put the ginger and garlic into the same oil. Stir and fry until
lightly browned. Now put in the
remaining ¼ tsp of turmeric and 1 tbs/
15 ml of the yoghurt. Stir and fry until
most of the liquid in the yoghurt

evaporates and the remaining particles
brown lightly. Add the remaining yoghurt 1 tbs/15 ml at a time, and cook in
the same way. Now put in the drained
dal, ½ tsp/2.5 ml salt and the chilli
powder (cayenne pepper). Stir to mix.
Sauté the *dal* for 1 minute.

Heat the oven to 325°F/170°C/gas
mark 3.

Bring 5 pints/3 litres/12 cups of
water to a rolling boil. Add 1 tbs/ 15 ml
of salt and stir. Now put in the drained
rice and bring to a boil again. Boil
vigorously for 5 minutes or until the
rice is about three-quarters cooked. It
should retain a slim, hard, inner core.
Drain the rice and empty half of it into
a wide, oven-proof casserole-type pan.
Cover the rice with the cooked *dal*.
Cover the dal with the remaining rice.
Spread the *ghee* and the browned
onions over the rice. Sprinkle the
lemon juice and milk, fresh coriander
(Chinese parsley), mint, green chillies
and *garam masala* over the top. Cover
tightly, first with foil and then with a
lid and place in the oven for 30
minutes.

Stir gently to mix before serving.

FROM THE HOUSEHOLD OF NAWAB SHAH
ALAM KHAN
FLAKY PAN BREAD
Paratha

One of the best unleavened breads of
India, these *parathas* should be cooked
on an Indian *tava*, a slightly concave
cast-iron plate, or else in a cast-iron
frying pan. They can be served with
kebabs, with Hyderabadi or North
Indian sauced meats and all the *bhaji-*

type vegetable dishes such as Cauliflower with dried Chillies and Mustard Seeds, Spicy Potatoes, Stir-fried Aubergine (Eggplant) and Stuffed Okra.

If you have access to *chapati* flour (page 196), available at Indian grocers, you may use 1 lb/450 g of it instead of the two suggested flours.

Makes 8 parathas
½ lb/250 g/1¾ cups plain white or unbleached white flour
½ lb/250 g/1¾ cups wheatmeal or wholewheat flour, sifted
1 tsp/5 ml salt
extra flour, wheatmeal or white, for dusting
about 8 fl oz/250 ml/1 cup *ghee* or melted butter

Put the two types of flour and salt into a bowl. Slowly add about ½ pint/300 ml/1¼ cups of water to get as soft a dough as posible. Knead the dough for 10 minutes. Cover and set aside for 4 hours.

Knead the dough again, using extra flour if it is sticky. Divide the dough into 8 balls. Set 7 aside and work on the eighth.

Set a *tava* or cast-iron frying pan to heat over a lowish flame.

Dust your work surface with flour. Put 1 ball of dough on it and flatten it into a patty. Roll it out until it is about 7 in/18 cm in diameter. Smear the surface of the *paratha* with about 1 tsp/2.5 ml of *ghee*. Now lightly dust a little flour over the *ghee*. Starting from the edge farthest away from you, begin rolling the *paratha* tightly towards you. You will now have a long 'snake'. Coil the 'snake' around itself tightly, spiral-ling upwards. Push down the spiral to form a patty. Dust the patty lightly with flour and roll it out into a round that is about ⅛ in/0.25 cm thick and roughly 7½ in/20.5 cm in diameter.

When the *tava* is well heated, slap the *paratha* onto it. Let it just sit for 30 seconds or so. Now lift it up slightly and dribble about 1 tsp/5 ml of *ghee* under it. Make a wad out of some absorbent kitchen paper (paper towel) and press down on the *paratha*, turning it slightly each time you do this. Cook the *paratha* this way for 2–3 minutes or until the bottom has reddish-brown patches. Dribble 1 tsp/5 ml of *ghee* on top of the *paratha* and turn it over. Press again with the wad of absorbent kitchen paper (kitchen towel), turning the *paratha* a bit each time you do so. Cook the second side for about 3 minutes or until it too has reddish-brown patches. When the *paratha* is done, wrap it quickly in aluminium foil. Make all *parathas* this way.

Note: the *parathas* may be stacked together wrapped in aluminium foil. This entire wrapped packet can then be heated in the oven set at 350°F/180°C/gas mark 4 for 10–15 minutes, just before you eat.

BILKIZ ALLADIN'S
SESAME CHUTNEY
Til Ki Chutney

Another everyday chutney that even finds its way to the breakfast table in Hyderabad along with Indian-style scrambled eggs, *papadum*, minced meat and tea.

Serves 6

2 oz/50 g/½ cup sesame seeds

enough well-packed fresh green
  coriander (Chinese parsley) to fill a
  glass measuring jug to the 2 fl oz/
  62 ml/¼ cup level

enough well-packed fresh mint leaves
  to fill a glass measuring jug to the
  2 fl oz/62 ml/¼ cup level

5 fresh, hot green chillies, coarsely
  chopped

3 tbs/45 ml tamarind paste

½ tsp/2.5 ml salt

Put the sesame seeds in a small cast-
iron frying pan over a medium flame.
Stir and toast them until they turn a
few shades darker. Put into a clean
coffee grinder or other spice grinder
and grind as finely as possible.

Put the ground sesame seeds
together with all the other ingredients
and 3 fl oz/90 ml/5 tablespoons of water
into the container of a food processor
or blender. Blend as smooth as
possible.

YOGHURT CHUTNEY
Dahi Ki Chutney

Here is a simple yoghurt relish that
seems to appear at all meals in
Hyderabad.

Serves 6

¾ pint/450 ml/2 cups plain yoghurt

¾ tsp/4 ml salt

freshly ground black pepper

3 tbs/45 ml very finely chopped onions

1 tsp/5 ml very finely grated, peeled
  fresh ginger

1 tsp/5 ml very finely crushed garlic

2 tbs/30 ml very finely chopped fresh
  mint leaves

2 tbs/30 ml very finely chopped fresh
  green coriander (Chinese parsley)

pinch red chilli powder (cayenne
  pepper)

Put the yoghurt in a bowl. Beat lightly
with a fork or a whisk until smooth
and creamy. Add all the other
ingredients except the red chilli powder and mix well. Sprinkle the chilli
powder over the top as a garnish.

TAMIL NADU
AND
KARNATAKA

The children, large-eyed moppets with dark blue-light blue uniforms and coconut oiled hair, are sitting cross-legged on the sand in the breezy shade of casuarina trees. They are on a school excursion. Having inspected, with required awe, the carved granite temples built at Mahabalipuram on Tamil Nadu's eastern shore some one thousand two hundred years ago, they are about to embark upon the exceedingly pleasant business of eating their lunches.

One girl opens up a newspaper bundle to reveal a second package made out of banana leaf. She smooths out the newspaper with her tiny hands, transforming it into an instant tablecloth. Then she undoes the second package to reveal two spongy *idlis* shaped like small flying saucers. To make them, a batter of ground, parboiled rice and split peas (*urad dal*) was left to ferment overnight. In the morning, when it was a mass of tiny, seething bubbles, it was poured into a whole tree of madeleine-like moulds and steamed. The small, fluffy cakes that formed in the vapour could, of course, have been eaten instantly with a coconut chutney but, for the child going on a trip, they were dipped into oil to prevent them from turning sour in the hot sun and then dipped again into *milagai podi*, a glorious mixture of roasted and coarsely ground seasonings such as sesame seeds, coriander seeds, red chillies and split peas (*urad* and *chana dals*). It is only in the South that tiny amounts of roasted or fried split peas are used as seasonings to give a warm, nutty – and recognizably South Indian – flavour to a host of foods.

A second child, her braided hair tied up in two loops with crisp ribbons, has opened up her tiffin-carrier and is using a spoon to tuck into yoghurt rice – or curd rice, as they say here when speaking in English. The preparation of this dish has been nothing short of ingenious. In the morning, freshly cooked slightly soft rice was mixed with milk and a few spoons of yoghurt. Then the combination was seasoned with mustard seeds, *urad dal* and red chillies, popped quickly in hot oil, as well as fresh bits of green coriander, green chillies and ginger.

As the child peered at massive elephants carved out of granite rocks or monkeys caught in playful poses on a stone frieze, the contents of her tiffin-carrier were going through a metamorphosis. The same heat that might have soured the first child's *idlis* had precautions not been taken, were working to the benefit of the second child by turning the milk in her container into yoghurt. A dish that was half-prepared when the child left home in the early morning was, by noon, the glorious, cooling, soothing, perky rice salad of the South, called *thayir saadam* in Tamil Nadu and *masuru anna* in Karnataka.

These two states, even though separated by differing languages, share a common heritage of foods, especially of foods that are basically vegetarian. There are, of course, many area specialities. Karnataka in justly renowned for its *bisi bela huli anna*, an inspired, hot and tart porridge of rice, split peas and vegetables. The Mysore palace kitchen has been known to produce superb, garlic-flavoured *idlis* as well *as anay pad wade*, large, 'elephant-foot' *wadas* (a kind of fried bread), all nice and brown on the outside and yellow with turmeric inside; and its *soppu pallya*, a dish of delicately steamed spinach, enriched with thick milk and flavoured with mustard and cumin seeds, is as good as is its *kosimbir*, a salad of cucumbers and raw but well soaked *moong dal*.

Still, there are more similarities than anything else. Rice is the king of grains in both states. No meal is possible without it making an appearance in one or many forms. Many people here are vegetarians. Grains and split peas form the core of their diet. Those who might tend to dismiss these staples as 'poor man's food' or as lacking in possibilities of excitement and variety, have only to spend a few days in the South to see how, with grinding, pounding, fermenting, steaming, poaching and frying, these humble, basic grains and split peas can be transformed into slinky fresh noodles, such as *sevai* (how I long to have some right now!), and into delicate, shimmering, sweet jellies, such as the *hulbai* of Mysore.

Vegetarian diets are by no means confined to the poor. Just north of Mahabalipuram, on the same Bay of Bengal coastline, is Tamil Nadu's capital city, Madras. Here, in a fashionable district, is a sprawling house set within a large, flower-filled, walled compound. A prosperous Iyengar Brahmin family, all vegetarians, is seated around the dining table, waiting for breakfast. The morning has begun, as all mornings do, with a bath and prayers. An anxious discussion about trees is in progress. A cyclone, one of many that tyrannize this shore, has just passed through. Venerable old trees have been up-ended, including a precious sandalwood tree. Just as in England all swans belong to the monarch, in India all sandalwood trees belong to the government. Can it be saved? Or should woodcutters be called in to saw it up? Just then, coffee arrives. Its odour has been haunting the house for some time.

South Indians are serious coffee-drinkers who generally begin by buying the beans of their choice. 'I would like an equal mixture of Peabody beans and Plantation A beans,' I once heard a lady ask in a coffee store. The beans are bought raw. They can then be roasted, either in the store or at home.

The Iyengar family has a large coffee-roaster in its pantry. It consists of a roller with a handle sitting on a narrow, box-shaped brazier. Early in the morning, while the dew still lingers on the cascading bougainvillaea, the brazier is filled with lighted charcoal. The roller heats up. Coffee beans are emptied into it and a servant begins to turn the handle. First a single coffee bean crackles, then a few more, until they build up to a cacophonous crescendo. The roasted beans are spread out to cool and then ground in an old, hand-cranked grinder attached to the wall.

South Indians here make strong, filtered coffee. But they do not drink it strong, preferring to mix it with lots of hot milk. The proportions vary from house to house. Sometimes there is as little as twenty percent coffee and at other times it is a neat balance of half and half. Before the coffee can be poured into individual glasses or cups, there is one more ritual to be performed, that of pouring the mixture from a height from one vessel to another in order to raise a nice head of froth!

Served with the coffee that morning are *dosas*. To call a *dosa* a pancake would be to do it no justice at all. At its best, it is a glorious, thin round – golden-red, crisp and smooth on one side, white, lined with concentric ridges and slightly yielding on the other. Made out of almost the same batter, both *dosas* and *idlis* are the breads of the South, as nourishing and digestible (due to the fermentation process) as they are delicious. They may be eaten with butter and honey, or with chutneys, or they may be stuffed with a spicy blend of potatoes and onions.

Their batter requires that rice and *urad dal* be soaked and ground separately, the former to a satiny paste, the latter to a light foamy one. This can only be done in an *attu kal*, a massive grinding stone in two parts, one with a hole in its centre and the other, an egg-shaped object designed to fit into the hole and do the actual grinding. Because of their weight, *attu kals* are permanently fixed in kitchen verandhas, courtyards and pantries, gracing the location where they are placed with all the strength and soft roundness of Henry Moore's sculptures.

With changing times, electrically run 'wet grinders' have been invented. The Iyengar family has one. Made out of both stainless steel and stone, half primitive, half modern, these practical grinders can be seen whirring and spinning in wealthier homes and in the kitchens of southern restaurants.

Simple vegetarian lunches in both Tamil Nadu and Karnataka consist of three courses, each eaten with rice. I once watched a thousand people eat such a lunch. It was at the medieval Krishna temple in Udipi, on India's west coast. I had heard that many of the cooks who worked in South Indian restaurants across the country were trained in the temple and that the training was nothing formal. Since the temple opened its dining hall doors to all who wished to enter – and between two and five thousand people entered daily – the cooks learned by just being around.

It did not surprise me that a temple was associated with good food. At the Varadharaja Temple in Kanchipuram (Tamil Nadu), after worshipping before the diamond- and gold-encrusted statues of Vishnu, the Preserver, and Laxshmi, his consort, I had been rewarded, so to speak, with the holy food, the famous Kanchipuram *idli*, a long, savoury loaf of rice, and *moong dal*, flavoured with the haunting tastes of cumin, coarsely crushed peppercorns and dried ginger. I suspect that the gods knew that I had timed my visit carefully so as not to miss the distribution of their 'lunch'. The Balaji Temple in Andhra Pradesh similarly offers *akkaravadisal*, a gorgeous, thick rice pudding, delicately flavoured with cardamon, saffron and edible camphor and dotted generously with almonds, cashews and raisins. No devotee considers leaving without at least some of it in his possession.

When I visited the Udipi temple, it had its own cowshed with 400 cows, vast storage halls filled with yellow, green and orange gourds suspended from the ceiling like colourful mobiles (they last over a year this way) and, in the kitchen, Brobdingnagian vessels of copper and brass large enough to hold several of me standing up. Paddles stood nearby for stirring. Parboiled rice was steaming in one pot, *sambar* in another. For the *sambar*, *toovar dal* had been boiled with turmeric. When it was soft, the solids – as happens with all dried beans – had settled to the bottom. The thin broth at the top, a kind of vegetarian stock, had been ladled off to make the *rasam*. Some pieces of white pumpkin were poached in thin tamarind water and then added to the thick *dal*. Sambar powder, a ground spice mixture that includes red chillies, *chana dal*, coriander seeds and fenugreek, was mixed in and the dish perked up with mustard seeds and curry leaves popped in hot oil. The *sambar* was ready. For the soupy *rasam*, the *dal* broth was mixed with tamarind water and its own spice mixture containing lots of ground black pepper, red chillies and cumin. Chopped green coriander was scattered and left to float on the top.

To feed all those who entered the pillared dining hall, banana leaves had been laid out on the floor as plates. Pairs of temple attendants, each carrying a good-sized pot between them, doled out the first course consisting of long beans cooked with mustard seeds and red chillies, rice and *rasam*. The watery *rasam* wet the rice just enough so that it could be scooped up with the palm and eaten. More rice was served for the second course, this time with dollops of *sambar*. The last course was rice, pickles, yoghurt and *papadums*. Southern meals tend to end this way: hot, fiery courses followed by bland and soothing ones.

The first shift rose to its feet and filed out. I lingered a bit and then headed towards an outside corridor. I had barely reached it when I heard a senior attendant call out, 'Haa, haa, haa!' There was a loud thundering of hooves. I glanced sideways to see a whole heard of cows, all 400 of them, I suspect, come leaping and charging down the corridor, up the steep temple steps, and into the dining hall. I was pinned to a wall, expecting fully to be gored or mashed. The cows were considerate. They left me alone and proceeded to eat up all the banana leaves, after which service they left the way they had come, their exist somewhat less energetic than their entrance. The hall was washed down quickly and a second shift allowed in through the portals just fifteen minutes after the first one had vacated it.

Vegetarian meals, using the same basic theme of rice, *rasam, sambar* and yoghurt, can, in the right hands, become much more elegant and elaborate. I remember one such lunch in Madras where the hostess, a superb cook, had prepared some choice dishes. We were served *usali*, an unusual pilaf made with *toovar dal*. The *dal* had been soaked, coarsely crushed and then steamed and crumbled. This base was then stir-fried with a host of ingredients – mustard seeds and peanuts added their nuttiness, green peppers and onions added a certain freshness, while green chillies and lime juice provided the necessary punch and tang. All the flavours were beautifully balanced. We were also served *rasavangi*, a kind of heady *sambar* with the tiniest of egg-shaped aubergines (eggplants) bobbing about in it; *vendaka curry* (currently, 'curry' seems to be the Tamil word for a dry, unsauced dish!), delightfully crisp fritters made by dipping cut okra sections into a spicy, chickpea flour batter and frying them; *keerai poricha kootu*, a kind of thick, soupy stew of *toovar dal*, spinach and fresh coconut, followed by the most exquisite dish of the day, *rasawade*, savoury *urad dal* doughnuts, immersed in a *rasam* just long enough to soften them and to soak up all its tart and fiery flavours. We ended the meal with some calming yoghurt rice. On that hot day, even the family dog stood up on its haunches and begged for some.

Not everyone in these two states in vegetarian. The fisherwomen on the coast near Udipi and Mangalore wait with the seagulls for the trawlers to come in. Most of the expensive fish, such as the seer and pomfrets, are bought for resale. But mackerel and sardines are cheap and plentiful. Some of these they keep for themselves. The plump mackerel are frequently slashed, rubbed with a mixture of tamarind paste, red chillies, ginger and garlic and then fried slowly in oil. Called *bangude puli munchi*, they are absolutely scrumptious. Mangaloris also enjoy *kori ruti*, a dish of spicy chicken – its sauce a creamy amalgam of tamarind, coconut, cardamom, cinnamom and cloves – served on a bed of thin, crisp rice cakes. The cakes begin to soften as soon as they start soaking up the sauce. That is the moment to devour the dish – when the *ruti* is half crisp and half soft.

South-east of Mangalore are the cool and stunning highlands of Coorg. The rising and falling tracts of land are covered with terraces of rice fields, open glades, bamboo thickets, acres of cardamom – and lots of coffee.

Coffee had been introduced to India's west coast by the Arabs. Moplas, Muslim Keralites, carried it inland to these hills where it thrived happily. In the nineteenth century, most homes scattered across the lonely hills had their own banana trees, betel nut palms, tanks stocked with fish, vegetable patches and coffee gardens. In the 1850s the English decided to clear acre upon acre of land and plant coffee on a large scale. Today, it is the tall, handsome, warrior race of Coorgis who own some of these plantations. The Coorgis hunt and fish as they have always done and are known to enjoy a dish of partridge pie – a hang-over from colonial times – just as much as some of their own delicacies, such as the wonderful stew of young bamboo shoots and jungle mushrooms eaten with *otty*, a flat rice bread.

At a recent Coorgi lunch with a family now settled in Bangalore, I was fortunate enough to be offered *pandi curry*, an absolutely gorgeous hot-and-sour, almost pickle-like pork stew. It was served with *kadambutte*, round rice balls, the likes of which I had never seen in India before. To make them, pounded rice – it had the texture of very coarse semolina – was cooked with water and coconut milk until it had turned into a sticky dough, at which point, while it was still hot, it was rolled into balls about 1½ inches (4 cm) in diameter with the aid of wet hands, and steamed. The combination of the tart stew, the balls that were just perfect for absorbing the sauce, and *mangay pajji*, a salad of yoghurt and ripe mangoes, was quite breathtaking.

I found one of the most interesting chicken dishes of the region in the Chettiyar community. Traders, merchants and money-lenders by profession, the Chettiyars of Chettinad (about 250 miles south of Madras) have travelled the seas freely since ancient times, doing business in Vietnam, Hong Kong and

Indonesia and running thriving plantations in Malaysia, Sri Lanka and Burma. Quick to adapt themselves to changing political climates, they are now expanding their businesses within India and have already turned their eyes westward towards the Middle East.

Their wealth is enormous, and what is more the Chettiyars are very comfortable and open about it. They are known to begin collecting dowries for their daughters at birth, literally filling one room with stainless steel utensils, one with copper, one with brass, one with aluminium, one with glass, one with china, one with wood (from coconut graters to furniture), one with stoneware (pickling jars), another with bedding (20 mattresses and 101 pillows are considered adequate), yet another with electric gadgets – to say nothing of the strong-room filled with gold and silver vessels. There are, of course, houses (one to house the dowry), land, shares, money, and jewels – the last described to me as sets of 'diamonds and red [rubies], diamonds and green [emeralds], diamonds and blue [sapphires] . . .' and so on. Oh yes, there are also toys – such as gold rattles – for the next generation.

Being a shrewd business community, they see to it that the girls marry their cousins so that the wealth does not stray far from home, and in fact, if one plays one's cards right, it all comes back. It was one such charming, disarming – and, in many ways, simple and traditional – family that set before me a feast of over twenty dishes.

Banana leaves had been laid out on the French-polished dining table. On it were placed small servings of dishes such as fried fish (*meen varuval*); fried meatballs made with a very creamy paste of meat, cashews, poppy seeds, coconut and fennel seeds (*varuval kola*); chicken cooked in spicy tamarind water (*koli kulambu*); and meat cooked with roasted coriander seeds and tomatoes (*kari kulambu*). There were mixed vegetables cooked with the second water used for washing rice (*mandi*), freshly made vermicelli, nicely seasoned with mustard seeds and *urad dal* (*idi appam*), as well as dishes of banana flowers, banana stems, dried mango, plus *rasam* and assorted pickles and sweets. And there was the chicken dish that I thought was just perfect.

They called it Chettinad fried chicken. It was one of the simplest stir-fried dishes – and so good that it almost took one's breath away. Chicken, with its skin, was cut up into small pieces and rubbed with a little salt and turmeric. Oil was then heated in a wok. Some of the traditional seasonings of the area, mustard seeds, *urad dal*, fennel seeds, red chillies, were thrown in. Chopped onion was added and fried. Now the chicken pieces were put in and stir-fried with frequent sprinklings of salted water. Within about ten minutes the chicken was golden brown – and cooked. It was heavenly. And so easy to prepare.

RECIPES FROM TAMIL NADU AND KARNATAKA

MYSORE SPINACH WITH DILL
Soppu Pallya

This dish comes from the palace in Mysore. It is very elegant – and very delicious. It may be served with both Indian and Western meals. It goes particularly well with Chettinad Fried Chicken, Plain Rice and Mango Salad.

Serves 3–4
1½ lb/700 g fresh spinach
2 oz/50 g/½ cup chopped dill
½–¾ tsp/2.5–4 ml salt
4 tbs/60 ml/⅓ cup double (heavy cream)
1 tbs/15 ml *ghee* or vegetable oil
¼ tsp whole black mustard seeds
⅛ tsp whole cumin seeds
1 whole dried, hot red chilli

Separate the spinach leaves and wash them well. Holding a good handful, cut them, crosswise, at ½ in/1 cm intervals.

Put the spinach and dill in a large pan. Cover and cook on a medium-low heat. The spinach will cook in its own juices. Stir once or twice and cook for about 20 minutes or until the spinach is tender. Remove the lid and add the salt and the cream. Turn the heat up a bit and boil away most of the liquid, stirring as you do so. They should be just enough liquid left to keep the spinach moist.

Heat the *ghee* in a small frying pan over a medium flame. When hot, put in the black mustard seeds. As soon as the mustard seeds begin to pop (this just takes a few seconds) put in the cumin seeds.

A few seconds later, put in the red chilli. When the chilli starts to darken, empty the contents of the frying pan into the pan with the spinach. Stir to mix.

CAULIFLOWER WITH DRIED CHILLIES AND MUSTARD SEEDS
Poriyal

This stir-fried dish cooks in 10 minutes and is amazingly good. It has a lot of whole chillies in it, but is not at all hot. The chillies, because they are unbroken, do not give out their heat, lending only the delicate flavour of their red and green skins.

You could serve this cauliflower dish with almost any Indian meal.

Serves 4–6
1½ lb/700 g, 1 head of cauliflower, yielding about ¾ lb/350 g of flowerets
5 tbs/75 ml/½ cup vegetable oil
¼ tsp ground asafetida
1 tsp/5 ml whole black mustard seeds
1 tsp/5 ml skinned *urad dal* (page 200)
2 whole dried hot red chillies

6 hot, whole fresh green chillies
¼ tsp/4 ml salt
2 tbs/30 ml grated fresh coconut
  (optional – page 197)

Cut the cauliflower into small, delicate
flowerets. No flowerets should be
longer or wider than 1½ in/4 cm.
Longer stems of flowerets may be cut,
crosswise, into rounds.

Heat the oil in a wok, *karhai* or frying
pan over a medium-high flame. When
hot, put in the asafetida. A second later,
put in the black mustard seeds. As soon
as the mustard seeds begin to pop (this
takes just a few seconds), put in the *urad
dal*. As soon as the *dal* turns reddish,
put in the red and green chillies. When
the red chillies start to darken, put in
the cauliflower. Stir for 1 minute. Now
add the salt and 1 tbs/15 ml of water.
Stir and cook for 1 minute. Add
another 1 tbs/15 ml of water if it looks
dry. Keep doing this for the next 4
minutes, adding in all about 6 tbs/90 ml/
½ cup of water. Cover, turn the heat to
low and cook for about 5 minutes or
until the cauliflower is just tender.
Remove the lid and dry off any liquid.
Add the coconut, if you wish, and stir.

Note: the whole chillies should only
be eaten by those who know what they
are doing.

MRS MALATI SRINIVASAN'S
MYSORE SPLIT PEAS WITH WHOLE SHALLOTS
Mysore Sambar

Sambars, eaten all over the South with
many local variations, are soupy dishes,
made with *toovar dal*. They are meant to
be eaten with Plain Rice and are quite
fiery. The only way to lessen their heat
is to put fewer red chillies in the spice
mixture – or *sambar* powder – with
which they are seasoned. This way you
can control the heat as well as the
flavour. A recipe for *sambar* powder
follows this one. As side dishes you
could serve Cauliflower with Dried
Chillies and Mustard Seeds, Stir Fried
Aubergine/Eggplant or Stuffed Okra.

Serves 6
6 oz/175 g/1 cup skinned *toovar dal*
  (page 200)
½ tsp/2.5 ml ground turmeric
3 tbs/45 ml vegetable oil
3½–4 oz/90–100 g/1 cup small shallots,
  peeled (large ones may be halved,
  lengthwise)
4 tbs/60 ml/⅓ cup tamarind paste
  (page 203)
1½ tsp/7.5 ml salt
2 tbs/30 ml *sambar* powder (next recipe)
1 tbs/15 ml *ghee* or vegetable oil
½ tsp/2.5 ml whole black mustard
  seeds
6–10 fresh or dried curry leaves

Pick over the *toovar dal* and wash it in
several changes of water. Drain. Put
the *dal* in a heavy-based pan. Put in
1¾ pints/1 litre/4¼ cups of water and
the turmeric. Bring to a simmer.
Cover, leaving the lid slightly ajar,
lower the heat and simmer gently for
1½ hours. Stir a few times during the
last 30 minutes.

Meanwhile, heat the 3 tbs/45 ml of
oil in another pan over a medium
flame. When hot, put in the shallots.
Stir and sauté them until they are
lightly browned. Now add ¾ pint/
450 ml/2 cups of water, the tamarind

paste, salt and *sambar* powder. Stir and bring to a simmer. Cover, lower the heat and simmer gently for about 10 minutes or until the shallots are tender.

Once the *dal* has finished cooking, add it to the pan with the shallots. Stir to mix and simmer for 5 minutes.

Heat the *ghee* in a small frying pan over a medium flame. When hot, put in the black mustard seeds. As soon as they begin to pop, put in the curry leaves. Stir them once and then empty the contents of the frying pan into the pan with the *sambar*.

MYSORE SAMBAR POWDER

The proportions which I have given make a very hot, traditional *sambar*. If you wish to make a medium-hot *sambar*, put in just 1½ tbs/22.5 ml of dried whole red chillies. For a mild *sambar*, put in just 7–8 of them.

Makes enough to fill a 6 fl oz/175 ml/¾ cup jar
2 tsp/10 ml vegetable oil
3 tbs/45 ml whole coriander seeds
2 × 1-in/2.5-cm cinnamon sticks, broken up
⅓-in/0.5-cm cube of solid asafetida (just break off a lump with a hammer)
⅛ tsp whole fenugreek seeds
3 tbs/45 ml or less (see note above) whole, dried hot red chillies
2 tbs/30 ml skinned *chana dal* (page 200)
4 tbs/60 ml/⅓ cup dessicated, unsweetened coconut
15–20 fresh or dried curry leaves

Heat 1 tsp/5 ml of the oil in a small, cast-iron frying pan. When hot, put in the coriander seeds, cinnamon, asafetida and fenugreek. Stir until the coriander seeds turn a shade darker and emit a roasted aroma. Empty into a bowl. Put the red chillies into the same frying pan. Stir and roast until they start to darken. Put them into the bowl as well. Now put the remaining 1 tsp/5 ml of oil in the pan. Put in the *chana dal*. Stir and fry until it turns reddish. Put it into the bowl. Put the coconut and curry leaves into the frying pan. Stir and roast them until the coconut turns a light brown. Put them into the bowl with the spices and mix.

Let the spices cool. Now put them, in batches, if necessary, into the container of a clean coffee grinder or other spice grinder. Grind. The mixture should remain slightly coarse. Put in a tightly sealed bottle and use as needed.

AJIT BANJERA'S
'PICKLED' MACKEREL OR BLUEFISH
Bangude Puli Munchi

The fish is not really pickled – it is just prepared in a tart and hot sauce. India's coastal waters are filled with short, plump mackerels. Sometimes they are roasted right on the beach and eaten with a vinegar sauce – at other times they are taken home by the fishermen, given a few deep gashes on both sides, marinated in a mixture of tamarind, red chillies, ginger and garlic and then cooked slowly in oil. It is this recipe that I have adapted here. Instead of cooking the fish in a pan, I have filleted and grilled (broiled) it. The result is quite wonderful. I have used much less red chilli powder (cayenne pepper) than would be used in Mangalore, the home of this dish. My fish is quite mild. You could use just about as much as you can bear.

Almost any filleted fish may be used. Mackerel and bluefish are ideal – but fillets of sole, herring, plaice, turbot and red snapper would also work very well.

You could cut up the fish and serve it as part of an Indian meal with rice, a *dal* and vegetable or you could do what we sometimes do, have it with Yoghurt Rice and a green salad – an unorthodox but very satisfying combination.

This recipe may be doubled or tripled quite easily.

Serves 2
½ tsp/2.5 ml salt
about 1 lb/450 g, 2 filleted pieces of mackerel or bluefish (see note above)
1½ tbs/22 ml oil
2 tbs/30 ml tamarind paste (page 203)
about ¼ tsp red chilli powder (cayenne pepper)
1 tsp/5 ml finely crushed garlic
1 tsp/5 ml finely grated, peeled fresh ginger
fresh green coriander (Chinese parsley), chopped

Sprinkle the salt evenly over the meaty side of the fish fillets. Spread some aluminium foil over your grilling (broiling) tray and rub it with about ½ tbs/7.5 ml of oil. Lay the fish pieces, skin side down, over the oiled area and set aside for 10 minutes.

Meanwhile, prepare the marinade. Put the tamarind paste, red chilli powder (cayenne pepper), garlic, ginger and remaining 1 tbs/15 ml of oil in a small bowl and mix well.

Rub the marinade evenly over the top of the fish and set aside for 1 hour.

Preheat your grill (broiler). When hot, put the fish under it and cook for about 8 minutes or until it is lightly browned and just done.

Just before serving, sprinkle with chopped fresh green coriander (Chinese parsley).

MRS SEETHA MUTHIAH'S
CHETTINAD FRIED CHICKEN
Koli Uppu Varuval

This particular quick-cooking, stir-fried dish is made by the Chettiyar community of Tamil Nadu. It is best cooked in a wok or *karhai*, though a frying pan would do. It may be served at almost all Indian meals and goes particularly well with Mysore Spinach with Dill, Cauliflower with Dried Chillies and Mustard Seeds, Plain Rice and Mysore Split Peas with Whole Shallots.

Serves 4
3 lb/1.4 kg chicken
1 tsp/5 ml salt
¼ tsp ground turmeric
4 tbs/60 ml/⅓ cup vegetable oil
½ tsp/2.5 ml whole black mustard seeds
½ tsp/2.5 ml skinned *urad dal* (page 200)
½ tsp/2.5 ml whole fennel seeds

5 whole dried hot red chillies
3 oz/75 g, 1 medium-sized onion,
  peeled and chopped

Cut the chicken, with skin, into small serving pieces as one might for Chinese food. (Wings, back, neck and innards maybe used for other purposes or frozen for making stock.) The breast should first be split in half. Each half should be cut into 6–8 pieces. Thighs should be halved. So should drumsticks. A heavy cleaver will do the job. Rub ¾ tsp/4 ml of the salt and the turmeric on the chicken and set aside for 15 minutes.

Put the remaining ¼ tsp/ of salt in a bowl with 3 tbs/45 ml of water and set aside.

Heat the oil in a wok or *karhai* over a medium-high flame. When hot, put in the mustard seeds. As soon as the mustard seeds begin to pop (this takes just a few seconds), put in the *dal*. As soon as the *dal* turns red, put in the fennel seeds and the red chillies. When the red chillies start to darken, put in the chopped onion. Stir and fry the onion until it browns lightly. Now put in the chicken pieces. Stir and fry the chicken for about 5 minutes. Start sprinkling a little salted water at a time from the bowl over the chicken and keep stirring and frying on a medium-high flame. Fry the chicken for about 10–13 minutes. All the salt water should be used up, and the chicken should be cooked through and slightly browned.

Take the chicken out of the oil with a slotted spoon and serve.

FROM THE WINDSOR PALACE HOTEL IN
BANGALORE
YOGHURT RICE
Masuru Anna

Families take this on picnics, children take it to school for lunch, it is a very popular food on train journeys and many meals all over the South end with its calming taste. Yoghurt Rice – called Curd Rice by English-speaking Southerners, is a simple, gentle dish, soothing in its texture and quite perky in its seasonings. It is always served at room temperature and may, at Western meals, be served as a rice salad and at Indian meals with Chettinad Fried Chicken and Green Beans with Coconut.

Serves 4
6 oz/75 g/1 cup long-grain rice
8 fl oz/250 ml/1 cup plain yoghurt
¾ tsp/4 ml salt
1–2 fresh, hot green chillies
½-in/1-cm cube of fresh ginger,
  peeled
1 tbs/15 ml vegetable oil
½ tsp/2.5 ml whole black mustard
  seeds
⅛ tsp skinned *urad dal* (page 200)
8–10 fresh or dried curry leaves
2 dried hot red chillies
1 tbs/15 ml finely chopped fresh green
  coriander (Chinese parsley)

Pick over the rice and wash it in several changes of water. Drain. Cover it by about 2 in/5 cm of water and leave to soak for 20–30 minutes. Drain.

While the rice is soaking, put the yoghurt in a bowl and add the salt. Beat lightly with a fork or whisk until it is smooth and creamy.

Bring 5 pints/3 litres/12 cups of water to a rolling boil in a big pan. Drop in the rice, stir and allow the water to come to a boil. Boil vigorously for about 12 minutes or until the rice is not only cooked but is slightly soft. Drain and put in a bowl. Add the yoghurt immediately, while the rice is still hot, and mix gently.

Chop the green chilli very, very finely. Cut the ginger into very fine slices. Stack a few of the slices at a time over each other and cut them first into very fine strips and then cut the strips into minute dice.

Heat the oil in a small frying pan or small pan over a medium flame. When hot, put in the mustard seeds. As soon as the mustard seeds begin to pop, put in the *urad dal*. When the *dal* turns red, put in the curry leaves and red chillies. When the red chillies start to darken, lift up the frying pan and pour its contents over the rice. Sprinkle the green chilli, ginger and fresh green coriander (Chinese parsley) over the rice as well and mix. Do not refrigerate. Serve the dish at room tempeature.

RICE PANCAKES
Dosas

Various breads and pancakes made with rice flour are a speciality of the South. The *dosa*, one such pancake, may be eaten with chutneys or pickles, it may be stuffed with spicy potatoes or it may be eaten with Mysore Split Peas with Whole Shallots. *Dosas*, because they are fermented, are light and easy to digest – and are served at breakfast, for snacks, and at main meals as well.

Makes 18 dosas
12 oz/350 g/2 cups long-grain rice
3 oz/75 g/½ cup skinned *urad dal* (page 200)
1 tsp/5 ml salt
about 6 fl oz/175 ml/¾ cup vegetable oil

Pick over the rice and wash it in several changes of water. Drain. Put in a bowl. Cover with water by 2 in/5 cm and leave to soak for 6 hours. Drain.

Pick over the *dal* and wash it in several changes of water. Drain. Put in a bowl. Cover with water by 2 in/5 cm and leave to soak for 6 hours. Drain.

Put the rice into the container of a food processor or blender. Blend until it breaks up into tiny, semolina-like grains. Slowly add about 6 fl oz/175 ml/ ¾ cup of water, pushing the batter down with a rubber spatula whenever necessary. Empty the rice batter into a bowl. Clean off your electric gadget and put the drained *dal* into it. Blend as finely as possible. Slowly add about ¼ pint/150 ml/⅔ cup of water 1 tbs/ 15 ml at a time. Keep the machine running until the *dal* is very light and frothy. Empty the *dal* batter into the bowl with the rice batter. Add 1 tsp/ 5 ml of salt and mix gently. Cover the bowl loosely with an overturned plate and put it in a warm place for about 20–22 hours. The batter should become a mass of tiny bubbles. In very hot weather this might happen faster. Once the batter has fermented, thin it out with about 8–10 fl oz/250–300 ml/ 1–1¼ cups of water. It should flow like crêpe batter.

Get everything ready to make your *dosas*. You will need a non-stick frying pan or a very well seasoned, cast-iron frying pan. You will also need a

A TASTE OF INDIA

measure – like a ladle, that will give you about 3 fl oz/75 ml/⅓ cup of batter at a time, a small bowl with the oil in it, a teaspoon, a spatula, a round soup-spoon and a plate with a cover in which you can keep the *dosas* after they are cooked.

Put 1 tsp/5 ml of oil in your frying pan and let it heat over a medium-low flame. Stir your batter and remove about 3 fl oz/75 ml/⅓ cup from it, emp-tying it into the very centre of the frying pan. Immediately place the rounded bottom of the soupspoon on the centre of the blob of batter and, using a continuous spiral motion, spread it outwards till the pancake measures about 6 in/15 cm. Dribble another 1 tsp/5 ml of oil over the pan-cake and spread it out gently with the spatula. Cover and cook for about 2½ minutes or until it is golden on the bottom. Turn over and cook the other side, uncovered, for about 2 minutes. Put the *dosa* in a plate and cover. Make as many *dosas* as you need. Leftover batter may be refrigerated.

RANI VIJAYA DEVI'S
CUCUMBER SALAD WITH MOONG DAL
Kosambri

This Mysore-style salad is crisp and refreshing. Nothing is cooked, not even the *dal*. You may serve it with any Indian meal.

Serves 4
1½/40 g/¼ cup skinned *moong dal* (page 200)
7 oz/200 g, 2 small or 1 large cucumber

2 tbs/30 ml finely grated fresh coconut (page 197)
2 tbs/30 ml chopped fresh green coriander (Chinese parsley)
1 tbs + 1 tsp/20 ml lemon juice
½ tbs/2.5 ml salt
½ tsp/10 ml vegetable oil
¼ tsp whole black mustard seeds
¼ tsp skinned *urad dal*, picked over (page 200)
1 whole, dried hot red chilli, broken into 2 pieces
5–6 fresh or dried curry leaves

Pick over the dal and wash it in several changes of water. Leave to soak for 5–8 hours. Drain.

Peel the cucumber and cut it into ¼-in/0.5-cm thick slices.

Put the dal, cucumber, coconut, fresh coriander (Chinese parsley), lemon juice and salt in a bowl. Mix.

Heat the oil in a small frying pan over a medium flame. When hot, put in the mustard seeds. As soon as the mustard seeds begin to pop (this takes just a few seconds), put in the *urad dal*. When the *dal* turns red, put in the red chilli and curry leaves. As soon as the red chilli starts to darken, pour the contents of the frying pan, oil and spices, into a bowl with the salad. Stir to mix and serve at room temperature.

MRS BIDAPA'S
MANGO SALAD
Mangay Pajji

This particular recipe comes from a Coorgi family. The sald is sweet and sour and can act as a delicious cooler at all Indian meals.

162

Serves 4–6

about 1 lb/450 g, 1 large ripe mango or
two smaller ones

1 tsp/5 ml whole black mustard seeds

8 fl oz/250 ml/1 cup plain yoghurt

1 fresh hot green chilli, very finely
chopped *or* ⅛–¼ tsp red chilli
powder (cayenne pepper)

1 tbs/15 ml finely grated fresh coconut
(optional)

1 tsp/5 ml sugar

¼ tsp salt

2 tsp/10 ml vegetable oil

1 whole dried hot red chilli

1 small shallot, peeled and thinly sliced

Peel the mango. Cut the flesh into
½-in/1-cm cubes.

Put ¾ tsp/4 ml of the mustard seeds
into the container of a clean coffee
grinder or other spice grinder. Grind.

Put the yoghurt in a bowl. Beat
lightly with a fork or whisk until
smooth and creamy. Add the ground
mustard seeds, the green chilli, coconut (if using it), sugar and salt. Add
the mango and stir it in.

Heat the oil in a small frying pan
over a medium flame. When hot, put
in the remaining ¼ tsp of mustard
seeds. As soon as the mustard seeds
begin to pop (this just take a few
seconds), put in the red chilli. When it
starts to darken, put in the shallot. Stir
and fry the shallot until it gets slightly
brown. Now empty the contents of the
frying pan into the bowl with the
mango. Stir to mix and serve at room
temperature or cold.

KERALA

Heaven must be a bit like Kerala, an ancient strip of lush, tropical land that slithers sensuously down the coast of south-western India. Devout Hindus, Muslims, Christians and Jews live in harmony here, the steeples and spires of their age-old temples, mosques, churches and synagogues all aspiring to some common goodness, side by side.

Blessed not only with the winds of tolerance but with temperatures that hover around the constantly balmy mark and plentiful rain, the land in Kerala produces with the enthusiasm of a pampered hothouse. When Ibn Batuta, an Arab traveller, traversed this region in the fourteenth century, he found that 'the whole way by land lies under the shade of trees and in the space of two months journey, there is not one span free from cultivation; everybody has his garden and his house is firmly planted in the middle of it.'

The gardens, then as now, are kitchen gardens which do not sit neatly and demurely on one side of the house as a European herb garden might, but encircle it with some abandon. Houses often disappear entirely within their verdant, forest-like foliage. Black pepper vines clamber tenaciously up mango trees, the peppercorns huddling together in bright green clusters like bunches of embryo grapes. Nutmeg fruit hang like tennis balls, ready to split open and offer both their nuts and their special bonus, curls of tangerine-coloured mace. Cinnamon, clove and tamarind trees compete for a view of the sky while cardamom stays close to the ground, hugging its mother bush. There are ginger and turmeric plants as well, sending fingers of their tuberous rhizomes out into the cool, dark earth. Above all, there are the two trees that give the foods of Kerala their very special character – the sweetly aromatic curry leaf tree (murraya koenigii) and the arching, swaying coconut palm.

It has been these spices that have lured traders into Kerala's warm waters since antiquity. The port of Cranganore (called Muzuris by Pliny) saw the ships of the Phoenicians, of King Solomon, of the Syrians under the Selucids, the Egyptians under the Ptolemies, the Greeks, Arabs, Romans and Chinese. Fleeing Christians, led it is believed by St Thomas, sought refuge here in the first century AD and then remained to form the thriving Syrian Christian community. Early Jewish settlers came here in the same century, fleeing Roman persecution. They stayed on and prospered. Arabs, long-time traders, built their first mosque in Cranganore in the seventh century, in the life-time of the Prophet Muhammad. The Chinese under the T'angs followed soon after with a trading post in Quilon.

In 1494, Pope Alexander VI divided the 'undiscovered' world into two halves. (Indian school children have hooted with laughter at this for as long as I can remember.) Spain was given the world west of the Atlantic, and Portugal the east. Vasco Da Gama hitched up his sails and after circling the Cape of Good Hope, landed in Kerala at the port of Calicut (known for its calicoes) in 1498. The local ruler, the Zamorin, agreed to trade. 'In my country there is an abundance of cinnamon, cloves, pepper and precious stones. What I seek from thy country is gold, silver, coral and scarlet [cloth],' he said quite reasonably.

This innocent offer started up a whirlwind of violence and colonization in which, using the name of God, king and country, Europeans – Portuguese, Dutch, French and English – tripped over each other in unseemly haste to capture and hold the lucrative spice trade.

The English won out, at least until Indian independence several centuries later, capturing a lion's share not only of the trade but of India itself. In 1683 they set up a factory at Telli-chery. This port city was to serve as an entrepot for black pepper from the surrounding north Kerala region and its name was to become synonymous with the heady, pungent aroma of the best pepper in the world.

What we call 'black' pepper is laboriously hand-picked while still green and then spread out on palm leaf mats to dry in the

sun. Here it shrivels, darkens and turns into its more recogniz-
able self. For the less aromatic white pepper, the berries are
picked when they are almost ripe. They are then soaked and
milled to remove the outer hulls.

Needless to say, this King of Spices, used in the past to pay
tributes and ransoms and now a part of everyday cooking
throughout the world, is used generously in Kerala's own dishes.

To sample these dishes, I have travelled freely across the state,
starting from the seas that produce the prawns (shrimps) that go
into picking jars, up the backwaters and lagoons that are
inhabited by crabs and otters, past palm-lined terraces where
reluctant ducks are herded from one flooded rice field to the
next, higher up into the Cardamom Hills where black pepper,
cardamom and ginger flourish, where lemon grass grows wild
and where decorously pruned tea bushes sit under the shade of
taller trees, and even higher up where forest-covered mountains
of luxuriant evergreen beauty sprout ebony, rosewood, sandalwood and teak, all to be bull-dozed by the most charming bull-
dozer on earth, the elephant.

The foods I have eaten on these travels have been nothing
short of magical, varying not so much from town to town as
from community to community, with many dishes common to all
groups. Let me give some examples.

It is Easter Sunday morning in a hamlet on the outskirts of
Kottayam. From a small, thatched building, which has nothing
more than a simple wooden cross to distinguish it as a church,
emerge men and women in white sarong-like *mundus*. They have
worshipped, segregated by sex, in a pewless church. Families
separate and, balancing themselves with accustomed sureness,
work their way home along the narrow embankments that separate paddy fields. These are Syrian Christians and they are
going home to an Easter feast.

The homes, with their pitched roofs, are old and fashioned
entirely out of carved wood. Many line a green, meandering
canal, part of an intricate system of inland waterways reaching
all the way down to the distant sea. One family enters through
the garden gate. Jasmines perfume the path to the front door.
Soon everyone will sit down to a mouthwatering breakfast.

Much of the work has already been done. Fires were lit early
in the morning with palm fronds and coconut husks. The 'stew',

or 'shtew' as they sometimes call it, is ready. Chicken and potatoes have simmered gently in a creamy white sauce flavoured with black pepper, cinnamon, cloves, green chillies, lime juice, shallots and coconut milk. Mounds of shallots and coconuts are used in the cooking. One slender girl in a turquoise and white checked *mundu* has spent the early morning with a basket of shallots, peeling and slicing them with the utmost, patience. Another girl handles the coconuts. First she hacks them into equal halves with a hooked cleaver and a practised hand. Then, sitting side saddle on a stool-shaped coconut-grater, she reduces the halves to snowy shreds in a matter of minutes. It is all in the wrist, she says, as she rests with a cup of filtered coffee.

The stew will be eaten with *appams* (or 'hoppers' as the English called them), a combination that compares, in an earthy sort of way, with caviar and champagne. It is quite magnificent. I find myself lusting for it in such an irrational manner that I am now convinced that while I might *look* like a dyed-in-the-wool North Indian, my soul is Southern.

Appams – *kallappams* or *wellayappams* to be more exact, as there is actually a whole family of them – are rice flour pancakes designed miraculously to have soft, thick, white spongy centres and thin, golden, crisp, lacelike edges.

To achieve this delightful balance of textures, a special rice flour – made by rhythmically pounding both ordinary and par-boiled rice in huge mortars – is used. This is then mixed with a little sugar, a little cooked rice paste and the tapped sap from palms – the alcoholic beverage, toddy. The last acts as a ferment-ing agent. The batter sits all night, seething and bubbling. Next morning, it is thinned out with coconut milk.

A small amount is ladled out into a heated and oiled two-handled wok known here, not too surprisingly, as a *cheena chatti* or 'the pot from China'. (The ancient Chinese may have come here for black pepper but, in fair exchange, they left behind their woks, cleavers, plates, pickling jars and designs for roofs and river-craft.)

In a cool corner of the kitchen is a rounded terracotta pot known simply as a *chatti*. Its contents, *meen vevichathu* – fish in a fiery red chilli sauce – were cooked three days ago and left unrefrigerated. At weddings, two or three dozen such pots filled with the same dish are cooked up to a week in advance and just brought to a boil every night. Nothing spoils. In fact, the taste of the fish improves and, as rules of hospitality require, there is always plenty for the unexpected guest. The secret lies partly in the pot. Terracotta breathes and keeps the fish air-cooled.

What really preserves the fish and gives the *vevichathu* its characteristic (and quite delicious) sour and smoky flavour is *kodampoli* (garcinia indica), also known as 'fish tamarind', the sour rind of a fruit that is first sunned and then arranged on shelves of bamboo slats set over kitchen wood stoves to dry slowly. After a meal is over, extra firewood and rice husks are thrown into the fire. Smoke billows upwards to blacken the rind and hasten the smoking process. The kitchen is also blackened but that is accepted, quite rightly, as a minor inconvenience.

Besides the chicken and fish, there is also red meat, *erachi olarthiathu*. Beef (it could be lamb as well) has been boiled with roasted coriander seeds, red chillies, cloves, cumin, onions, garlic, ginger, fried coconut chips and a little vinegar. Then, with the water reduced, the meat is almost fried dry in a little oil that has been flavoured with sliced shallots and the highly aromatic curry leaves. Beef is eaten freely in Kerala. It is the only Indian state where, perhaps in defence to its high population of Christians, Muslims and Jews, the slaughter of cows is not banned.

Vegetables from the garden are cooked simply and quickly. A *thoran* is being made with shredded green papaya. Papayas, like the massive jackfruit, are treated as vegetables when they are green and as fruit when they ripen. The technique of making a *thoran* is very interesting. A ball of seasonings, some ground and some crushed – green chillies, cumin seeds, garlic, shallots, turmeric and coconut – is buried under a mound of finely shredded papaya in a wok. A little water is added and the wok covered so the vegetable cooks gently in delicious natural juices. Within ten minutes it is ready. Sesame oil is heated separately in a wide *urali*, a cross between a wok and a wide frying pan. In it are thrown mustard seeds, a little raw rice (it makes a wonderfully nutty 'spice'), sliced shallots, red chillies and curry leaves. As soon as the seasonings begin to pop, sizzle and brown, the papaya and the coconut mixture are emptied over them and given a final, vigorous stir. That is all there is to it.

No meal here is complete without rice, and it is puffing up in a *kozhul* or a narrow-necked urn. This is parboiled rice, its exist-ence in the South preceding Uncle Ben by many centuries, and it comes from the family's own fields some distance away. A clear distinction is made in Kerala, as indeed in the whole South, between 'raw' rice – which is the usual white, milled variety – and 'boiled' rice, which has been parboiled and dried. Far from being a mechanized process, parboiling is done in courtyards and fields, often under the watchful supervision of the house-hold women.

Until now, the family has sustained itself on coffee alone, coffee that was served before church services in the early morning.

Impelled by hunger, and successive waves of heady kitchen smells, the children begin to mill around the dining table. Adults follow on their heels. But before breakfast is served, the lady of the house ambles into the store-room and confronts the pickles.

They sit in neat rows, some hiding in massive Ali Baba-style jars of ancient origin. Which is it to be? There are whole green mangoes in brine, flavoured with mustard seeds and fenugreek powder, pickled prawns, pickled meat cubes, limes pickled with ginger, bitter gourds pickled with garlic and tamarind, citron pickled with garlic and ginger and *ada manga*, almost black in colour, dried mangoes pickled in sesame oil and dark vinegar. The last is selected. Not much is left as it is quite the family favourite.

The food begins to stream in. Besides the stew and *appams* and meat and fish and rice, there are delicious little morsels that appear out of nowhere – fried banana slices, crunchy yam crisps, prawns in coconut milk and the chestnut-like seeds of jackfruit flavoured with chillies, garlic, cinnamon and fennel.

The meal is to end simply – but divinely – with thick, creamy yoghurt (the cow outside takes full credit) laced with *paani* from Kottayam. *Paani* is Kerala's nectar and its best kept secret. It is the maple syrup of the south-west, the honey made without any assistance from bees, by boiling down tapped toddy until it is a thick, irresistible, golden syrup.

After feasting with the Syrian Christians, I decide to clear my palate with fresh passion fruit juice and move on to the Thiyyas. Thiyyas are Hindus and, by ancient tradition, professional toddy-tappers. It is they who shimmy up coconut and palmyra palms to collect the sap that turns into *paani*. Thiyya society is matriarchal, their line of inheritance moving somewhat like the knight in chess – to the side and then down – with a man required to bequest his wealth not to his own offspring but to those of his sister.

Many dishes are common to all Keralites, *appams* being one of them. The Thiyya family I visit have long given up toddy-tapping for the more earthbound pleasures of medicine and business. They too eat *appams*, sometimes with 'stew', sometimes – with egg mixed into the batter – with sugar and thick coconut milk, and sometimes with the North Kerala speciality *meen kootan* or 'fish in coconut sauce'.

This is no ordinary coconut sauce. Fresh coconut has been hand-ground (as no machine in my kitchen can manage) to a silken paste. It has been put into a terracotta *chatti* along with ginger, green chillies, curry leaves, bits of tart green mango and seer, a fish with firm, white flesh. The vessel is not stirred as it cooks, just shaken. When we eat the fish with our *appams*, we come across bits of the mango – little starbursts of sourness in a sea of cream. It is superb.

There is lamb 'stew' at this meal as well, served with *neiphathal*, a star fish-shaped fried bread made with ground rice, and there is pumpkin *pachadi*. For this, ground mustard seeds and ginger have been mixed into plain yoghurt. Then, cooked pumpkin is folded in as well and the mixture left overnight in a pickling jar to 'mature'.

For dessert, there is *prathaman*, as delicious pudding made by boiling *mung dal* with coconut milk and then flavouring it with raw palm sugar, cardamom and ginger powder. Sprinkled like nuggets in the pudding are fried cashews, raisins and little coconut chips.

My next stop is Trivandrum, the capital of the state. Here, as the sun dips into the Arabian Sea, I loll in the superb Ashok Kovalam Beach Resort hotel, sipping gimlets made with Indian gin and lime cordial. Soon after I keep my rendezvous with some Brahmin families who offer me *kalan* – green plantains stewed in buttermilk, and *olan*, little squares of ash gourd (winter melon) poached with lentils and yoghurt. These treats are followed by the equally exquisite offerings of the beautiful, willowy women of the warrior caste, the Nairs, who serve split peas cooked with coconut milk, '*dal* curry', and *kootu*, a unique melange of mixed vegetables, coconut and dried beans.

Once again I move on, this time to the port city of Cochin. There is much here to intrigue visitors: little green islands, set like jewels amidst the lagoons and backwaters, where coconut husks are transformed into coir; the sixteenth-century synagogue which has floors of blue and white Chinese tiles; the St Francis Church where Vasco da Gama was once buried (he has been moved to Portugal since) and where records are kept of every 'heathen' and 'savage' that was converted by changing denominations of Christians – Catholic, Dutch Reform and Anglican; and the wholesale spice markets that make one sneeze and sneeze again as one passes them.

There is another shrine in Cochin, a living shrine that most visitors miss. He is an elderly gentleman who happens to be Jewish and a complete charmer. I decide to pay him a visit. He does not live in the historic Jewish quarter known as Jew Town. He has prospered and lives in the 'newer' sea-facing suburb of airy colonial mansions settled in the 1500s, Fort Cochin.

I catch him munching on a mouth-puckeringly sour Indian gooseberry (emblic myrobalan). 'My family,' he says with a twinkle, 'are Baghdadis and we came here *very* recently. Only about two hundred years ago. Before long, even we, like our earlier counterparts, were speaking the local language, Malayalam. Of course, it was pidgin Malayalam, with words of Portuguese, Spanish, Dutch and English thrown in. And we have completely succumbed to Kerala's passion for hot and sour foods. Many of the young people have now emigrated to Israel. But they keep writing to us to send parcels. Italian hoodlums at the Rome airport once tried stealing such a parcel. They left pickled mangoes and smoked tamarinds scattered over hallways in utter disgust.'

The foods of these Iraqi Indian Jews are a fascinating blend of the Middle East and Kerala. A Friday evening meal might include *mahasha*, a Baghdadi speciality consisting of vegetables such as tomatoes, green peppers, onions and aubergines (eggplants) stuffed with minced (ground) meat, rice and nuts, as well as 'green chilli chicken', which no one but a Keralite could dream up. The last calls for a chicken, 1½ pounds (700 grams) shallots, ¼ pound (100 grams) hot green chillies, 1 tablespoon ground red chillies and a lump of sour tamarind – certainly enough 'heat' to, well, clear the head.

Breakfasts for all Keralites, whatever their religion, might turn up *appams*, or *uppama*, a vegetable and semolina pilaf or an amazing hot 'cereal' known as *pootu*.

Pootu was served to me for the first time many years ago. I had spent the preceding winter's night in the courtyard of a small temple, being mesmerized by Kerala kathakali dancers who strutted, leapt and swayed in front of a flickering oil lamp. By the time the rosy glow of dawn had hit the makeshift stage, Good had prevailed over Evil and the dancers – all male – were ready to slip out of their towering headdresses, take a few puffs of their cigarettes and head home.

I, too, was ready to head home, which, that week, happened to be a tiny rest house in the village of Cheruthuruthy, north-east of Cochin. But before I could fling myself on my bed, I had to eat. I was starved.

The kitchen staff were barely up when I marched in. As I was the sole paying occupant, everyone scurried around, anxious to please. Would I like fried eggs and toast? Good grief, no! (What did they take me for? A north Indian memsa'b?) Did they have anything else? Well, they did have their *pootu* . . . That was it. It would be *pootu*.

I took my place, my solitary place, in the airy dining room. Five minutes later a section of bamboo, about two inches wide, appeared on a plate. The waiter lifted it up and pushed a rod into its top opening. What came out, like marrow from a bone, was a cylinder of hot, steaming *pootu*, to be eaten with milk and tiny, sweet-sour bananas. I became a hopeless addict on the spot.

To make *pootu*, 'raw' and parboiled rice are first crushed until the grains resemble coarse semolina. This flour is then mixed with grated coconut, stuffed into the hollow of a bamboo and steamed in an upright position. These aromatic bamboo steamers are now fast disappearing, to be replaced by more functional aluminium tubes. However, the *pootu* still tastes good.

Mopla fishermen, who are Muslims, enjoy eating their *pootu* with well-spiced meat. They will not touch pork but favour beef and shellfish with a passion. A tiny Mopla lady, her head covered with a long, white scarf and her ears festooned with earrings along their entire length, leads me into her kitchen where she will prepare my lunch. There is to be a prawn *pullao* (pilaf) which, I am told, must be eaten with fried prawns. Water, perfumed with cardamom pods, cinnamon sticks and cloves, is on the boil. Rice is dropped into it, partially boiled, and then drained. Prawns have already been cooked with chillies, ginger, poppy seeds, coconut milk and lime juice. The rice and prawns are then layered, along with crisply fried onions and fried cashews, in a large pot and left to steam together briefly. When the lid is removed, the smell of the *pullao* perfumes the whole kitchen.

Moplas are not the only fishermen in Kerala. Further down the coast is the fishing village of Vizhingam where about a hundred families, all 'Latin Christians', live along sandy lanes. The men go out to sea in slim catamarans made out of five logs tied together. ('Maran' means 'log' and 'kettu' means 'to tie'.) The catamarans seem so frail and the sea so vast and ruffled. Yet, they streak forth in the middle of the night, catching the currents as they have done for centuries, travelling ten miles, sometimes fifteen, and returning with meagre or hefty catches of sardines, mackerel, pomfret, seer, prawns and squid. Squid used to sell cheaply once. But now the Japanese market offers bags of hard currency.

The fish is auctioned off on the beach by the village women almost as soon as it comes in. A tenth of the catch will go to the church which stands on the shore, keeping a watchful eye on the comings and goings of the fishermen. The fishermen keep an eye on the church, too. They want all the protection it can give. The sea can be treacherous.

The seer and pomfret and prawns will fetch a good price, ending up in the kitchens of the rich in the forms of *meen pappaas*, fish cooked with curry leaves and coconut milk, or *meen molee*, fish cooked with onions, tomatoes and coconut. Sardines are running at the moment and are therefore cheap. They will go into hundreds of humble terracotta pots to be cooked simply with lots of red, red chilli powder and *kodampoli*, the smoky 'fish tamarind'. The fishermen might eat this themselves, with some whole chillies to bite on as a relish, fresh tapioca *thoran* to provide the starch, and a nice, large bottle of alcoholic toddy to ease the aching of tired bones.

RECIPES FROM KERALA

MRS S. MATTHAI'S
GREEN BEANS WITH COCONUT
Payaru Thoran

There is a very slim, rounded, long bean – almost 1 ft/30 cm long – that is available in many Indian and Oriental grocery stores. It is sometimes known as the asparagus bean, or as *lobhia* or, in Malayalam, the language in Kerala, as *payaru*. If you can find it, do use it. It has a delicate but fairly assertive flavour that is quite delicious (I love eating it raw as well.) On the other hand, almost any green beans may be used – French beans, flat green beans and the more common rounded green beans. If the beans are on the tougher side, it might be a good idea to parboil them quickly first by cutting them, and dropping them into boiling water for 1 minute or so and then draining them.

Thorans may be made with shredded cabbage, spinach, even carrots and peas, if you like. Whatever vegetable you use, cut it into small pieces or shreds so it cooks quickly.

In this dish, raw rice is used very interestingly as a spice. You may serve this versatile *thoran* with almost any Indian meal.

Serves 6
1 lb/450 g green beans
1 oz/25 g, 1 good-sized shallot, peeled and very coarsely chopped
1–2 fresh, hot green chillies, cut into 2–3 pieces each
2 cloves garlic, peeled
3 oz/75 g/1 cup grated fresh coconut
1 tsp/5 ml ground cumin seeds
¼ tsp ground turmeric
5 tbs/75 ml/½ cup vegetable oil
1 tsp/5 ml whole mustard seeds
2 tsp/10 ml uncooked white rice
10–12 fresh or dried curry leaves
1 whole, dried, hot, red chilli
about 1 tsp/5 ml salt

Lay several beans down together, trim their ends and then cut them, crosswise, into ¼-in/0.5-cm rounds. Do all the beans this way. Put the shallots, green chillies, garlic, coconut, cumin and turmeric into the container of a food processor or blender. Grind to a coarse consistency. Decant into a bowl.

Heat the oil in a large frying pan or wok over a medium-high flame. When hot, put in the mustard seeds and rice. When the mustard seeds begin to pop and the rice swells and turns golden (this just takes a few seconds), put in the curry leaves and the red chilli. When the chilli swells and darkens (this also takes just a few seconds) put in the green beans. Stir and fry them for 2–3 minutes. Now make a hole in the centre of the mound of beans and put the coarsely ground spices there. Cover up the spices with the beans and sprinkle salt evenly over the top. Add 2 tbs/30 ml of water to the pan and cover immediately. Turn the heat to low and cook for 10 minutes or until the beans are tender. Mix well and serve.

This *thoran* may be made a couple of hours ahead of time and reheated.

VEGETABLES COOKED WITH SPLIT PEAS
Kootu

All kinds of vegetables – pumpkin, carrot, spinach, string beans – are combined with *chana dal* in Kerala to make a very nourishing dish which most of northern India has never heard of – *kootu*. Even the texture of the dish is very Southern – neither wet, like a *dal*, nor dry but something in between so it can be eaten with rice. Yoghurt dishes and Plain Rice are almost always served with it, especially by Kerala's vegetarians. In the following recipe I use potatoes and cabbage.

Serves 6
3 oz/75 g/½ cup skinned *chana dal* or
   yellow split peas (page 200)
10 oz/275 g, 3 smallish potatoes
¼ tsp ground turmeric
¼ tsp ground red chilli powder
   (cayenne pepper)
about 1 lb/450 g, half of a medium-
   sized green cabbage, cored and
   shredded
2 fresh, hot green chillies, cut into very
   fine rounds
about ½ tsp/2.5 ml salt
4 oz/100 g/1 cup grated fresh coconut
   (page 197)
1 tsp/5 ml ground cumin seeds
2 tbs/30 ml vegetable oil
½ tsp/2.5 ml whole mustard seeds

½ tsp/2.5 ml skinned *urad dal*, if
   available (page 200)
½ tsp/2.5 ml uncooked, white rice
1 hot, dried, red chilli, broken into 2
   pieces
10 fresh or dried curry leaves

Pick over the *chana dal* and wash it in several changes of water. Drain. Put it in a small, heavy pan. Add 12 fl oz/ 350 ml/1½ cups of water and bring to a boil. Turn heat to low, cover partially and cook for about 1 hour or until the *dal* is tender but not mushy. Make sure that the water does not evaporate entirely. Add 1–2 tbs/15–20 ml of hot water if necessary. Set the *dal* aside. Wash the potatoes and peel them if they are old otherwise leave them with their skins on. Dice into ½-in/1-cm cubes.

Put the potatoes in a wide pan along with ¾ pint/450 ml/2 cups of water, the turmeric and chilli powder (cayenne pepper). Bring to a boil. Cover, lower the heat and simmer for 7–8 minutes or until the potatoes are almost tender. Now put in the cooked *dal*, the cabbage, green chillies and salt. Cook, stirring gently over a moderately high heat until the cabbage is just tender and just a little liquid is left in the bottom of the pan.

Put the coconut and cumin seeds in the centre of the pan and cover with the cabbage and potatoes. Cover with a lid, turn heat to low and steam for 2 minutes.

Heat the oil in a small frying pan. When very hot, put in the mustard seeds, then the *urad dal* and rice. When the *urad dal* reddens and the rice turns golden, put in the red chilli and the curry leaves. As soon as the chilli darkens, empty the contents of the small frying pan into the pan with the vegetables. Gently stir the vegetables.

PRAWNS/SHRIMPS COOKED WITH COCONUT MILK
Konju Pappaas

I love this dish with a passion. Give it to me with a bowl of Plain Rice and I will not ask for anything more.

There are two ingredients here that may be hard to find. Do not let that stop you from cooking it as I will suggest alternatives. The first ingredient is *kodampoli*, a sour, smoky tamarind that balances the creamy sweetness of the coconut milk. Lemon juice may be used in its place. The second ingredient is fresh curry leaves. If you cannot get them, use the dried ones and leave out the step that calls for the fresh ones.

I often make this dish when I am entertaining as most of the work can be done ahead of time. The sauce can be made and the prawns (shrimps) peeled well before the guests arrive. Then all I do 5 minutes before we sit down to eat is heat the sauce, fold the prawns (shrimps) into it so they cook through and then pour in the coconut milk.

If you want the dish to end up by being mildly hot, use ¾ tsp/4 ml of chilli powder (cayenne pepper). The sauce may taste quite fiery before the prawns (shrimps) and coconut milk are added but the final result will be fairly mild.

Serves 6
2 lb/900 g unpeeled, uncooked medium-sized prawns (shrimps) without heads or 1½ lb/700 g peeled prawns (shrimps)

2 tbs/30 ml whole coriander seeds
¼ tsp whole fenugreek seeds
1 tsp/5 ml whole black peppercorns
10 dried curry leaves (you do not need these if fresh ones are available)
1 tbs/15 ml fish tamarind (*kodampoli*) cut into slivers the width of a pencil or 2 tsp/10 ml lemon juice
5 tbs/75 ml/½ cup vegetable oil
1 tsp/5 ml whole black mustard seeds
10 fresh curry leaves, if available
1 medium-sized onion, peeled, cut into half lengthwise and then cut crosswise into half rings
5 cloves garlic, peeled and cut into fine slivers
1 tsp/5 ml peeled and finely grated fresh ginger
2 tbs/30 ml bright red paprika
¾ tsp/4 ml red chilli powder (cayenne pepper)
½ tsp/2.5 ml ground turmeric
about ¾–1 tsp/4–5 ml salt
3 whole fresh, hot green chillies
14 fl oz/400 ml/1¾ cups fresh or tinned unsweetened coconut milk (page 198)

If the prawns (shrimps) are not peeled, peel them. Devein the prawns (shrimps) (page 203). Wash them quickly and pat them dry. Cover and refrigerate.

Heat a small, 5-in/12.5-cm, cast-iron frying pan (a crêpe pan will do) over a medium flame. When hot, put in the coriander seeds, the fenugreek seeds and the peppercorns. Stir them about for 1 minute or so until they are lightly roasted. Remove from the heat. Put them into the container of a spice grinder or coffee grinder along with the dried curry leaves (if you are using them). Grind as fine as possible. Wash the fish tamarind slivers (if using them) under running water and then soak them in about half a teacup of water for 5 minutes. Drain. Heat the oil in a 10-in/25.5-cm frying pan or in a wide pan over a medium flame. When hot, put in the mustard seeds. As soon as the mustard seeds begin to pop put in the fresh curry leaves, if you are using them. Stir once and put in the onion and garlic. Stir and fry until they are lightly browned. Add the ginger. Stir and cook for another few seconds. Now put in ¾ pint/450 ml/1¾ cups of water, the paprika, red chilli powder (cayenne pepper), turmeric, salt, whole chillies, the ground spice mixture and either the drained fish tamarind or lemon juice. Bring to a boil. Turn the heat to medium-low and simmer vigorously for 5 minutes. Turn off the heat. (This sauce base may now be kept for several hours.)

Five minutes before you want to eat, heat the sauce in the frying pan over a fairly high flame. As soon as it begins to bubble, put in all the prawns (shrimps). Stir them around until they just turn opaque. Stir the coconut milk and pour it in. Keep stirring the contents of the frying pan. When the coconut milk is heated through and the first bubbles begin to appear, turn off the heat and serve.

MRS BABU ABRAHAM'S
FISH IN A CREAMY SAUCE
Meen Molee

This dish is a favourite at parties in Kerala and is often served with rice or bread. (You could also serve it with a crusty loaf of French or Italian bread.) It is frequently much hotter than I have made it. You can make it more or less hot, according to your taste. In Kerala, the fish that was used for this *molee* was the firm-fleshed seer. Haddock, halibut, cod, scrod, monk fish, or bream all make good substitutes. Buy thick fillets or use fish steaks. The choice of cut is crucial as the dish needs thick chunks of fish that won't disintegrate easily. Buy thick fillets or use 'steaks' of fish that have been cut crosswise.

Serves 6
3-in/7.5-cm piece of fresh ginger, peeled
6 fresh hot green chillies
7 cloves garlic, peeled
1 tbs/15 ml flour
1¼ pints/750 ml/3 cups thin coconut milk (page 198)
4 tbs/60 ml/⅓ cup vegetable oil
9 oz/250 g, 3 medium-sized onions, peeled, cut lengthwise into half and then cut crosswise into fine slices
¾ tsp/4 ml turmeric
¼–½ tsp red chilli powder (cayenne pepper)
about ½ tsp/2.5 ml salt
1 lb/450 g/3 cups, 3 medium-sized tomatoes, chopped
1¾ lb/800 g haddock or halibut fillets, cut at least 1½ in/4 cm thick
½ pint/300 ml/1¼ cups thick coconut milk (page 198)

Chop 2 in/5 cm of the ginger coarsely. Take 3 of the green chillies and chop them coarsely. Put the chopped ginger, chopped green chillies and garlic into a container of a food processor or blender along with 4 tbs/

178

60 ml/⅓ cup of water. Blend until you have a somewhat coarse paste. Take the remaining 1 in/2.5 cm of ginger and cut it crosswise into very fine slices. Stack up the slices, a few at a time and cut into very fine strips.

Cut small slits down the middles of the 3 remaining green chillies. Put the flour in a bowl. Slowly add the thin coconut milk, mixing well as you do so. Strain, if lumps form.

Heat the oil in a large wok or wide pan over a medium flame. When hot, put in the sliced onions, the strips of ginger and the whole, slit green chillies. Stir and fry until the onions just start to brown, this takes about 2 minutes. Now add the paste from the food processor or blender. Stir and fry for about 5 minutes. Add the turmeric and chilli powder (cayenne pepper) and stir once or twice. Now put in the thin coconut milk, salt and tomatoes. Mix and stir gently until the sauce comes to a boil. Let the sauce cook on a medium flame for about 10 minutes or until the tomatoes have softened and the sauce has reduced a bit. Stir as this happens.

Cut the fish into pieces about 2½ in/6.5 cm square and slip them into the sauce. Turn the heat down a bit to allow the fish to poach gently. Ladle the sauce over the fish as it does so. It should take about 10 minutes to cook through. Pour in the thick coconut milk. As soon as bubbles begin to appear in the sauce, turn off the heat.

Lift the fish pieces carefully out of the pan and put in a serving dish. Put over the sauce.

MRS K M MATHEWS
CHICKEN STEW
Kozhi Shtew

In Kerala, this superb stew may be made with chicken, goat or lamb and potatoes, hard-boiled eggs and potatoes or with just potatoes. It is soothing and heavenly in all its forms. If you are using tinned coconut milk, it is particularly easy to prepare.

Traditionally, such stews are eaten at breakfast with *appams* – those deliciously spongy pancakes. Plain Rice combines equally well and may be served instead of *appams*. On the side you could serve Moghlai Spinach and Dry Cauliflower.

If this stew tastes very 'Western' in its seasonings – cloves, cinnamon, and black pepper (many people compare it to Irish stew) – remember that these are Kerala's spices, not those of the Western world. They grow in the back gardens of many private homes. In Kerala, these spices are left whole in the stew. They are just pushed to the side of the plate at mealtime. If this seems bothersome to you, then take the spices out of the pan just after you have fried them. Tie them up in a muslin or cheesecloth bundle and drop them back into the stew when you add the thin coconut milk. The bag can be removed when the stew is cooked.

If you wish to substitute lamb for chicken, get stewing lamb with bone preferably from the neck and shoulder. Cook it for about 50 minutes before adding the potatoes and then continue as for Chicken Stew.

Serves 4–5

3 lb/1.4 kg chicken, skinned and cut
    into reasonably small pieces
5 tbs/75 ml/½ cup vegetable oil
1½ tsp/7.5 ml whole black peppercorns
3×4-cm/1½-in cinnamon sticks
10 whole cloves
8 whole cardamom pods
1 lb/450 g, 3 good-sized onions, cut in
    half lengthwise and then cut
    crosswise into fine half rings
1½-in/4-cm piece fresh ginger, peeled,
    sliced and then cut into fine slivers
1 tbs/15 ml flour
6 whole, fresh hot green chillies slit
    slightly down their centre
1 pint/600 ml/2½ cups thin coconut
    milk (page 198)
1 lb/450 g, 3 medium-sized potatoes,
    peeled and cut lengthwise into 1-in/
    2.5-cm thick 'fingers' ('thick fries')
about 1½ tsp/7.5 ml salt
1 tbs/15 ml lime or lemon juice
1 tbs/15 ml coconut or any other
    vegetable oil
4 tbs/60 ml peeled and finely sliced
    shallots
15 fresh or dried curry leaves
½ pint/300 ml/1¼ cups thick coconut
    milk (page 198)

When cutting up the chicken, cut the breasts into 6 pieces and each leg into 3 or 4.

Over a medium flame, heat 5 tbs/ 75 ml/½ cup of oil in a large, wide-based casserole pan. When hot, put in the peppercorns, cinnamon sticks, cloves and cardamom pods. Stir once and add the onions and ginger. Sauté until the onions are translucent. Put in the flour and stir it around for 30 seconds. Add the green chillies, chicken and thin coconut milk. Bring

to a boil. Cover, turn the heat to low and simmer for 10 minutes. Add the potatoes and the salt and stir. Bring to a boil. Cover, turn the heat to low and simmer for 20 minutes or until the chicken and potatoes are tender. Stir in the lime juice.

Heat the coconut oil in a small frying pan over a medium flame. When hot, put in the sliced shallots. Stir and fry the shallots until they are lightly browned. Put in the curry leaves and stir for a second. Pour the contents of the frying pan into the chicken stew. Stir the thick coconut milk and add it to the stew as well. Bring to a simmer, stirring gently all the time. As soon as the first bubbles appear, turn off the heat. (If you reheat the stew, stir it gently so it does not curdle. Turn off the heat when it just begins to bubble.)

THE KODAR'S
GREEN CHILLI CHICKEN

This superb dish comes from the Jewish Community in Cochin where it is often served for the Friday night dinner, accompanied by Plain Rice or slices of bread. I happen to think that it is scrumptious with *appams* as well. I have modified the recipe only to the extent of using fewer green chillies and shallots and less red chilli powder (cayenne pepper). It may be made a day ahead and refrigerated. Its flavour improves as it sits.

Tamarind is sold by most Indian grocers. If you cannot find it, use fresh lemon juice instead and leave out the boiling water.

Serves 4

3 lb/1.4 kg chicken, skinned and cut into small serving pieces

1 oz/25 g, a walnut-sized lump of tamarind or 2 tbs/30 ml lemon juice

1 tsp/5 ml salt

1½ tsp/7.5 ml sugar

12–15 fresh or dried curry leaves

½ lb/225 g/2 cups shallots, peeled and finely sliced

6–7 cloves garlic, finely chopped

1½-in/4-cm cube fresh ginger, peeled and finely chopped

7 fresh, hot green chillies, 5 cut into fine rings and 2 cut into long slivers

6 oz/175 g/1 cup, 2 small tomatoes, chopped

½ tsp/2.5 ml ground turmeric

¼–½ tsp red chilli powder (cayenne pepper)

When cutting up the chicken, cut the breasts into 6 pieces and each leg into 3 or 4.

Break up the tamarind into smaller pieces and put in a cup or small bowl. Cover with 4 fl oz/125 ml/½ cup of boiling water and set aside for 1–2 hours. Mash up the tamarind and then sieve the pulp into another bowl. Discard the leftovers from the sieve. Mix the sieved pulp with a quarter of the salt and all the sugar. Set aside. Over a medium-high flame, heat the oil in a heavy, casserole-type pan. When hot, put in the curry leaves. Let them sizzle for a couple of seconds. Then add the shallots, garlic, ginger and the 5 chillies cut into rings. Stir and fry for 5–6 minutes or until the shallots have browned lightly.

Now put in the tomatoes. Keep stirring and frying for another 4 minutes or until the tomatoes have turned soft and have started to brown. Add the turmeric and chilli powder (cayenne pepper) and give a quick stir. Now put in the chicken and the remaining salt. Give the chicken a stir. Add ½ pint/300 ml/1¼ cups of water and bring to a simmer. Cover tightly, turn the heat to low and cook for 20 minutes. Stir the chicken once during this time.

Add the slivers of green chilli, cover again and cook for another 5 minutes. Remove the lid. Stir the tamarind mixture and pour it in. Stir the chicken gently to mix. Turn the heat to medium and cook, uncovered, for 10 minutes so the sauce can reduce a bit. As it does so, keep spooning the sauce over the top of the chicken. Take care that the chicken does not stick to the bottom of the pan.

Spoon off some of the surplus fat from the top of the dish before you serve it.

MRS K M MATHEW'S
DAL CURRY – DAL WITH COCONUT MILK
Molaghashyam

In Kerala, *toovar dal*, with its earthy taste and colour is mellowed somewhat by the addition of coconut or coconut milk. Curry leaves and browned shallots perk it up and give the dish its characteristic Kerala taste.

This delicious *dal* may be served with almost any Indian meal and goes particularly well with Green Chilli Chicken and Green Beans with Coconut and rice.

181

Serves 6

7 oz/200 g/1 cup skinned *toovar dal* or
    yellow split peas (page 200)
⅛ tsp ground turmeric
1 tbs/15 ml peeled and very finely
    chopped shallots
1 tsp/5 ml ground cumin seeds
3–4 whole fresh, hot green chillies, slit
    down their middles
4 tbs/60 ml vegetable oil or 2 tbs/30 ml
    coconut oil and 2 tbs/30 ml *ghee*
½ tsp/2.5 ml whole black mustard
    seeds
10–12 fresh or dried curry leaves
1–2 whole, hot, dried red chillies
    broken up into 2–4 pieces each
2 tbs/30 ml peeled and finely sliced
    shallots
2 cloves garlic, peeled and finely
    chopped
5 oz/150 g, 1 medium-sized tomato,
    chopped
¾–1 tsp/4–5 ml salt
½ pint/300 ml/1¼ cups, tinned or
    fresh, unsweetened coconut milk
    (page 198)

Pick over the *dal* and wash it in several
changes of water. Drain. Put it in a
heavy-based pan and add 1½ pints/
900 ml/3¾ cups of water as well as the
turmeric. Bring to a boil. Turn the
heat to low and cover, leaving the lid
slightly ajar. Simmer the *dal* for about
45 minutes. Now put in the chopped
shallots and ground cumin. Stir, cover
in the same way as before and cook for
another 15 minutes. Add the green
chillies and cook for 10–15 minutes or
until the *dal* is tender. If the *dal* seems
too thick at any point, add up to 4 fl oz/
125 ml/½ cup of boiling water. The
dal, at this stage, should be like a
thick, paste-like soup. Leave on a very

low heat as you complete the final step.

Heat the oil in a small frying pan
over a medium flame. When hot, put
in the mustard seeds. As soon as the
mustard seeds begin to pop, (this takes
just a few seconds), put in the curry
leaves and the red chillies. When the
red chillies darken (this happens
almost immediately), put in all the
sliced shallots and garlic. Stir and fry
until the shallots turn a reddish-brown
colour. Now add the tomato pieces.
Stir and fry until they soften.

Pour the entire contents of the small
frying pan into the *dal*. Add the salt
and mix. Add the coconut milk and
stir in.

The *dal* may be cooked several
hours ahead of time and then
reheated.

KUNYA AMINA'S
PRAWN/SHRIMP PILAF
Konju Pullao

The Muslim Moplas of Kerala like to
serve this pilaf for lunch. Perhaps it is
their passion for the crustacean that
started it, but it seems the done thing
to eat it with more of the same – fried
prawns (shrimps)! We are not obliged
to carry matters that far. I sometimes
serve the pilaf as I might a pasta, with
a crisp, green salad. At other times I
make an okra or spinach *pachadi* to go
with it and also serve some fresh
spring onions (scallions).

Serves 6

1 lb/450 g unshelled, uncooked,
    medium-sized prawns (shrimps)
    without heads or 14 oz/400 g

uncooked, shelled prawns (shrimps)
15 oz/425 g/2½ cups Basmati or other
  long-grain rice
1-in/2.5-cm cube of fresh ginger,
  peeled and coarsely chopped
5 fresh, hot green chillies, coarsely
  chopped
7–8 cloves garlic, peeled
6 tbs/90 ml/½ cup vegetable oil
1 oz/25 g/¼ cup raw cashew nuts split
  in half, lengthwise
5 oz/150 g, 1 large onion, peeled, cut in
  half, lengthwise and then cut
  crosswise into very fine half rings
1 tsp/5 ml ground cumin
6 oz/175 g, 2 small tomatoes, chopped
4 fl oz/125 ml/½ cup plain yoghurt
1½ oz/40 g/½ cup freshly grated
  coconut
1½ oz/40 g/½ cup unsweetened
  coconut milk, fresh or tinned (page
  198)
¾ tsp/4 ml salt
10 whole cloves
2-in/5-cm cinnamon stick
5 whole cardamom pods
2 tsp/10 ml salt

Peel the prawns (shrimps), if they are
unshelled and devein them. Rinse
them off and pat them dry. Cover and
refrigerate.

Pick over the rice and wash it in
several changes of water. Put the rice
in a bowl. Cover with water so it comes
to about 2 in/5 cm above the rice and
leave to soak for 30 minutes. Strain
and leave in the strainer.

Put the ginger, green chillies and
garlic into the container of a blender
or food processor. Add 4 tbs/60 ml/⅓
cup of water and blend, pushing down
with a rubber spatula whenever necessary. Line a plate with absorbent
kitchen paper (paper towel) and set it
beside you.

Heat the oil in a wok or a large
frying pan over a medium flame.
When hot, put in the cashew nuts. Stir
them about. As soon as they turn
golden (this happens very fast),
remove them with a slotted spoon and
put them on one half of the absorbent
kitchen paper (paper towel). Put the
onions into the same oil. Stir and fry
them until they are reddish brown and
crisp. Remove them with a slotted
spoon and put them beside the cashew
nuts on the paper.

Put the paste from the blender or
food processor into the oil. Add the
cumin. Stir and fry for about 2
minutes or until all the liquid is absorbed. Add the tomatoes. Stir and fry
them, still on a medium heat, until
they soften and begin to darken. Add
the yoghurt. Stir and fry until all the
water from the yoghurt disappears
and you can see the oil in the bottom
of the pan. Now put in the grated
coconut and stir for a few seconds. Put
in the coconut milk and ¾ tsp/4 ml salt.
Cook, stirring all the time, for about 1
minute or until the sauce thickens a
bit. Put in the prawns (shrimps). Stir
once and turn off the heat. Put the
half-cooked prawns (shrimps) and
their sauce into a heavy, oven-proof
pan. Preheat the oven to 325°F/170°C/
gas mark 3. Bring about 5 pints/2.75
litres/3 quarts of water to a boil in a
large pan. Add the cloves, cinnamon,
cardamom and 2 tsp/10 ml salt. When
the water is at a rolling boil, drop in
the rice and give it a stir. Cook the rice
for exactly 6 minutes. Drain the rice in
a colander and put it on top of the
prawns (shrimps). Spread the cashew

nuts and fried onions on top of the rice. With a chopstick or the handle of a long spoon make a well, for the steam to come out, in the centre of the rice, about 1 in/2.5 cm in diameter, going from the top, all the way down to the bottom of the pan. Cover tightly, first with foil and then with the lid of the pan. Put in the oven and bake for 20 minutes or until the rice is just done. Stir gently before serving.

VASANTINAZARETH'S
HOPPERS – RICE PANCAKES
Appams

I have often said that if a French crêpe were to marry a crumpet or an English muffin, they would probably become the proud parents of *appams*. *Appams* are a special kind of pancake made out of a leavened rice batter. They are thick, soft, white and spongy in the centre and crisp and lace-like along their golden edges.

There is nothing quite as gorgeous as steaming hot *appams* and they remain one of my favourite Indian pancakes. What makes them especially attractive is that they are really very easy to make. If you can make a crêpe, you can make an *appam*. Time *is* required for the soaking of rice and the fermentation of the batter but this is time that the cook can spend twiddling his or her thumbs.

In Kerala, a special two-handled cast-iron wok is used for making *appams*. I do not happen to have such a utensil and I find my well seasoned, large, Chinese wok perfectly adequate. If you do not have a wok, use a crêpe pan. You will not get the traditional *appam* form but you will still end up with a good pancake. Also, I find that my electric blender makes a better batter than my food processor. The recipe here is not the traditional one requiring the hand-pounding of two different types of rice, toddy for fermentation and cooked rice paste for added texture. This is a much simplified recipe worked out by a Keralite in a Washington DC kitchen. The results, you will find, are superb.

There are many ways to eat an *appam*: smear it when hot with butter and jam and eat for breakfast or dessert; put fine ground sugar and thick coconut milk on it and eat it with a meal or as a snack or as a dessert; use it as a bread and eat it with Chicken Stew or Green Chilli Chicken; oh yes, you can also eat it with butter and honey, which is what I was doing just a few minutes ago. The *appam* seems designed to absorb juices whether they be buttery and sweet or hot and savoury. The batter for *appam* is most amenable. It lends itself to busy schedules with the utmost flexibility. Once you have made the batter you may refrigerate it overnight and use it the next morning. You can also, wonder of wonders, freeze it. Just allow it to thaw completely and come to room temperature before you start cooking.

Makes about 16 appams
1 lb 2 oz/500 g/3 cups long-grain rice such as Carolina (perfumed rice, such as Basmati is not suitable)
14 fl oz/400 ml/1¾ cups unsweetened coconut milk, fresh or tinned (page 198)

1½ tsp/7.5 ml active dry yeast granules
3 tbs/45 ml sugar
3 medium-sized eggs, at room
   temperature
½ tsp/2.5 ml salt
about 4 fl oz/125 ml/½ cup extra warm
   water or coconut milk
about 6 tbs/90 ml/½ cup vegetable oil

Put the rice in a bowl and wash it in several changes of water. Drain. Add enough water to the rice to cover it by 1½ in/4 cm and leave to soak for at least 8 hours or overnight.

Drain the rice and put in a blender. Add the 14 fl oz/400 ml/1¾ cups of coconut milk and blend until you have a fine paste. There will be very fine granules in the paste but that is as it should be. Empty the paste out into a bowl.

Put the yeast and 1 tbs/15 ml of the sugar into a cup. Add the 4 tbs/60 ml of warm water and mix. (The water should be about 100°–115°F/38°–46°C). Set aside for about 10 minutes for the fermenting action to start. Add the yeast mixture to the batter in the bowl and mix it in. Cover the bowl with a plate and leave it in a warm place for 6 hours.

Beat the eggs lightly. Add the salt and the remaining sugar. Mix. Add this mixture to the batter. Stir. Add about 4 fl oz/125 ml/½ cup of warm water or coconut milk to the batter to produce a consistency perhaps just a little bit thicker than a crêpe batter.

Got everything ready for making the *appams*: set up your wok and keep its cover handy; you will need a pastry brush or a wad of cloth; put the oil in a small bowl; keep near you the bowl of batter, a measure or ladle that will hold a tiny bit less than 3 fl oz/85 ml/⅓ cup, an a spatula that works well in the wok; you will also need a deep dish to hold the *appams* as they get made and some foil to wrap them in if you are not eating them immediately.

Put on a low flame under the wok and let it heat a bit. Dip the pastry brush or the cloth wad in the bowl of oil and brush a 7-in/18-cm circumference with it in the centre of the wok. Stir the batter gently. Ladle just a little less than 3 fl oz/85 ml/⅓ cup of batter into the centre of the wok. Quickly pick up the wok by its two handles (if it has only one handle, wear an oven glove (mitten) and put your second hand where the second handle might have been). Tilt the wok around, just as you would for crêpes, so the batter covers about a 6 in/15 cm diameter. Cover and cook for about 3½ minutes on a low heat. The bottom and edges of the *appam* should barely turn golden and the centre should be pale and spongy. Eat immediately, if possible. Otherwise put the *appam* in a deep dish, cover and make the rest of the *appams*.

Leftover *appams* may be wrapped tightly in foil and refrigerated. Heat foil packet in a moderately hot oven 400°F/200°C/gas mark 6 for about 10 minutes.

SPINACH AND YOGHURT
Cheera Pachadi

Pachadis may be made with all manner of vegetables and fruit, including okra pumpkin, semi-ripe pineapple and green mangoes. They add sparkle and zest to meals, serving as a cross between a relish and a vegetable dish.

Pachadis go well with most Indian meals but this one goes particularly well with Prawn/Shrimp Pilaf.

Serves 6
5 tbs/75 ml/6 tablespoons vegetable oil
1 tsp/5 ml whole cumin seeds
1 tsp/5 ml skinned *urad dal* (page 200)
8–10 fresh or dried curry leaves
1 whole, hot, dried red chilli, broken into 2–3 pieces
4 tbs/60 ml/⅓ cup peeled and finely sliced shallots
2–3 fresh, hot green chillies, sliced into very fine rounds
1 oz/25 g/⅓ cup grated fresh coconut (page 197)
5 oz/150 g/2 well packed cups spinach leaves, finely sliced
about ½ tsp/2.5 ml salt
¾ pint/450 ml/2 cups plain yoghurt

Heat the oil in a wok or a medium-sized frying pan over a medium flame. When hot, put in the cumin seeds and *urad dal*. As soon as the *dal* turns red-dish, put in the curry leaves and red chilli. When the red chilli darkens (this just takes a second), put in the shallots and green chillies. Stir and sauté until the shallots turn golden. Add the coconut and stir once. Now put in the spinach and salt. Turn the heat down a bit. Stir and sauté the spinach until it is tender, adding a little more water if you think there is any danger of the spinach browning.

Put the yoghurt in a bowl. Beat lightly with a fork or a whisk until it is smooth and creamy. Add the contents of the wok or frying pan. Mix well and serve at room temperature or cold.

MRS MADHAVAN'S
OKRA WITH YOGHURT
Vendakay Pachadi

This *pachadi*, similar to the spinach one, is made with fried okra. I am including it only because I find it utterly delicious and simple to make. You could also make it with pumpkin, as my hostess did. Just boil cubes of pumpkin in a little water flavoured with turmeric and red chilli powder (cayenne pepper). Boil until the water gets aborbed. Then put the pumpkin pieces into seasoned yoghurt as you would the okra.

Serves 4–6
1 tsp/5 ml whole, black mustard seeds
9 oz/250 g fresh okra
6 tbs/90 ml/½ cup vegetable oil
¾ pint/450 ml/2 cups plain yoghurt
½ tsp/2.5 ml peeled and finely grated fresh ginger
½ tsp/2.5 ml salt
1 hot, fresh, green chilli, finely chopped
pinch of ground asafetida (optional)
¼ tsp whole black mustard seeds
10 fresh or dried curry leaves
1 dried, hot red chilli, broken into 2 pieces

Put the 1 tsp/5 ml of black mustard seeds into the container of an electric coffee grinder or a spice grinder. Grind as fine as possible. Leave in the grinder.

Rinse the okra quickly and pat it dry. Cut off the tip and top crowns of the okra pods and then cut them cross-wise into ¼-in/0.5-cm thick rounds.

Heat the oil in a wok or frying pan over a medium flame. When hot, put in the okra. Stir and fry until the okra turns reddish brown in parts and is cooked through. Remove the okra with a slotted spoon and put in a plate lined with absorbent kitchen paper (paper towels). Strain off the oil in the pan and save it.

Put the yoghurt in a bowl. Beat it lightly with a fork or a whisk until it is smooth and creamy. Add the ground mustard seeds to the yoghurt as well as the ginger, salt, sugar and green chilli. Mix. Put the okra into the yoghurt and stir it in.

In a small frying pan, heat 2 tbs/ 30 ml of the oil that the okra was fried in over a medium flame. When hot, put in first the asafetida, then a second later, the whole mustard seeds. As soon as the mustard seeds begin to pop, put in the curry leaves and the red chilli. When the chilli darkens, pour the contents of the frying pan, oil and spices, into the yoghurt. Mix.

Serve at room temperature. You may also let the *pachadi* sit, covered and unrefrigerated, for a day and serve it the following day.

Note: the pieces of red chilli should only be eaten by those who know what they are doing!

BASIC RECIPES
AND
GENERAL NOTES

BASIC RECIPES

DAL WAFERS
Papar or *Papadum*

Called *papadum* in South India and *papar* in the North, these thin wafers are generally made out of split peas, such as *urad dal* or split mung beans, *moong dal*, though they could also be made out of potatoes or sago. They are served at nearly all vegetarian meals in India. Bengalis eat them towards the end of a meal with chutney; Southerners are known to crush them and eat them with rice, yoghurt and pickles while North Indians often serve them as appetizers with drinks. *Papadums* are bought partially prepared. All you have to do is cook them. There are two basic methods to choose from: frying or roasting. The traditional method is to deep fry them. This allows the *papadums* to expand to their fullest and turn very light and airy. This method does however, leave those who are nibbling the wafers with slightly greasy fingers. The second method is to roast the *papadums* directly over or under a flame. This way you end up with clean fingers and the *papadums* are less calorific. But the *papadums* do not expand as much and remain denser than the fried ones.

Papadums may be bought plain, dotted with black pepper, dotted with red pepper or flavoured with garlic.

You may serve *papadums* with drinks or with any Indian meal.

Serves 4

Frying Method

4 papadums
vegetable oil for deep frying

Break each *papadum* into 2 pieces.

Pour enough oil in a wok or frying pan to come to a depth of ¾in/2cm. Set the oil to heat over a medium flame. When hot, drop in a *papadum* half. Within seconds it will sizzle and expand. Remove the *papadum* with a slotted spoon and drain on absorbent kitchen paper (paper towels). Cook all the *papadums* this way.

Papadums should retain their yellowish colour and not brown. They should also cook very fast. Adjust your heat if necessary.

Roasting Method

4 papadums

Preheat your grill (broiler)

Put 1 *papadum* on a rack and place it about 3in/7.5cm away from the source of heat. Watch it carefully. It will expand in seconds. It will also pale and develop a few bubbles. Turn it over and expose the second side to the flame for a few seconds. Watch it all the time and do not let it brown or burn. Remove from the grill (broiler) when done. Make all the *papadums* this way. (When making *papadums* under a grill (broiler) it is not always necessary to turn them over. You will just have to use your own judgment here.)

If you happen to have a toasted sandwich maker (electric toaster oven) you may make your *papadums* in that. Just as you would under a grill (broiler). That is what, in fact, I do in my own house.

DEEP-FRIED PUFFY BREAD
Poori

These deep-fried breads puff up in hot oil like balloons. They are crispy-soft and may be eaten with almost all Indian meats, vegetables and split peas.

It is most economical – and safe to make *pooris* in a wok or an Indian *karhai*. You may use 8oz/225g/2 cups *chapati* flour to make the *pooris*. If you cannot find it, use the combination suggested below.

Makes 12 pooris and serves 4
4oz/100g/1 cup sieved, wheatmeal (wholewheat) flour
4oz/100g/1 cup plain flour (unbleached all-purpose flour)
½tsp/2.5ml salt
2tbs/30ml vegetable oil, plus more for deep frying
3½oz/120ml/½ cup water or milk

Put the two flours and salt in a bowl. Dribble the 2tbs/30ml of oil over the top. Rub the oil in with your fingers so the mixture resembles coarse bread-crumbs. Slowly add the water to form a stiff ball of dough. Empty the ball on to a clean work surface. Knead it for 10–12 minutes or until it is smooth.

Form a ball. Rub about ¼tsp of oil on the ball and slip it into a plastic bag. Set it aside for 30 minutes.

Knead the dough again, and divide it into 12 equal balls. Keep 11 of them covered while you work with the twelfth. Flatten this ball and roll it out into a 5–5½-in/12.5–13.5-cm circle. If you have the space, roll out all the *pooris* and keep them in a single layer, covered with cling film (plastic wrap).

Over a medium flame, set about 1in/2.5cm of oil to heat in a wok, *karhai* or small, deep frying pan. Let it get very, very hot. Meanwhile, line a platter with absorbent kitchen paper (paper towel). Lift up one *poori* and lay it carefully over the surface of the hot oil. It might sink to the bottom but it should rise in seconds and begin to sizzle. Using the back of a slotted spoon, push the *poori* gently into the oil with tiny, *swift* strokes. Within seconds, the *poori* will puff up. Turn it over and cook the second side for about 10 seconds. Remove it with a slotted spoon and put it on the platter. Make all the *pooris* this way. The first layer on the platter may be covered with a layer of absorbent kitchen paper (paper towel). More *pooris* can then be spread over the top. Serve the *pooris* hot.

FLAT WHOLEWHEAT BREAD
Roti

Makes 12 rotis
8oz/225g/2 cups *chapati* flour or 4oz/100g/1 cup sieved wholewheat flour mixed with 4oz/100g/1 cup plain white flour
additional flour for dusting

Put the flour in a bowl. Slowly add enough water so that you will be able to gather the flour together and make a soft dough. You will need about 6½ fl oz/190 ml/a good ¾ cup of water. Knead the dough for 7–8 minutes or until it is smooth. Make a ball and put it inside a bowl. Cover the bowl with a damp cloth and set it aside for 30 minutes.

If the dough looks very runny, flour your hands and knead for another few minutes. Form 12 equal balls and dust each one with a little flour. Keep them covered.

Set a *tava*, cast-iron griddle or cast-iron frying pan to heat over a medium-low flame. Allow at least 5 minutes for that. Keep some extra flour for dusting near you. Remove a ball of dough and flatten it between the palms of your hands. Dust it on both sides with flour. Roll it out, as thinly and evenly as you can, aiming for a 5½ in/13.5-cm circle. When the griddle is hot, slap the *roti* on to its heated surface. Cook for about 1 minute or until soft bubbles begin to form. Turn the *roti* over. (Most Indians use their hands to do this.) Cook for ½ minute on the second side. If you have a gas cooker, light a second burner on a medium flame and put the *roti* directly on it. Using tongs with rounded ends, rotate the *roti* so that all areas are exposed to the shooting flames. Take 5 seconds to do this. Turn the *roti* over and repeat for about 3 seconds. The *roti* should puff up. Put the *roti* on a plate and cover with a clean tea towel (dish towel). Make all *rotis* this way. If you have an electric stove, place the griddle and *roti* under a grill (broiler) for a few

seconds, until the *roti* puffs up. Serve hot.

PLAIN RICE
Saday Chaval

Serves 6
Basmati or any long-grain rice
    measured to the 15 fl oz/450 ml/2 cup
    level in a glass measuring jug.

Put the rice in a bowl and wash in several changes of water. Drain. Leave to soak in 2 pints/1.5 litres/5 cups of water for 30 minutes. Drain thoroughly.

Put the drained rice and 1 pint/600 ml/2⅔ cups of water in a heavy pan and bring to a boil. Cover with a very tight-fitting lid, turn heat to very, very low and cook for 25 minutes. Take the rice pan off the flame and let it rest, still covered and undisturbed, for another 10 minutes.

A YOGHURT DRINK
Lassi

One of the few drinks, other than water, that is drunk with meals in India. Lassi is very popular at breakfast, lunch and as a snack. It can be sweet or salty. If you wish to make sweet lassi, do not put in the salt or cumin. Instead, put in as much sugar as you like.

Serves 2
4 fl oz/125 ml/½ cup plain yoghurt
½ pint/300 ml/1¼ cup ice-cold water

½ tsp/2.5 ml ground roasted cumin
seeds
¼ tsp salt
¼ tsp finely crumbled, dried mint,
optional

Combine all the ingredients in the
container of an electric blender and
blend for 3 seconds. If you do not have
a blender, put the yoghurt in a bowl.
Beat with a fork or whisk until smooth
and creamy. Slowly add the water,
beating as you do so. Add all the other
ingredients and mix.

CARROT HALVA
Gajar Ka Halva

Serves 4
6 medium carrots
1¼ pints/750 ml/3 cups milk
8 whole cardamom pods
5 tbs/75 ml/½ cup vegetable oil or *ghee*
(page 201)
5 tbs/75 ml/6 tablespoons sugar
1 tbs/15 ml shelled, unsalted pistachios,
lightly crushed
½ pint/300 ml/1¼ cups double cream
(heavy cream), lightly whipped,
optional

Peel the carrots and grate them either
by hand or in a food processor. Put the
grated carrots, milk, and cardamom
pods in a heavy-bottomed pot and
bring to a boil. Turn heat to medium
and cook, stirring now and then, until
there is no liquid left. Adjust the heat,
if you need to.

Heat the oil in a non-stick frying pan
over a medium-low flame. When hot,
put in the carrot mixture. Stir and fry

until the carrots no longer have a wet,
milky look. They should turn a rich,
reddish colour. This can take 10–15
minutes.

Add the sugar, sultanas (golden
raisins), and pistachios. Stir and fry for
another 2 minutes.

This halva may be served warm or at
room temperature. Serve the cream
on the side, for those who want it.

SEMOLINA HALVA
Sooji Ka Halva

This very light, fluffy halva may be
eaten as a snack or at the end of a
meal. It is very popular with children.

Serves 6
1 pint/600 ml/2½ cups water
5 tbs/75 ml/½ cup vegetable oil or *ghee*
(page 201)
3 tbs/45 ml slivered, blanched almonds
11 oz/300 g/2 cups semolina
5½ oz/165 g/¾ cup sugar
2–3 tbs/30–45 ml sultanas (golden
raisins)
¼ tsp finely crushed cardamom seeds
(use a pestle and mortar to crush)

Put 1 pint/600 ml/2½ cups of water to
boil in a pan. Once it comes to a rolling
boil, let the pan sit on a back burner
over a low heat.

Heat the oil or *ghee* in a large, preferably non-stick frying pan over a
medium flame. When hot, put in the
almonds. Stir and fry them until they
turn golden. Take them out with a
slotted spoon and leave them to drain
on absorbent kitchen paper (paper
towels). Put the semolina into the same

oil. Turn the heat to medium low. Now stir and sauté the semolina for 8–10 minutes or until it turns a warm, golden colour. Do not let it brown.

Add the sugar to the pan and stir it in.

Very slowly, begin to pour the boiling water into the pan. Keep stirring as you do so. Take a good 2 minutes to do this. When all the water had been added, turn the heat to low. Stir and cook the halva for 5 minutes. Add the sultanas (golden raisins) and almonds. Stir and cook the halva for another 5 minutes.

This halva may be served hot, warm or at room temperature.

GENERAL NOTES

Amchoor Dried powder and slices made from sour unripe mangoes. My recipes call for only ground (i.e. powdered) *amchoor*. Amchoor gives foods a slightly sweet sourness. If unavailable, lemon juice may be substituted.

Asafetida *(Heeng)* A somewhat smelly brown resin used mainly for its digestive properties and its truffle-like flavour. It is available both in lump form and as a grainy powder. The lump is supposed to be purer. Break off a small chip with a hammer and crush it between two sheets of paper to make your own powder, if you wish.

Basmati Rice A fine aromatic, long grain rice grown in the foothills of the Himalaya mountains. If unavailable, any fine long grain rice may be substituted. Basmati rice should be carefully picked over and washed in several changes of water before being cooked.

Bengali *Garam Masala* see *Garam Masala*

Cardamom *(Elaichi)* An aromatic spice, generally sold in its pod. The green-coloured pods are more aromatic than the plumper, bleached, whitish ones. Some Indian grocers sell the seeds separately, a great convenience when grinding spice combinations such as *garam masala*. Many of my recipes call for whole cardamom pods. They are used as a flavouring and are not meant to be eaten. If a recipe calls for a small amount of ground cardamom seeds, pulverize them in a mortar.

Cardamom, Large Black *(Bari Elaichi)* They look like black beetles and have an earthier, deeper flavour than green cardamom. Use them only when the recipe calls for them. They can be ground whole, skin and all.

Chana Dal, see *Dals*

***Chapati* Flour** A very finely ground wholewheat flour found only at Indian grocers and used for making Indian breads. If unavailable, use suggested combinations of wholewheat or wheatmeal flour and plain flour/white flour.

Chickpea Flour Flour made out of chickpeas. In Indian shops it is known as gram flour or *besan*. It is also available in Britain in health food shops and in the United States in specialty stores where it is known as *farine de pois chiches*. I store mine in the refrigerator to discourage bugs.

Chillies, Fresh Hot Green *(Hari Mirch)* The fresh chillies used in India are 2–4in/5–10cm long and quite slim.

196

They are generally green but sometimes ripen to a red colour and may be used just as easily. Besides being rich in vitamins A and C, their skins give Indian food a very special flavour. If other varieties of chillies are substituted, adjustments should be made as they could be very mild in flavour, such as 'Italian hot peppers' or wildly hot, such as the Mexican *jalapeño*.

To store fresh chillies, do not wash them. Just wrap them in newspaper and put them in a plastic container or plastic bag. Any chillies that go bad should be thrown away as they affect the whole batch.

All chillies should be handled with care especially when cut or broken. Refrain from touching your eyes or your mouth and wash your hands as soon as possible after you finish with them.

If you want the flavour of the green chilli skin and none of its heat, remove its white seeds before cooking.

Chillies, Whole Dried Hot Red *(Sabut Lal Mirch)* These chillies are generally 1½–2½ in/3.5–6 cm long and quite slim. They too should be handled with care, just like the fresh hot green chillies. If you want the flavour of the chillies, without their heat, make a small opening in them and shake out and discard their seeds.

Chilli Powder, Red/Cayenne Pepper *(Pisi Hui Lal Mirch)* Indians refer to ground dried red chillies as red chilli powder. This is *not* the 'chilli powder' used in America to make Mexican 'chilli'. American 'chilli powder' is a spice mixture which includes ground cumin seeds. Because of this confusion, I

have been forced to write 'red chilli powder (cayenne pepper)', even though I'm aware that cayenne is a particular red chilli. For the purposes of this book, Indian red chilli powder and cayenne pepper may be used interchangeably.

Coconut, Grated Fresh When buying coconuts, make sure that they have no mould on them and are not cracked. Shake them to make sure that they are heavy with liquid. The more liquid the better. To break a coconut, hold the coconut in one hand over the sink and hit around the centre with the claw end of a hammer or the blunt side of a heavy cleaver. The coconut should crack and break into two halves. (The coconut water may be saved. It is generally not used in cooking but is very refreshing to drink.) Taste a piece of the coconut to make sure it is sweet and not rancid. Prise off the coconut flesh from the hard shell with a knife. If it proves to be too obstinate, it helps to put the coconut halves, cut side up, directly over a low flame, turning them around now and then so they char slightly. The woody shell contracts and releases the kernel.

Now peel off the brown coconut skin with a potato peeler and break the flesh into 1-in/2.5-cm pieces (larger ones if you are grating manually). Wash off these coconut pieces and either grate them finely on a hand grater or else put them in an electric blender or food processor. Do not worry about turning them into pulp in these electric machines. What you will end up with will be very finely 'grated' coconut, perfect for all the Indian dishes that require it.

Grated coconut freezes beautifully and defrosts fast. I always grate large quantities whenever I have the time and store it in the freezer for future use. (In America, excellent frozen grated coconut is available in some Mexican and Asian grocery stores. It is frozen in flat rectangles and defrosts very fast. It may be used in all my recipes that call for grated fresh coconut and may also be used to make coconut milk.)

Coconut Milk, Fresh Fill a glass measuring jug up to the ¾ pint/450ml/2 cup mark with grated coconut. Empty it into a blender or food processor. Add ½ pint/300ml/1¼ cups very hot water. Blend for a few seconds. Line a sieve with a piece of muslin or cheesecloth and place it over a bowl. Empty the contents of the blender into the sieve. Gather the ends of cloth together and squeeze out all the liquid. This is Thick Coconut Milk if the recipe calls for both thin and thick coconut milk. You should get about 12 fl oz/350 ml/1½ cups. To make Thin Coconut Milk, repeat the process with the coconut dregs and fresh hot water once or twice until you have the amount you require. If the recipe calls simply for Coconut Milk then follow the instructions for Thick Coconut Milk.

Coconut Milk, Tinned Excellent quality tinned coconut milk is sold by most grocers who stock East Asian, South Asian or Latin American foods. You may use this in all my recipes. Make sure to buy *un*sweetened coconut milk. When you open the tin, stir its contents first as the cream tends to

rise to the top. If the recipe calls for thin and thick coconut milk, go about it this way: buy two tins, each roughly ½ pint/300ml/1¼ cups in capacity. For the Thin Coconut Milk, open one tin and scoop off the cream which rises to the top. Set the cream aside. Pour the remaining liquid into a measuring jug to make the required quantity. For the Thick Coconut Milk, open the second tin and stir its contents. As you happen to have a little extra coconut cream handy, this may be added to the contents of the second tin to make it extra rich.

Coconut Milk made from Creamed Coconut Creamed coconut is available fairly easily in Great Britain and in some Indian shops in Europe and the United States. It, too, may be used to make coconut milk. Put 5 (level) tbs/75 ml/½ cup in a bowl. Slowly add ¼ pint/150ml/⅔ cup of hot water and mix well. You should get about 8 fl oz/250 ml/1 cup of coconut milk. This may be used in any recipe that calls for Coconut Milk or Thick Coconut Milk. Where Thin Coconut Milk is required, put 5 tbs/75 ml/½ cup in a bowl and slowly add ½ pint/300ml/1¼ cups of hot water. This should give you about 12 fl oz/350 ml/1½ cups of thin coconut milk.

Coriander, Fresh Green/Chinese Parsley (*Hara Dhania*) One of India's favourite herbs, this is used both as a seasoning and a garnish. Just the top leafy section is used.

To store fresh green coriander, put it, unwashed, roots and all, into a container filled with water, almost as if you're putting flowers in a vase. The leafy section of the plant should not be in water. Pull a plastic bag over the coriander and the container and refrigerate the whole thing. It should last for weeks. Every other day, discard any yellowing leaves.

Coriander Seeds, Whole and Ground *(Dhania, Sabut* and *Pisa)* These are the round, beige seeds of the coriander plant. You may buy them already ground or you can buy whole seeds, and grind them yourself in small quantities in an electric coffee grinder. I like to put my home-ground coriander seeds through a sieve but this is not essential.

Ground coriander seeds, if stored for long, begin to taste a bit like sawdust. It is best at this stage to discard them and start with a fresh batch.

Coriander and Cumin Seed Mixture, Ground *(Dhana Jeera* Powder) This combination of roasted and ground coriander and cumin seeds, in the proportion of 4 parts to 1 part, is used in Gujarat and Maharashtra.

To make it, put 4 tbs/60 ml/⅓ cup of whole coriander seeds and 1 tbs/15 ml of whole cumin seeds into a small cast-iron frying pan and place the pan over a medium flame. Stir the seeds and keep roasting them until they turn a few shades darker. Let the seeds cool somewhat. Put the seeds into the container of a coffee grinder or other spice grinder and grind as finely as possible. Store in an airtight container.

Cumin Seeds, Whole and Ground *(Zeera, Sabut* and *Pisa)* Whole seeds keep their flavour well and may be ground very easily in an electric coffee grinder when needed. You may also buy the seeds in their ground form.

Cumin Seeds, Roasted and Ground *(Bhuna Hua Zeera)* Put 4–5 tbs/60–75 ml of whole cumin seeds into a small cast-iron frying pan and place the pan over a medium flame. Stir the seeds and keep roasting them until they turn a few shades darker. Let the seeds cool somewhat. Put the seeds into the container of a coffee grinder or other spice grinder and grind as finely as possible. Store in an airtight container.

Cumin Seeds, Black *(Shah Zeera, Siyah Zeera* or *Kala Zeera)* A caraway-like seed with a flavour that is more refined and complex than that of the ordinary cumin. As it is expensive, it is used in small quantities. If you cannot find it, use regular cumin seeds as a substitute.

Curry Leaves, Fresh and Dried *(Kari Patta)* The highly aromatic curry leaves are shaped rather like bay leaves and are sold in India while still attached to their stems. Indian housewives and cooks use them only when they are fresh, pulling them off their stems just before they throw them into the pot. Only the dried leaves are available in most Western cities though I notice that some grocers in Great Britain are now beginning to import them, fresh and on the stem, from Africa. There are sections of India, such as the South, where curry leaves flavour more than half the dishes. Use the fresh leaves whenever you can find them; otherwise resort to the less flavourful dried ones.

Dals (Dried Split Peas and Beans)
Technically, a *dal* is really a dried, split pea though, even in India, the word is used rather loosely at times for all pulses (legumes) – dried beans and split peas. Most split peas are sold in India in two forms, skinned and unskinned. It is the skinned variety, also known as 'washed', 'white' or '*dhuli dal*', that is used in this book.

Chana Dal This is very much like the yellow split pea although it is smaller in size and sweeter in flavour. It is used as a spice in South India. Make sure you buy the skinned, split variety.

Masoor Dal A hulled, salmon-coloured split pea, this is also known as red split lentils. If buying from an Indian shop, make sure you buy the skinned variety.

Moong Dal Split *moong dal* or mung beans are sold both hulled and unhulled. My recipes call for only the skinned, all-yellow variety, also known as 'white' or 'washed'.

Toovar Dal Also known as *toor dal* and *arhar dal*, this hulled, ochre-coloured split pea has quite a dark, earthy flavour. Make sure you buy the skinned variety, sometimes called 'washed' or 'white'. Some shops sell an oily *toovar dal*. Here the *dal* has been rubbed with castor oil which acts as a preservative. The oil needs to be washed before the *dal* can be used. None of my recipes call for the oily *dal* though you may use it if the plain kind is not available.

Urad Dal For this book, only buy the 'washed' or 'white' dal, i.e., the skinned variety. This rather pale *dal* is used in the South for all kinds of savoury cakes and pancakes.

Fennel Seeds (Sonf) These seeds look and taste like anise seeds, only they are larger and plumper. They may be roasted (see the method for roasting cumin seeds) and used after meals as a mouth freshener and digestive. To grind fennel seeds, just put 2–3 tbs/45 ml into the container of a clean coffee grinder or other spice grinder and grind as finely as possible. Store in an airtight container.

Fenugreek Seeds (Methi) Yellow, square and flattish, these seeds are meant to soothe the intestinal tract. They have a slightly bitter flavour and should not be allowed to burn.

Fish Tamarind (Kodampoli) This sour rind of a special fruit – garcinia indica – is dried over wood smoke to make a black, sour, smoky seasoning that is particularly good with fish. It is used frquently in the cooking of Kerala. Before it is used, it should be rinsed off, sliced, and then given a quick soak for a few minutes to soften it a bit. If you cannot find it, use *kokum*, an unsmoked version of a fairly similar seasoning that is used further up the same West coast. It, too, needs to be rinsed off, sliced and soaked briefly. If you cannot find either *kodampoli* or *kokum*, lemon juice may be used as suggested in the specific recipes.

Garam Masala There are hundreds of spice mixtures in India, each used for different dishes in different ways. *Garam masala* is a highly aromatic mixture that is often sprinkled over the top of dishes that have almost finished cooking. There are many recipes for it. Here is mine. Take 1 tbs/15 ml cardamom seeds, 1 tsp/5 ml each whole black cumin seeds, whole cloves and black peppercorns, as well as about ⅓ of a nutmeg and a 2-in/5-cm cinnamon stick. Put them all into the container of a clean coffee grinder or other spice grinder and grind as finely as possible. Store in an airtight container.

To make **Bengali *Garam Masala***, put 3×1-in/2.5-cm cinnamon sticks, 15–20 whole cardamom pods and 8 whole cloves into the container of a clean coffee grinder or other spice grinder and grind as finely as possible. Store in an airtight container.

Ghee This is butter that has been so well clarified that you can deep fry in it. Because it is totally free of all milk solids, it does not need refrigeration. *Ghee* has a very special, nutty taste. If you have access to Indian shops, my own advice would be that you buy ready-made *ghee*. The Netherlands, for example, exports an excellent quality which many Indian shops buy in bulk and then package in their own bottles. If you cannot buy ready-made *ghee*, here is how you go about making your own: take 1 lb/450 g/2 cups of the best quality unsalted butter that you can find. Put it in a heavy, smallish pan and let it melt over a low flame. Soon it will begin to simmer. Let it simmer on a low heat for about 45 minutes (timing really depends upon the amount of water in the butter), or until the milky solids turn brownish and either cling to the sides of the pan or else fall to the bottom. Because you have to boil all the water away without letting the butter brown, you must watch it, especially towards the end of the cooking time. Now strain the *ghee*

through a quadrupled layer of cheesecloth. Homemade *ghee* is best stored covered in the refrigerator.

Ginger, Dried, Ground *(Sont)* This is the ginger that is dried and ground (powdered), the same that you might use to make gingerbread. It is available in supermarkets.

Ginger, Fresh *(Adrak)* Known sometimes as ginger 'root', this is really a rhizome with a refreshing pungent flavour. Its potato-like skin needs to be peeled before it can be chopped or grated. To grate ginger, use the finest part of a hand grater. You should end up with a paste.

When buying ginger, look for pieces that are not too wrinkled and have a taut fresh skin. If you use ginger infrequently, you can 'store' it by planting it in somewhat dry sandy soil. Water infrequently. Your ginger will not only survive but may sprout fresh knobs. If you use ginger frequently, store in a cool airy basket along with your onions and garlic.

Karhai This is the Indian wok and may be made out of cast-iron or stainless steel. It is excellent for stir frying and its rounded bottom makes it very economical for deep frying.

Kodampoli, see Fish Tamarind

Mango Many shops sell 'ripe' mangoes that are actually unripe and quite hard. You may ripen them yourself at home by wrapping them individually in newspaper and then storing them either in hay or in a basket. When they are ripe they should be very slightly soft to the touch and should begin to smell like mangoes. There should however, be no black spots on them. Once they are ripe they can be refrigerated.

Masoor Dal, see *Dals*

Moong Dal, see Dals

Mustard Oil *(Sarson Ka Tel)* This yellow oil, made from mustard seeds, is quite pungent when raw, and sweet when heated to a slight haze. It is used all over India for pickling. In Kashmir and Bengal it is also used for everyday cooking and gives the foods of those regions their very special character. If you cannot find it, any other vegetable oil may be substituted. You might consider the rather unorthodox use of virgin olive oil. It has as much character and 'kick' as mustard oil, though of course the taste is completely different.

Mustard Seeds, Whole Black These tiny dark round seeds, sometimes quite black, sometimes reddish-brown, are used throughout India for pickling and for seasoning everything from yoghurt to beans. They have a dual character. When popped in hot oil, they impart an earthy sweetness. However, when they are ground, they turn nose-tinglingly pungent and slightly bitter. Indians have developed a taste for this bitterness and consider it to be very good for their digestive systems. If you wish to cut down on the bitterness, use only freshly-bought black mustard seeds or use yellow mustard seeds.

Mustard Seeds, Whole Yellow These are commonly available and may be substituted for black mustard seeds should the latter prove elusive. They are less bitter and milder in flavour.

Mysore Sambar Powder, see *Sambar Powder.*

Nigella Seeds *(Kalonji)* These seeds are sometimes known, inaccurately, as onion seeds. They are little tear-shaped black seeds used throughout all of India for pickling. Some North Indian oven breads are dotted with them and in Bengal they are used commonly for cooking vegetables and fish.

Panchphoran (5-Spice Mixture) This very Bengali spice combination contains whole cumin seeds, whole fennel seeds, whole nigella seeds (*kalonji*), whole fenugreek seeds, and a tiny aromatic seed known in Bengal as *radhuni*. As *radhuni* is generally unavailable outside Bengal, even Indians, in India, use black mustard seeds as a substitute. You may buy ready-mixed *panchphoran* or you can put it together yourself by mixing 2 tsp/10 ml of whole cumin seeds, 2 tsp/10 ml of whole black mustard seeds, 2 tsp/10 ml of whole fennel seeds, 1 tsp/5 ml of nigella seeds (*kalonjui*) and ¾ tsp/4 ml of whole fenugreek seeds. Store in an airtight container.

Papadum Also called *papar*. These Indian wafers are generally made out of split peas and flavoured with red pepper, black pepper or garlic. *Papadums* made with sago flour or potato flour are also very popular in India.

Keep what you do not use in a tightly sealed tin.

Poppy Seeds, White *(Khas Khas)* These tiny white seeds can became rancid so they should be kept in a tightly closed bottle and stored in a cool place. You may even freeze poppy seeds. Blue poppy seeds are never used in India.

Prawns/Shrimps, how to Peel and Devein Pull off the dangling legs as well as the head if it is there. Next, peel the shell from the body. Pull off the tail separately. To devein, make a shallow incision along the length of the prawn, right where the backbone would be if the prawn had one – all the way from head to tail. Here you will see a thread-like vein, often filled with black or green or yellow substance. Pull this out. If you do not find it, so much the better. Place all the peeled and deveined prawns in a bowl and wash them quickly under cold running water. Pat dry.

Pulses/Legumes, see *Dals*

Rice Flour Also called rice powder, it has the same texture as corn flour and is sold in India and oriental grocery stores.

Saffron I have used only 'leaf' saffron here – the whole dried saffron threads. Find a good, reliable source for your saffron, as there is a great deal of adulteration.

***Sambar* Powder, Mysore** A south Indian spice mixture (page 158).

Sesame Seeds *(til)* I used the beige, unhulled seeds. They have a wonderful nutty flavour especially after being roasted.

Tamarind *(Imli)* This is the bean-like fruit of a tall tree. When ripe, it is peeled, seeded and compressed into brick-like shapes.

To make tamarind paste: break off ½lb/225g from a brick of tamarind and tear into small pieces. Put in a stainless steel or a non-metallic bowl covered with ¾pint/450ml/2 cups of very hot water, and set aside for at least 3 hours or overnight. (In an extreme case when you need to use it instantly, you may simmer the tamarind for 10 minutes.) Set a sieve over a stainless steel or non-metallic bowl. Empty the soaked tamarind and its liquid into the sieve and push as much pulp through with your fingers or with the back of a wooden spoon as you can. Put whatever tamarind remains in the sieve back into the soaking bowl. Add 4floz/125ml/½ cup of hot water to it and mash it a bit. Return it to the sieve and try to extract some more pulp. Do not forget to collect all the thick, strained paste clinging to the bottom of your sieve. This quantity will make about 12floz/350ml/1½ cups. (Whatever tamarind remains in your sieve may be used for polishing brass!) Tamarind paste freezes well and will also last a good 2–3 weeks in the refrigerator. As long as it has no mould on it, you may use it.

Tava A slightly curved cast-iron griddle used in India for making breads. A cast-iron frying pan may be substituted.

Toovar Dal see *Dals*

Turmeric A rhizome of the ginger family with bright yellow flesh. Generally, only ground turmeric is available. It is made by boiling, drying and grinding the rhizome. In India it is considered an antiseptic.

Urad Dal see *Dals*

White Radish (*Mooli*) Long white radishes are sold in India with their leaves and the combination of vegetable and leaf is often cooked together. If you cannot find *mooli* with its leaves, substitute round or oval red radishes and their leaves.

RECIPE INDEX

A TASTE OF INDIA

RECIPE INDEX

INDEX

with fresh green
  coriander 107–8
chickpea flour 196
  stew with dumplings
  28–9
chilli 58, 196–7
  cauliflower with
    mustard seeds and
    dried 156–7
  chicken in a green sauce
    139–40
  chicken stew 179–80
  fish in a Bengali sauce
    123–4
  fish in a creamy sauce
    178–9
  green, chicken with
    180–81
  green peppers in a
    sesame seed sauce
    137
  Kashmiri red, lamb with
    108–9
  lamb cooked in the
    Kolhapuri style 88–9
  lamb with onions and
    mint 140–141
  Mysore *sambar* powder
    158–9
  prawns with mustard
    seeds 125–6
  quick kebabs 140
  roasted *moong dal* with
    spinach 122–3
  spicy crabs 124–5
  tomato chutney 127
chilli powder 197
China 62, 96, 166, 168
Chinese parsley, *see*
  coriander leaves
chingri maachher jhal 125–6
Chowpatty Beach 82
Christians 165, 166,
  167–70, 172, 174
chutney 100
  sesame 144–5
  tomato 127
  walnut 110
  yoghurt 145
  see also relishes
Cochin 172, 180
coconut 168, 197–8
  cucumbers with fresh

90–91
fish in a packet 68
green beans with 175
potatoes with tomatoes
  86
coconut milk 198
  chicken stew 179–80
  dal curry 181–2
  fish in a creamy sauce
    178–9
  hoppers 184–5
  prawns cooked with
    177–8
  tomato with 84
coffee 149, 153
cold summer soup with
  cucumbers and tomato
  65
Coorg 153
coriander leaves 198–9
  Bhopali fish with green
    seasonings 48
  chicken in a green sauce
    139
  fish in a packet 68
  lamb or chicken with
    107
  lamb with onions and
    mint 140–41
  sesame chutney 144 5
coriander seeds 199
corn cooked with milk 67
crabs, spicy 124–5
Cranganore 166
Crawford Market,
  Bombay 81
cream: carrot halva 194
cucumber, cold summer
  soup with tomato and
  65–6
  in relish, with tomato
    and onion 31–2
  salad with *moong dal* 162
  with fresh coconut
    90–91
cumin seeds 199
  diced potatoes with
    turmeric and 67
curd rice 160
curry leaves 169, 171, 199
  dal curry 181–2

dahi ki chutney 145

dahi shorba 83
Dakor 57
dal curry 181–2
Dal Lake 95, 98
dal wafers (*papadums*) 77,
  132, 191–2, 203
dal with coconut milk
  181–2
dalcha 130, 141–2
dals 200
date jaggery 115
Deccan hills 75, 77
deep-fried puffy bread
  (*poori*) 34, 35, 96, 192
Delhi 11–31, 38, 113, 130
delicious fried morsels
  120–21
dhana jeera powder 199
dhaniwal korma 100, 107–8
dhoklas 57, 72–3
diced potatoes with
  turmeric and cumin
  67–8
dill: carrots with 42
  chicken in a green sauce
    139
  Mysore spinach with
    156
Divali 33, 75
do piaza 140–41
dosas 149–50, 161–2
dry cauliflower 45–6
dumplings, chickpea flour
  stew with 28–9
Dwarka 58

East India Company
  113–14
eggplant, *see* aubergine
eggs: hard-boiled, in a
  tomato sauce 138

farasvi bhaji 85–6
fennel seeds 200
  mushrooms with ginger
    and 104
fenugreek leaves: chicken
  in a green sauce 139
fenugreek seeds 200
fish 40, 79, 111–12, 152,
  173–4
  Bhopali, with green
    seasonings 48

INDEX

tava 204
tea 95, 96
Tellichery 166
Thiyyas 170–71
thoran 169, 174, 175–6
Tibet 94, 96
til ki chutney 130, 144–5
tomato: and onion with
   yoghurt 91
   chutney 127
   cold summer soup with
    cucumbers and 65
   in relish, with onion and
    cucumber 31–2
   potatoes with 86
   puréed vegetables 66
   rice with spinach and 90
   sauce for hard-boiled
    eggs 138
   with coconut milk 84
tomato kut 133, 138–9
tomato palak bhat 90
tomato saar 84
toovar dal 38, 60, 61, 65,
   77, 200
   cold summer soup with
    cucumbers and
    tomato 65
   dal curry 181–2
   Mysore split peas with
    whole shallots 157–8
Trivandrum 171
trout 99
tsoont vaangan 104–5
turmeric 204
   diced potatoes with
    cumin and 67–8
turnips, red kidney beans
   cooked with 99, 109

Udipi 151–2
urad dal 200
   green beans cooked with
    split peas 85–6
   rice pancakes 161–2
Uttar Pradesh 33–55, 78

vegetables 97–8
   cooked with split peas
    176
   delicious fried morsels
    120–21
   puréed 66
vendakay pachadi 186–7
Vizhingam 174

waazwaan 101–2
wafers (*papadums*) 77, 132,
   191–2, 203
walnut chutney 110
Wankaner 60
water chestnuts 95
wheat 94
white radish 204

yakhni 95, 97, 98
yakhni pullao 31
Yamuna River 11, 12, 14
yoghurt: chicken in a
   green sauce 139
   chutney 145
   drink 193–4
   hot soup 83
   lamb or chicken with
    fresh green coriander
    107–8
lussi 33, 193–4
   mango salad 162–3
   okra with yoghurt
    186–7
   rice 148, 151, 160–61
   sauce for aubergine
    44–5
   sauce for potatoes and
    peas 47–8
   smoked aubergine with
    73–4
   spinach and 185–6
   tomato and onion with
    91
   walnut chutney 110
   with apple 54–5

Zoroastrianism 62

**Photographic
Acknowledgements**

Food Photography

The publishers would like
to acknowledge the
following people and
organisations for their
help:

Joss Graham, Oriental
Textiles, 10 Eccleston
Street, Londond SW1, for
supplying Indian textiles
and artefacts; The
General Trading
Company, 144 Sloane
Street London SW1, for
supplying Indian
artefacts; Gwyneth
Antiques, 56 Ebury Street,
London SW1, for
supplying a Kashmiri rug;
Liz Hippisley for the
styling; Moya Maynard for
preparing the dishes.